ALFRED

WARRIOR KING

In the island in the river
   He was broken to his knee:
And he read, writ with an iron pen,
That God had wearied of Wessex men
And given their country, field and fen,
   To the devils of the sea.

G.K. Chesterton, *The Ballad of the White Horse*

ALFRED
WARRIOR KING

JOHN PEDDIE

SUTTON PUBLISHING

First published in 1999 by
Sutton Publishing Limited · Phoenix Mill
Thrupp · Stroud · Gloucestershire · GL5 2BU

British Library Cataloguing in Publication Data
A catalogue record for this book is available from the British Library

ISBN 0 7509 2105 6

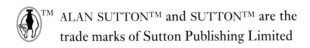

™ ALAN SUTTON™ and SUTTON™ are the
trade marks of Sutton Publishing Limited

Typeset in 11/15pt Ehrhardt.
Typesetting and origination by
Sutton Publishing Limited.
Printed in Great Britain by
Butler & Tanner, Frome, Somerset.

Contents

Introduction

> History is lived forward but is written in retrospect. We know the end before we consider the beginning and we can never wholly recapture what it was to know the beginning only.
>
> C.V. Wedgwood, *William the Silent*

The shadow of things to come revealed itself in AD 787, the year in which the King of the West Saxons, Brihtric, 'took to wife, Eadburh, daughter of King Offa'. It was early autumn and the people, in the words of Aethelweard the chronicler, were out in the fields 'making furrows in the grimy earth' in an atmosphere of 'supreme tranquillity'. The land was at peace with itself and with its neighbours. Indeed, as the annalist relates in a strikingly descriptive phrase, the richly fertile downland of the coastal shore was bathed in such contentment 'that even the burden-bearing frame of the oxen placed their necks under the yoke in dearest love'.[1] It was an idyllic scene but it was soon to be shattered when a look-out on the cliff tops sighted three unidentified ships breasting the horizon and heading in the direction of land. Whatever the intention of these vessels, whether they were hostile or friendly or plying for trade, it was the duty of the coast guard to notify the king's reeve of their arrival. He hied himself away immediately for that purpose, for the royal representative was coincidentally visiting a nearby town, possibly Dorchester, 'and then the reeve rode thither and tried to compel them to go to the royal manor, for he did not know who they were; and then they slew him'.[2] The unhappy reeve, Beaduheard was his name, had had the misfortune to challenge, on behalf of his royal master, the first Danish raiders recorded as landing in England.

It is conceivable that this incident was followed by many more such landings but, as they were minor in scale and perhaps becoming commonplace, they went unrecorded by the compilers of contemporary chronicles. The first main strike against the island, as recorded by the *Anglo-Saxon Chronicle*, occurred in the summer of 793, when a Viking force of undefined size but savagely professional in its behaviour descended upon the monks of Lindisfarne Abbey, in north-east England, and put many of its occupants to the sword. The raiders destroyed the church and several of its relics, ravaged the surrounding countryside and robbed the community of many of its substantial treasures. When word of the catastrophe reached Alcuin, Bishop of York, he wrote in sympathy to the abbot of the monastery. At the same time he felt it right to remind him of the generally declining moral standards of the church fraternity and its unseemly craving for a worldly life. His letter can have done little to bring the abbot consolation in the midst of his misery. 'Be not dismayed by this calamity,' Alcuin adjured his underling, 'for God chastiseth every son whom he receiveth.'[3]

Following upon the Lindisfarne disaster, which clearly boded little good for the future, no further raid was chronicled for a period of some thirty years, but after 832, when 'the heathen devastated Sheppey', the tempo of the attacks increased sharply, mainly against the Wessex coastline. Within a further twelve months, King Egbert of Wessex was fighting 'against 25 ships' companies[4] at Carhampton; and great slaughter was made there, and the Danes had possession of the place of slaughter'.[5]

Then, two years later, a 'great pirate host' came to Cornwall to ally itself with the Cornish Britons against Egbert of Wessex. Again, the pace had hastened. From the onset, this was plainly much more than a pirate raid. Its very scale suggested that it was aimed at the outright defeat of Egbert and the destruction of his army and, *ipso facto*, the occupation of at least part of the West Saxon kingdom. On this occasion Egbert was ready for them: he met them in battle east of the Tamar and decisively defeated the combined force at Hingston Down in Devon. The resolve and military strength displayed by Egbert at this battle, together with the severity of his handling of its aftermath, had an important outcome. It left the Cornish Britons thoroughly chastened and for many years they remained markedly reluctant to contribute to any further military adventures of this nature. Alfred, when at the nadir of his fortunes, was later to benefit from this reluctance.

The nature and severity of the Viking raids against Anglo-Saxon England were now about to enter a significantly different dimension. Until now it had been realistically possible to define them as piratical raids, but from the mid-ninth century onwards they appear to take on a different character, combining their hunger for Danegeld with the occupation or neutralisation of tactical targets. The year 851 was the turning point, for it was then that,

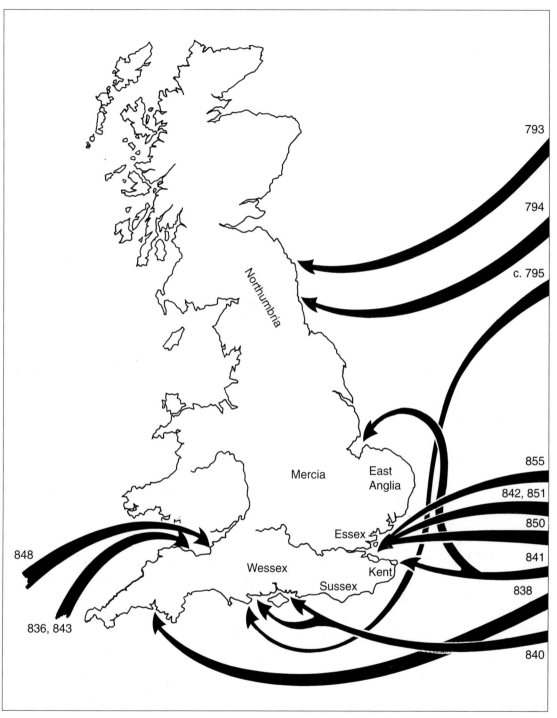

Early Viking raids against Britain were focused on Northumbria but during the ninth century they became more widespread. (Aardvark Illustration)

the heathen stayed in Thanet over the winter. And the same year, came 350 ships to the mouth of the Thames, and stormed Canterbury, and put to flight Beorhtwulf, King of Mercia, with his levies, and then went south . . . over the Thames into Surrey.[6]

This brief entry conceals a lot of facts. The Isle of Thanet, in those times, was still separated from mainland Kent by the Wantsum Channel, a waterway which, at its southern extremity, permitted access from the English Channel at Richborough, near Deal. Its northern entry point lay at Reculver, in the Thames estuary. The Wantsum was popularly used for both transit and for shelter by continental shipping serving the Thames estuary and the east coast of Britain. By this means the light craft of the day, plying to Britain from the continent (including Scandinavia, it should be noted), were enabled to avoid the heavy, frequently storm-ridden, waters of the North Sea by following a course through the safer continental coastal waters before tackling the short Channel crossing to Kent. In this light the strategic importance of the Wantsum does not need stressing and the events of 851 must be regarded as deeply significant. The 'heathen' occupation of Thanet secured the Wantsum. The follow-up force of 350 ships, mentioned by the *Chronicle* and probably carrying some 7,000 foot soldiers, then passed through the waterway to enter the Thames estuary, where, having first removed any possibility of intervention from Mercia, north of the Thames, they moved south to storm Canterbury and neutralise the people of East Kent.

Plainly this operation was not unplanned and the Kentishmen reacted sharply but belatedly to it. It was not until the following year that they responded, when the combined *fyrds* of Kent and Surrey, commanded respectively by ealdormen Ealhhere and Huda, crossed the Wantsum and landed on Thanet in an unsuccessful effort to rid themselves of the 'heathen host'. Both men were killed in the fighting 'and there were many slain and drowned on either side'. There is no evidence that the West Saxons made any further attempt to regain their lost territory. On the contrary, in 855, we learn that 'the heathen' had occupied the Isle of Sheppey. By this move the Danes extended their grip on the Thames estuary, including the riverway itself, and created a situation whereby they could commence forays against East Saxon territory, on the north bank of the estuary, without fear of hindrance.

We are not told who masterminded these operations. Clearly they were so systematically structured that they could not have happened fortuitously. The name of Ragnaar Lothbrok is frequently mentioned as a possible author of the

Regions and peoples of Britain, c. 850. (Aardvark Illustration)

plan (see Appendix A). Certain it is that, some ten years later, when a great Danish host landed in East Anglia 'and took winter quarters' there, Lothbrok's three sons, Ivar, Halfdan and Ubba, all featured largely in the operations which then ensued, their task having been made infinitely easier by the creation of a Danish firm base astride the Thames estuary and in the Wantsum waterway. Within five years the great Saxon kingdoms of East Anglia, Northumbria and Mercia had tumbled before them, their peasant armies unable to counter the almost professional power and tactics of the Viking warbands.

It was at this moment, in 871, when the Saxon kingdoms of Britain had been subdued and Wessex had been long deprived of her eastern shires, that the Danish commanders determined on the conquest of Wessex. It was a decision that quickly brought Alfred to centre stage, together with his elder brother Aethelred, who died in the early fighting, thus allowing Alfred simultaneously to become king and commander-in-chief. His general lack of success, both before and after coming to the throne, which he appears to have ascended in the middle of a battle, was so pronounced that G.K. Chesterton felt able to write of him, in his *Ballad of the White Horse*,

> I am that oft-defeated king.
> Whose failure fills the land,
> Who fled before the Danes of old,
> Who chaffered with the Danes for gold
> Who now upon the Wessex Wold
> Hardly has feet to stand.

Sadly this was true. Subsequent to the battle of Ashdown in January 871, where he gained a great victory with his brother Aethelred, they jointly shared defeat at Reading, Basing and *Meretun*; finally, at Wilton, after succeeding to the throne, he was compelled by his enemy, Halfdan, to buy for Wessex a few years of peace. This is not surprising: he was still only twenty-three years of age and he had inherited from his predecessors an antiquated military machine – a largely peasant army, quite unsuited for tackling the new-style, highly mobile enemy now overrunning his homeland.

This work, *Alfred: Warrior King*, is a study of the young king's military campaigns, the military problems which beset him and the opposition which confronted him. It is not intended to be yet another history of the life and times of Alfred the Great, for this is a subject which, in the past one hundred years, ever since Plummer produced his pre-emptive volume in 1902,[7] has been copiously covered by a legion of respected scholars and historians, sometimes in very frank discussion. This is an arena into which I have entered only with great caution. There have also been published invaluable and innumerable papers which discuss almost every aspect of the king's life, ranging from the political purpose of his reception by Pope Leo IV in Rome, a city he visited as a boy of six in the year 853, to a medical diagnosis of the sickness, probably Crohn's disease, that struck him down at his wedding feast and continued to afflict him 'throughout his life'.[8]

In any study of the reign of Alfred the Great we are largely dependent upon two main sources for our facts. The first is a contemporary biography, *The Life of King Alfred*, compiled by Asser, a scholarly monk, and probably a bishop, of the great church of St David's in south-west Wales, from where he was recruited to the king's household in 885. The second source is the *Anglo-Saxon Chronicle*, which two distinguished historians, Plummer and Hodgkin, have surmised is largely a product of Alfred's times, inspired and overseen by him. Their opinions merit great respect. Hodgkin[9] saw it as a treatise not actually written at the king's dictation but delegated to clerics commissioned by him 'to collect what information they could about the history of his dynasty and its relation to the history of the island'. Plummer took a stronger stance:

> I do not mean that the actual task of compiling the *Chronicle* from earlier materials was necessarily performed by Alfred, though I can well fancy that he may have dictated some of the later annals which describe his own wars. But that the idea of a national *Chronicle* as opposed to merely local annals was his, that the idea was carried out under his direction and supervision, that I do most firmly believe.[10]

In fact, he mooted, perhaps slyly, that the fact that we believe Alfred to be 'Great' may in part be because he tells us so, but there was considerable purpose to the two annals the king inspired. The *Chronicle* was produced at a time of deep national crisis, in late 892 or early 893, when events on the continent had persuaded the third great Viking army, after an absence of some seven years, to abandon its pursuits there and recross the Channel to conduct a potentially more profitable campaign in England. It was an event that signalled the beginning of Alfred's concluding struggle with his Viking enemies. Although the outcome was indecisive during his lifetime, it was to set the stage for the unification of

England, a process he had begun in 878, after his defeat of Guthrum at the battle of Edington. It is probable, at this crucial moment of renewed conflict, that the *Chronicle* was actively circulated, directed mainly at the influential people of England. It would have provided a useful propaganda vehicle through which to emphasise the leadership and military qualities of the West Saxon king, who was seeking to enlist their total support.

The dating of Asser's *Life of King Alfred* is more obscure, although its origin clearly lies between 885, when Asser first arrived at the West Saxon court, and 894, in which year the biography comes abruptly to an end. It is said by some to have been written to complement the *Chronicle*, perhaps with Welsh leadership in mind, for the Welsh rulers had but recently submitted to Alfred and were now numbered among his subjects. Others suggest that the *Life* was not produced at any one time but that it was 'an imperfect conflation of several separate, shorter treatises on the king, all written at different times'. Whatever the timing of its production, there is one aspect of the work about which there can be no doubt: many of the events described in it, such as the early wars with the Lothbrok brothers and with Guthrum during the years 871–8, were matters of which Asser had no direct knowledge. At best they were recorded by him some fifteen years after they took place. It follows, therefore, that his information on these matters was second-hand, possibly drawn from the memories of members of the royal court who had played some part in them. In these circumstances it is impossible that he could not have turned for advice to his patron, Alfred, the senior protagonist. It may thus be judged that the flavour of the king's influence is present in both the *Life* and the *Chronicle* and that they should be read and interpreted in this knowledge.

Alfred's early setbacks, which tempted G.K. Chesterton to write about 'that oft-defeated king', were turned by him to good advantage when he was driven to seek shelter on Athelney. His time spent there enabled him to think, to assess the short- and long-term problems which lay ahead and to plan how they might be circumvented. He found space in which to contact his friends and to gauge the depth of the immediate support he might expect from them, and he was able to prepare and set in hand plans for the reconquest of his homeland. But more than this: his sojourn on Athelney allowed him the opportunity to examine his own performance and weaknesses. Alfred was a deeply religious man. Like Alcuin of York, he regarded many of the tribulations which now beset his people as a punishment for their religious failings. He was later to write,[11]

Remember what punishment befell us in this world when we ourselves did not cherish learning nor transmit it to other men. We were Christians in name only, and very few of us possessed Christian virtues.

The man who fled with the remnants of his army from Chippenham to the Somerset marshes, early in 871, was a different man to the one who emerged in the following spring to lead the West Saxons to victory at Edington. He had in the meantime discovered that vital sense of responsibility and moral courage without which no leader, whatever his status, can hope to succeed. It supports him through the crises of failure, steels him in the making or conveying of unpopular decisions, sustains him in the loneliness of command and carries him that bit further when lesser men might turn back.

CHAPTER 1

Alfred of Wessex

No great man lives in vain. The history of the world is but the biography of
great men.

Thomas Carlyle

Alfred the Great, if we are to believe Asser's biography (and there are some
eminent historians who do not do so in this connection), was born at the royal
estate at Wantage in the year 849,[1] 'in the district known as Berkshire, which is so
called from Berroc Wood, where the box tree grows very abundantly'. Whether or
not Berkshire lay within Wessex territory at that time is debatable. Within months
of Alfred's arrival in what was to prove a troublesome world, a great Danish army
of some 350 longships entered the 'mouth of the Thames, stormed Canterbury,
put to flight Beorhtwulf, King of Mercia, with his levies, and then went south
into Surrey', where they were halted and defeated in battle by his father,
Aethelwulf.[2]

Almost certainly Wantage was under Mercian rule until three or four years
after the young prince's birth, and it is notable that the ealdorman of Berkshire,
the loyal and worthy Aethelwulf, who held the same name as the king and fell
fighting gallantly for Wessex against the Danish stronghold at Reading in 871,
was subsequently carried back across the River Thames for burial in Mercia, his
homeland. Militarily Wantage had for many years been a Saxon settlement of
importance, strategically located where the Icknield Way crosses the Letcombe
Brook. The brook is a tributary of the Ock, itself a substantial tributary of the
Thames, which it joins on the southern outskirts of the ancient abbey grounds at
Abingdon. The royal *vill* where Alfred was first presented to his mother, Osburh,
is traditionally said to have stood on high ground at Belmont, north-west of the
present town centre, but no trace of its site remains to be seen today.

The details of Alfred's lineage, as set down by his biographer Asser, some time
between the years 885 and 894,[3] are almost overly fulsome. Much of what Asser

An eighth-century carved stone from Gotland, Sweden, depicting a Viking longship. Note the typical square sail, strengthened by cross stitching. (Antikvarisk-topografiska arkivet, Stockholm)

wrote in his biography of the king is thought to have been directed at the Welsh people, whose sympathy and support he was particularly striving to win. The reason for this, at the height of West Saxon war with the Vikings, is not difficult to perceive, for the coves and harbours of the western coastline of Wales, lying on the open flank of Wessex, were well used by Norsemen and Danes alike, not only to further their operations in the Irish Sea and northern England, but also as bases from which to extend their influence into north Cornwall and the Severn estuary.

There were, of course, others whom the king was trying to attract to his side and some of the antecedents Asser claims for his royal patron have clearly been inserted in order to display a common thread linking him to influential factions among the diverse population of England at that time. He is shown, for example, as descended both from Adam, a suggestion that would have appealed greatly to the Church, which overlaid many of the divisions of the country then hostile to him, and from the Norse god Woden, the source of wisdom and valour, and from whom the Northumbrian Anglo-Saxon houses of Deira and Bernicia claimed descent.[4] For his part, Alfred's visible origins were impeccable. He was the son of

Two views of a gold and niello ring, bearing the name of Alfred's father, King Aethelwulf. Twice actual size. (British Museum)

King Aethelwulf, himself the son of the redoubtable Egbert, who was descended from Ingild, the brother of Ine, the powerful lawmaking King of the West Saxons. On the distaff side, his mother Osburh, portrayed by Asser as a most religious woman, 'noble in character and noble by birth', was the daughter of one Oslac, variously described as butler or cupbearer to Aethelwulf, a rank of distinction, probably equivalent to that of chamberlain of the royal household. Oslac, it seems, was descended from two Jutish chieftains, the brothers Stuf and Wihtgar, who had been granted the Isle of Wight in the early sixth century by their uncle Cerdic, founder of Wessex.

Alfred was the youngest of five brothers, the others being Aethelstan, Aethelbald, Aethelberht and Aethelred. They had one sister, Aethelswith, who was later to marry Burghred, King of Mercia. Alfred's relationship with his brothers is obscure: details of their activities are rarely given by Asser and, other than Aethelbald, who is castigated for marrying his father's widow, Judith, and Aethelred, to whom reference is made generally when Alfred has also been mentioned, they are rarely referred to except in an oblique and deprecatory manner. On the other hand, 'his esteemed lord', Asser tells us,

was greatly loved more than all his brothers, by his father and mother – indeed by everybody – with a universal and profound love, and he was always brought up in the royal court and nowhere else. As he passed through infancy and boyhood, he was seen to be more comely in appearance than his other brothers, and more pleasing in manner, speech and behaviour. From the cradle onwards, in spite of all the demands of the present life, it has been the desire for wisdom, more than anything else, together with the nobility of his birth, which have characterised the nature of his noble mind; but alas, by the shameful negligence of his parents and tutors, he remained ignorant of letters until his twelfth year, or even longer.[5]

It is a strangely unpleasant paragraph in which the author, trying to enhance the image of his patron in the eyes of his readers, was prepared to scold the king's parents for 'shamefully' neglecting his education, and to criticise his brothers, despite the difficulties in comparison presented by a considerable difference in age, for being less lovable, less pleasing in manner, less intelligent and less ambitious than the young prince. Yet they were not guilty of neglecting their responsibilities to Wessex. Aethelstan, for example, ruled over the provinces of eastern Wessex, a task delegated to him by his father Aethelwulf, when the latter assumed the throne of Wessex from Egbert in 837. Aethelstan could not therefore have been a callow youth when we find him, with ealdorman Ealbhere of Kent, twelve years later, 'slaughtering a great Viking army at Sandwich'.[6] He captured nine enemy ships and put the others to flight but after this incident he disappears from Asser's pages entirely, and we can only assume he was killed in battle as a result of this or subsequent fighting. He predeceased his father by seven years, when Alfred was still in his infancy. Even in the knowledge that young princes in medieval times assumed their duties at an early age, it would not be extravagant to suggest that Aethelwulf's eldest son must have been about thirty years of age at the time of his death. Alfred, at that moment, would have been two years old.

Aethelbald succeeded King Aethelwulf to the throne of Wessex in 858. Seven years earlier he had participated at the battle of *Aclea*, where his father had resoundingly beaten a Danish war party that had penetrated deep into Surrey. Asser has little that is good to say of him and, as is related and discussed below, in his *Life of King Alfred*, he accuses Aethelbald of conspiring with Ealhstan, Bishop of Sherborne, in 855–6, to usurp his father's throne, while the king was away on a pilgrimage to Rome. Aethelbald died in 860, after reigning for two peaceful years and, perhaps because of this piece of good fortune, is said by Henry of Huntingdon to have been mourned by all of England. Asser makes no mention of any such popularity and is content simply to record the year of his death.

Six mortuary chests in Winchester Cathedral contain the oldest royal bones in England, including those of King Egbert. During the Commonwealth, all the bones were tipped out and jumbled up. (John Crook)

It was Aethelwulf's intention, according to the terms of his will, that Aethelbald should be succeeded to the throne by his fourth son Aethelred, and that Aethelberht, his third son, should remain as King of Kent, an appointment he had assumed about 855. This arrangement was, however, set aside on Aethelbald's death and Aethelberht assumed the kingship of all Wessex as well as Kent. He died in 866 and Asser wrote of him that 'he went the way of all flesh, to the great sorrow of his people . . . after governing in peace, love and honour for five years. Then, in the year of the Lord's Incarnation, 866, the eighteenth of King Alfred's life, Aethelred . . . took over the government of the kingdom of the West Saxons.'

The jumbled up skulls and bones of England's earliest monarchs. (John Crook)

Armed with these facts and dates, it is interesting to speculate on the relative ages of both Osburh and her sons at the time of their deaths for at first sight these are hard to reconcile. Aethelstan, as we have demonstrated, was probably no more than thirty years of age when he disappeared from historical view in about 853. He was thus born about 823 and would have been some twenty-eight years older than Alfred, who patently was a very late arrival in the Aethelwulf family. He himself did not die until 899, at the age of fifty, and nearly forty years after Aethelbald, thirty-three years after Aethelberht, twenty-eight years after Aethelred, who seemingly died of wounds received in the battle of *Meretun*, and eleven years after his sister Aethelswith, who passed away at Pavia in 888, while taking the traditional pilgrim's road to Rome.[7] These figures give a clear indication of the age difference between Alfred and the rest of his brothers and his sister. He was the youngest born by several years. It is thus not difficult to understand how Asser could write that 'he was greatly loved, more than all his brothers, by his father and mother – indeed by everybody – with a universal and profound love'. The child prince, 'brought up in the royal court, and nowhere else', would clearly have been the centre of much attention from both the royal family and courtiers alike.

Yet again, if we acknowledge, as we must, the clear difference in age and experience between Alfred and his brothers, we are forced to remind ourselves that we are discussing a period of history in which the average lifespan for men was 32.5 years (for women marginally less) and in which only 10 per cent of the population survived for fifty years.[8] Thus if we assume that Osburh bore Aethelstan when she was seventeen, she would have been, in this context, an elderly and unlikely forty-three or forty-four when she produced Alfred in 849, and fifty years of age in 856. This is the year by which she is judged already to have passed away, for it was then that Aethelwulf returned to Wessex from Rome, controversially bringing with him, as a child-bride, Judith, the young daughter of Charles the Bald, King of the Franks.

In the light of these statistics, our instinct must be to reject Asser's charming biographical depiction of Osburh encouraging her sons to read:

One day, therefore, when his mother was showing him and his brothers a book of English poetry which she held in her hand, she said: 'I shall give this book to whichever one of you can learn it fastest.' Spurred on by these words, or rather by divine inspiration, and attracted by the initial letter in the book, Alfred spoke as follows in reply to his mother, forestalling his brothers (ahead in years though not in ability): 'Will you really give this book to the one of us who can understand it the soonest and recite it to you?' Whereupon, smiling with pleasure, she reassured him and said 'Yes, I will.'[9]

This extract is not easy to comprehend. First, its implication is immediately to contradict Asser's earlier statement that the king's youthful education had suffered because of 'shameful neglect' by his parents, and secondly because the part depicted as played by his brothers must surely be questioned. If Osburh died in 856, as has been suggested, and if Alfred and his father were engaged in their pilgrimage to Rome for the greater part of the years 855–6, as we know them to have been, then Alfred must have been somewhere between three and six years of age when this incident took place. Correspondingly, at least two of his remaining brothers were in their middle to late twenties. Aethelberht had almost certainly succeeded Aethelstan as under-king of Kent and Aethelbald, who had accompanied his father to the battle at *Aclea* in 851, had probably already been designated successor to Aethelwulf. Aethelred cannot have been much younger than his elder brothers, for it will be recollected that Aethelwulf had not thought it wrong to nominate him as Aethelbald's successor to the throne of Wessex, rather than the older Aethelberht.

It stretches the imagination, therefore, to be asked to believe that these young men, enjoying a full life and doubtless involved in high matters of state, both political and military, with an accompanying sense of importance, would have considered competing in such a manner with a boy of such an age and in such circumstances. We are thus forced to search for other explanations. It is obviously not improbable that Asser distorted his biography of Alfred's life to show his patron in the best possible light; but another, more acceptable, answer is that Alfred (and perhaps Aethelred, although this must remain a matter of doubt) was the son of Osburh and that his elder brothers were the product of an earlier marriage by their father, Aethelwulf.[10]

When Alfred was aged four, King Aethelwulf sent him on a visit to Rome where, by the eighth century, visitors from England, frequently royalty, had become so numerous that a national hostel, known as the Schola Saxonum, had been opened in the neighbourhood of St Peter's. It was succeeded in the fourteenth century by the English College which is to be found today in the via Monserrato. The route the young prince would have followed, accompanied by a colourful caravanserai of courtiers, commoners and clerics, was well used but potentially hazardous. It would have been essential for his person to be well safeguarded, with arrangements where necessary for escorts to be provided by the various kingdoms through which he passed. The whole enterprise would have required careful preparation and liaison, and we are driven to question the reason for the dispatch of the boy to Rome at this precise moment.

We are already aware, from Asser's *Life*, which we must assume to have been written and published with King Alfred's approval, that because of 'the shameful negligence of his parents and tutors he remained ignorant of letters until his twelfth year, or even longer'. Thus it must be doubtful that the young boy went to Rome to be educated. Perhaps the explanation is to be found in Aethelwulf's seeming willingness to tinker with the laws of succession. If it were his aim that his throne should be occupied by all of his sons in turn, then he may have judged that this was the moment to consolidate such a process. This would have been particularly necessary if the young prince had been the child of a second marriage. In that event, his succession to the throne could well have been challenged by the male heirs of the sons of his earlier line. Thus Aethelwulf, by sending the young prince to Rome and arranging his reception and confirmation by Pope Leo IV, may have felt that he was ensuring his youngest son's position as the ultimate 'heir apparent'. The *Anglo-Saxon Chronicle* for the year 853 is intended to leave us in no doubt of Aethelwulf's intentions: 'King Aethelwulf sent his son Alfred to Rome. The lord Leo was the Pope in Rome, and he consecrated him king and stood sponsor for him at confirmation.'[11]

The Pope, for his part, was seemingly wary of involvement in any political ploy. Following his reception of the young prince, he wrote a letter in cautious language to Aethelwulf, in which he carefully underlined the stated purpose of the boy's arrival in Rome, namely, to visit the Holy City, and emphasised briefly the non-partisan nature of the ceremony of investiture which Alfred had attended to receive his purely Italian award:

We have now generously received your son Alfred, whom you were anxious to send at this time to the threshold of the Holy Apostle, and we have decorated him, as a spiritual son, with the dignity of the belt [sword] and the vestments of the consulate, as is customary with Roman consuls, because he gave himself into our hands.[12]

The two accounts of the ceremony in Rome are thus vastly different. The *Anglo-Saxon Chronicle* relates that Alfred 'was consecrated king' by Pope Leo IV. The Pope, on the other hand, states that the boy was decorated with the sword and vestments of the consulate, 'as is customary with Roman consuls'. In republican Rome consuls were the highest civic authority. More importantly, they were also selected as commanders of Rome's many armies and frequently held the highest military rank. At the time of Alfred's visit, however, the title had diminished to a degree where the grant of the rank to an individual was regarded as a decorative honour rather than as an appointment to rank. Leo IV's choice of words, perhaps recognising events of a deeper significance, of which he would doubtless have been made aware by his clergy, appear to be deliberately framed in order to deny the king any opportunity of attaching greater purpose to the occasion than the ceremony warranted.

Pope Leo IV died in 855 and was succeeded by Benedict III. It was perhaps for this reason, and because of his desire to establish a sound relationship with the new occupant of the influential papal throne, that Aethelwulf now decided to journey to Rome himself. He had much upon his mind. He set forth in great state, taking many splendid gifts with him. Asser relates that Alfred had by this time returned home and now accompanied his father on yet another visit. Whether or not this was so,[13] the *Annals of St Bertin*[14] make no reference to the young prince's presence in their record of Aethelwulf's arrival at the Frankish court, where Charles received the West Saxon king with honour, as he 'hastened' on his way to Rome. Charles, according to Bertin, 'presented him with everything belonging to the royal estate and had him escorted to the frontiers of his kingdom with the attendance fitted for a king'.

These were eventful, highly politically charged days for Aethelwulf. His second wife Osburh, if we accept the possibility of his remarriage, is allowed by chroniclers to slip quietly away, unheralded, out of the pages of their annals, before her husband's departure to the continent. It may be that she was by then already deceased for, by medieval standards, she would have attained the elderly age of fifty. On the other hand, it is clear that Aethelwulf was by now pursuing an entirely different political objective. If he were truly 'hastening to Rome' on his outward journey, as the *Annals of St Bertin* relate, he appears nevertheless to have spent some considerable time at the Frankish court. The reason for this delay emerged upon his return journey, for he now tarried a further several months with Charles the Bald until July, when Aethelwulf's betrothal to his host's daughter Judith was announced. She was just twelve years old, surprisingly young in modern eyes, but not so in the early medieval age. Aethelwulf did not take his road homewards until early autumn, after he had married his young bride, on 1 October, at the royal palace at Verberie.

The *Annals of St Bertin* have provided us with some detail of their marriage ceremony and their subsequent return to Wessex:

> when the diadem had been placed upon her head, Ingmar, Bishop of Reims, giving the blessing, he honoured her with the name of queen, which hitherto had not been customary with him and his people; and when the ceremony had been solemnised with royal magnificence on both sides and with gifts, he returned by ship with her to Britain, to the control of his kingdom.[15]

These lines, in their brief comment that Judith was honoured 'with the name of queen', were highly controversial. This was a practice not then recognised in Wessex, where the wife of the king was never referred to as 'queen' but simply as the 'king's wife', thus requiring her to be kept firmly in the background and devoid of governmental influence. It is more than likely that this condition to the marriage had already been discussed at length, during the outward leg of his journey to Rome, between Aethelwulf and Judith's father Charles. As may be imagined, details of their talks reached the ears of Aethelwulf's eldest son, Aethelbald, in whose hands the king had left affairs of state during his absence; angered by the change in the traditional laws of succession apparently agreed by his parent, Aethelbald is said to have plotted with his councillors, as well as Eanwulf, the ealdorman of Somerset, and Ealhstan, the powerful Bishop of Sherborne, to exile his father from Wessex upon his return to Britain.

Thus, there is a delightful wealth of understatement in the comment by the *St Bertin*'s annalist that Aethelwulf, after his marriage, returned to the 'control of his kingdom'. In truth, the control of his kingdom had been perilously close to slipping from his fingers for several months of his stay overseas. Indeed, some sources, in particular the *Liber Pontificalis* containing the life of Benedict III, record that Aethelwulf received warnings while visiting the Holy City that, because of the suspicion and anger he was arousing at home by his behaviour overseas, he was in direct peril of losing his throne. These rumours were to prove to be of real substance and he returned to a troubled homeland.

Asser, in his *Life of King Alfred*, written, we should remind ourselves, with the knowledge and support of the king himself, wrote about these events in sharp terms and described it as a 'disgraceful episode, contrary to the practice of all Christian men'.[16] A great many people, he wrote, ascribe this wretched incident, unheard of in all previous ages, to the bishop and the ealdorman alone, at whose instigation it is said to have taken place. There are many who also attribute it to arrogance on the part of King Aethelbald, because he was grasping in this affair and in many other wrongdoings, as I have heard from the reports of certain men, and as was demonstrated by the outcome of the . . . event.

Despite this stinging criticism by Asser of an 'iniquitous and grasping' Aethelbald, while in contrast speaking of Aethelwulf as a man of 'indescribable forbearance', the outcome of the dispute proved to be a nicely worked compromise which neatly avoided a heavy confrontation between king and councillors. It resulted in the division of Wessex, with the eastern province, smaller and more vulnerable, being 'assigned to the father' and the 'western part of the Saxon land, which had always been more important than the eastern', being assigned to the son.[17] The decision to divide Wessex in such a manner could only have been considered as a matter of the greatest import. Its separation into two districts was something that could not have been achieved and carried through without the unanimous approval of the *witan*, an advisory body of great collective power, made up of the most influential men of the West Saxon kingdom. Its membership was drawn from powerful Church leaders, aristocratic ealdormen and thegns of the shires, and many of those officers of the royal household who held positions of honour and trust as servants of the king. Decisions reached by such men can be judged to have been made in the best interests of the kingdom.

Clearly Aethelwulf, in the eyes of his royal councillors, had lost the argument, whether it had concerned his remarriage, a lack of policy consultation with his councillors or a supposed interference with the existing laws of succession, perhaps to the benefit of his youngest son, Alfred.

The appointment as ruler of the eastern province cannot have been received warmly by Aethelwulf, even though he was described as sharing the throne of Wessex with Aethelbald. He would have been well aware that, a little more than two years earlier, on the eve of his departure to Rome, a great Danish army had entered the Thames estuary and landed in force on the Isle of Sheppey. There, it had wintered on English soil, the first time a Viking raiding army had endeavoured to do so, threatening the sovereignty of Wessex by its presence and living off Danegeld extracted ruthlessly from the people of Kent and the prosperous Church estates surrounding Canterbury. Judith accompanied

Aethelwulf as he took up his appointment in these uneasy frontier shires. Her new husband had ordered that 'she should sit beside him on the royal throne until the end of his life'.

Aethelwulf died within two years of these events. He was at once succeeded to the throne by his son Aethelbald, who, upon becoming King of all Wessex, in the words of Asser, 'took over his father's marriage bed and married Judith, daughter of Charles, King of the Franks, incurring great disgrace from all who heard of it'.[18] Again one must take issue with the scribe for, despite his statement that Aethelbald incurred great disgrace from this action, it is clear that he retained the goodwill of his people for the remaining two and a half years of his life. Moreover in medieval times it was not unusual for a man to marry his mother-in-law, and Aethelbald does not appear to have incurred the disapproval of Charles the Bald for, after Aethelbald's death in 860 his young widow returned to Francia, where Charles welcomed her home with considerable warmth, accommodated her in the palace at Senlis and 'afforded her all the honour due to a queen'.[19] From this, we may assume that she had 'sat beside' Aethelbald's throne just as she had that of his father, that this was equally acceptable to the king's councillors as it had been previously and that there must have been good political reasons for it.

Enemy pressures, year upon year, were now crowding in upon Wessex. The *Anglo-Saxon Chronicle* refrains from revealing these in detail but the annal for 860, in an illuminating few lines, discloses how the traditional burial place of the West Saxon kings at Winchester, the political and religious capital of Wessex, had by then perforce to be abandoned, thus compelling another to be found, further from hostilities, deeper in the heart of Wessex. Thus, we are told, that in this year:

King Aethelbald passed away, and his body lies at Sherborne. And Aethelberht, his brother, succeeded to the entire kingdom. And in his reign a great pirate host landed and stormed Winchester. And against the host fought ealdorman Osric with the men of Hampshire and ealdorman Aethelwulf with the men of Berkshire and put the host to flight. . . . And that Aethelberht reigned five years and his body lies at Sherborne.[20]

Aethelwulf, their father, under-king of the eastern district of Wessex, was buried initially at Steyning, away from the problems of Thanet and the Kentish coast, and was later believed to have been reinterred by King Alfred at Winchester upon the return of more peaceful times. Aethelbald and, later, Aethelberht were buried

ANCIENT COFFIN LID
OBSERVE THE TWO INCISED CROSSES
INDICATING THE BURIAL OF AN
IMPORTANT PERSON. THIS LID
POSSIBLY COVERED THE BODY OF
KING ETHELWULF WHO WAS
BURIED HERE IN 858. HE WAS
SUBSEQUENTLY EXHUMED AND LATER
RE-INTERRED AT WINCHESTER NEAR
HIS SON KING ALFRED.

The coffin lid claimed to be from King Aethelwulf's tomb at Steyning church, Sussex. (H.C. Randall) at Sherborne, for Winchester had by the time of their deaths been devastated by a Danish army under Weland; Aethelred, who died in the field after defeat at the battle of *Meretun*, is said to have been carried to Dorset and buried at Wimborne Abbey.

It had been Aethelwulf's wish that he should be succeeeded to the throne by each of his sons in turn, according to their lineage. Fate decreed that his wish was to be surprisingly quickly achieved. This is not remarkable if it is recognised that Aethelwulf reigned over Wessex for some nineteen years (839–858) in an era when, as we have demonstrated, the length of life was limited and longevity was a rarity. His surviving older sons, by reason of the length of his reign, were thus relatively elderly men by the time they came to power. Their succession was virtually predictable. Aethelwulf, on the other hand, was equally concerned that the inheritance of Osburh's sons, the youngest of his progeny, should be similarly assured. Alfred's childhood visit to Rome, quickly followed by his father's own pilgrimage to the Holy City, emphasised Aethelwulf's anticipation of problems ahead for the two young stepbrothers of the older princes, and his concern for their heritage. In the event the departure of Aethelbald and Aethelberht from the scene, the circumstances of war and the youth of those of Alfred's nephews who might have competed with him for the kingship ensured Alfred's accession to the crown.

What then of the strange affair of Judith's marriage to Aethelwulf when, it should be remembered, the bride was in her thirteenth year and her consort was an elderly man who obviously could not have anticipated many more years of life? From the viewpoint of Charles the Bald, Judith would have been a valuable asset, a very marketable daughter, and he would presumably not have offered her hand to the West Saxon king unless, in modern parlance, he could have seen value for money. It has been suggested[21] that the West Saxons benefited because, as a result of the union, the two peoples became linked to the leading institutions of Western Christendom at a moment when their respective kingdoms were suffering relentlessly increasing attacks from pagan Viking raiders. It was only a few months after the wedding before Weland, a formidable Danish freebooter, was to abandon his base on the Seine, having made peace with the King of the Franks, to sail across the Channel and sack the West Saxon capital and religious centre of Winchester. Thus in these dangerous times both sides had much to offer each other, not only through Christian solidarity but in the very practical terms of military intelligence and defence techniques. Alfred's later pattern of river defence along the length of the Thames, interwoven with his burghal hidage system, owed much to Frankish military practice.

A painted block of stone, once part of a Saxon wall painting, reused within the foundations of the New Minster at Winchester. (Winchester Research Unit)

Anglo-Saxon longevity statistics underline another relevant fact: the early age of death for men and women reduced the period of contact between generations. Alfred's mother, as we have seen, interested herself in his education but even so he complained that 'by the shameful negligence of his parents and tutors he remained ignorant of letters until his twelfth year, or even longer'.[22] The age difference between himself and his elder brothers inevitably would have meant that the young prince spent his early days among the children of the court. With them he would have played and learnt boyish pursuits; with them, in due course, he would have passed through a school of arms, been instructed in the arts of the chase and developed the eye for country he was later to demonstrate as a soldier. In truth there would have been plenty of distractions to keep him from his books, but the age at which Alfred, in his own words, began to absorb his letters, his 'twelfth year', is in itself intriguing, for this was also the year of Aethelwulf's death. Following this, responsibility for his schooling probably fell fleetingly upon Aethelbald (858–860) but mainly upon Aethelberht (860–65), who occupied the throne between his young stepbrother's twelfth and seventeenth years. Almost certainly, as king, he would have delegated his duties in this regard to the scholars of the Church.

The ancient Coronation Stone at Kingston upon Thames, where no fewer than seven Saxon kings were crowned, including Alfred's son Edward the Elder. (David Hilliam)

The first whispers of the Christian faith had probably reached British shores as early as the first century AD, for the Roman invasion of these islands took place only four to five years after the crucifixion of Christ. Indeed, Aulus Plautius, the Roman general appointed by the Emperor Claudius to command the landings on the Kentish coastline in AD 43, was later required to sacrifice his career because his wife Pomponia Graecina, a convert, was charged in Rome with 'foreign superstition' and was referred to her husband for trial. In the custom of the time Plautius acquitted her but from that moment became responsible for her future behaviour and surrendered his public duties. In later years a Romano-Celtic church developed in Britain but it was pushed aside to the extremities of the west country by the arrival of the Anglo-Saxons during the so-called Dark Ages. Here it survived, particularly in Wales. In 596 Pope Gregory I sent to England a mission of several monks headed by Augustine, then prior of the monastery of St Andrew in Rome. A Northumbrian monk from the abbey at Whitby later narrated that Gregory had been persuaded to take this action from the moment when, before his pontification, he had sighted some fair-haired youths for sale in the slave market:

> God prompting him inwardly, he asked of what race they were. And when they replied, 'Those from whom they are sprung are called Angles,' he said, 'Angels of God.' Then he said, 'What is the name of the king of that people?' And they said, 'Aelle'; and he said 'Alleluia! for the praise of God ought to be there.'[23]

Augustine initially proved a somewhat reluctant missionary. He had proceeded only a short distance on his way when his courage failed him and he returned to Rome to request of His Holiness that he and his followers should be relieved of such a dangerous mission. Pope Gregory inspired him to set forth again and in the event Augustine discovered that he had worried unduly. King Aethelberht of Kent, who came to meet him upon his arrival, not only provided his mission with protection but gave him the authority to preach and make converts. It was not long before the great majority of the people of Kent had adopted Christianity and the next 250 years saw its vigorous development. The Church, operating inside the disciplines set by the papacy, became a unifying and influential force within an island until then divided into dynastical kingdoms.

The constitutional results of this were quickly noticeable, for rulers were soon surrounded by bishops and clergy whose worldly, as well as spiritual, knowledge was superior to that of both the rulers and their ministers. They had a virtual monopoly of the art of writing and access to seats of learning. Through their energies and the work of the early missionaries a system of organised education began to emerge, initially based on schools founded for the instruction of children selected to train for holy orders. The work of the Church in this regard was greatly strengthened in 664 when Theodore arrived to take over the see of Canterbury. He had been carefully and personally selected for the appointment by the Pope and was, in the words of the early English historian Bede,[24] writing in 731, 'a man of proven integrity, learned in both sacred and secular literature and in Greek and Latin'. He was the first archbishop to have dominion 'over the entire Church of the English'. Bede commented that Theodore, with his assistant Hadrian, attracted a large number of students, into whose minds they poured the waters of wholesome knowledge day by day. In addition to instructing them in the holy Scriptures, they also taught their pupils poetry, astronomy and the calculations of the church calendar. In proof of this, some of their students, still alive today, are as proficient in Latin and Greek as in their mother tongue. Never had there been such happy times as these since the English settled in Britain; for the Christian kings were so strong that they daunted all the barbarous tribes. The people eagerly sought the new-found joys of the kingdom of heaven and all who wished for instruction in the reading of the Scriptures found teachers ready at hand.[25]

The halcyon, non-secular days of the English Church of the mid-eighth century were not, however, to survive for many more decades. Alcuin of York, a friend of the powerful Charlemagne and an adviser to him on religious matters, wrote a lengthy letter to Higbald, Bishop of Lindisfarne, after the sacking of the monastery by Viking raiders in 793. He first commiserated with the monks for the calamity which had struck them and then he added that it was truly not something which had happened by chance but was a 'sign that it was well merited by someone'. In those times it was widely believed that disasters were visited upon people either because of their sins and omissions or as a test of their character and faith. Alcuin now called upon the Lindisfarne community to examine its behaviour, and his words point to a decline in the previously high moral standards of the missionary Church.

Do not glory in the vanity of raiment: this is not a glory to priests and servants of God, but a disgrace. Do not in drunkenness blot out the words of your prayers. Do not go out after luxuries of the flesh and worldly avarice, but continue steadfastly in the service of God and in the discipline of the regular life, that the most holy fathers, which begot you, may not cease to be your protectors . . . Be not degenerate sons of such great fathers. Yet be not destroyed by this calamity. God chastiseth every son whom he receiveth . . .[26]

The growing scale of Viking piratical raids at this time had a devastating effect on the work of the great religious institutions and, consequently, upon the administration of both Church and State, for the literate clergy were the natural civil servants of government. The disruption created by the raiders not only impeded the spread of Christianity but lowered the level of literacy and negated

The late Saxon church at Bradford-on-Avon. (John Mennell)

the significant advances which had been made during the first half of the ninth century. The learning of Latin had become of considerable importance not only to the Church, since scriptures and services were in this language, but also to the State, since many official documents and charters of the eighth and ninth centuries were compiled in it.

The reversal of this advance and the impact of the consequential decline in administrative and educational standards is clearly exemplified in a study of a total of fifty-two ninth-century charters,[27] forty-four of which had been compiled in Canterbury. The calligraphy of those written in the first half of the century was immaculate and the knowledge of Latin adequate for the task. The situation in the cathedral writing office during the following thirty years or so, after the calamitous arrival of the great Viking army in 851, was greatly changed and reflected the severity of the attack which the cathedral suffered at that time and of others which followed in its wake. Clerical competence was pitifully low, knowledge of Latin was poor and standards of spelling and script were little better. The dimension of the crisis then facing the Church, with which the future of the State was so closely intertwined, becomes revealed when it is appreciated that by the year 873, when Kent had virtually succumbed under Viking domination, there appears to have been only one scribe active at Canterbury and he was a man of poor performance and failing eyesight.[28] As the blows rained down upon these important centres of Church teaching and administration, the very future of Christianity in Britain came to be questioned and charters, by which rights were granted, frequently contained the proviso, 'so long as the Christian faith should continue to exist in Britain'.

It is thus not surprising that Aethelwulf and Osburh should have found it difficult to provide the levels of education which Alfred was later to complain had been missing from his upbringing. He was perhaps setting himself high standards for the times in which he lived but it is easy to picture his determination that, while he occupied the throne, neither the levels of learning and administrative efficiency he set for himself and his staff, nor the educational achievements of his children, should be limited by lack of proper teaching. He had plans for the reorganisation of government, the reshaping of the laws of the kingdom and the restructuring of its defensive system. He appreciated that he could do little of this work of reconstruction until he had provided himself with a 'civil service' that could read and write, and he had created within his kingdom a widespread basic literacy which would help convey his legislation to his subjects. In other, more military terms, until he had created an efficient command and control network. In his *Prose Preface to Gregory's Pastoral Care*, Alfred has given us what is sometimes considered to be an overstated description of the situation that confronted him when he ascended the throne:

> Learning had declined so thoroughly in England that there were very few men on this side of the Humber who could understand their divine services in English, or even translate a single letter from Latin to English; and I suppose that there were not many beyond the Humber either. There were so few of them that I cannot recollect a single one south of the Thames when I succeeded to the kingdom.[29]

His remedy was significant and underlines his clear intention to establish political and military control of his kingdom. With meticulous care he selected 'many nobles of his own nation and boys of humbler birth and formed them into a school' attached to the royal household. This establishment, which was also attended by his young sons, was intended to provide a leavening of administrators for his government. The king did not end his educational drive here. He next made it known to his senior officials, particularly his personal representatives, the ealdormen and reeves of the shires, that they would be required to surrender their appointments if they failed to learn how to read and write. As a result, nearly all of them, many of whom had been illiterate since childhood, 'applied themselves in an amazing way how to read, preferring rather to learn this unfamiliar discipline, no matter how laboriously, than to relinquish their offices of power'. He then endeavoured to move one stage further. He announced to Werferth, Bishop of Worcester, his wish, perhaps to be achieved by the revival of cathedral schools throughout the country, that the children of all free men should be literate in their native tongue.[30] This appears to have been an overly ambitious desire, for there is no evidence to show that it was achieved.

Alfred could not set his reforming programme in hand until he lifted Danish pressure against Wessex by defeating Guthrum at *Ethandun* in 878; from that moment forward, he re-established his position on the throne, with all the authority which that implied, and regained firm control of the royal estates and finances. As soon as this had been done, one of his first actions was to provide a monastery at Athelney, where he gathered together monks of a variety of nationalities. He appointed as its first abbot John, the monk who had befriended him when he sought shelter on Sheppey after his flight from Chippenham. His next act was to establish a second monastery, as a residence for nuns, close to the east gate of Shaftesbury. Here he installed his daughter Aethelgifu as abbess. He then endowed both institutions with 'estates of land and every kind of wealth'. When these affairs had been settled, in the words of his biographer, he then asked himself 'what more he might add that would be more in keeping with his holy resolve'.

Thus it was at this moment, at the beginning of the 880s, when he was rather more than thirty years of age, that Alfred began his powerful drive to reorganise the governmental affairs of his kingdom. It was an appropriate moment. The Danes had been driven from his kingdom, albeit they were to return, and he was once again receiving 'the riches which accrued to him annually from every form of taxation and were assigned to the treasury'. Alfred gave detailed instructions as to how this wealth was to be spent. One half was to be devoted to secular affairs and he instructed that this should be divided into three equal parts and paid out, first to his fighting men[31] and to the staff of the royal household; next to his craftsmen, an international group whom he had recruited for their skill in many arts, to help with the design and construction of religious buildings, shrines and reliquaries; and lastly to foreigners of all races who came seeking his patronage. In an increasingly troubled world, this last, seemingly charitable act, would have enabled Alfred to keep abreast of the ebb and flow of events across the Channel in continental Europe.

The second half of his riches Alfred earmarked to be spent in the service of God. He divided the sum into four parts and disbursed one part 'to the poor of every race who came to him'; another part he devoted to the maintenance of the two monasteries he had founded and to the welfare of those who served within them; a third part he set aside for the maintenance of the school he had by this time established within the royal court. Alfred's final allocation, at a time when he was seeking political friends, both at home and abroad, may be judged to have been money well invested: he employed it to make grants to monasteries in Mercia and other Saxon kingdoms with a further provision, should his resources permit, for further subsidies to be paid to religious houses 'in Wales and Cornwall, Gaul, Brittany, Northumbria, and sometimes even in Ireland'.

Having thus arranged the manner in which the revenue of his kingdom should be disbursed, the king next turned his mind to his personal commitment to God, to whom he vowed to allocate, in a similar way, 'one half of his mental and bodily effort, both by day and night'. He at once encountered a difficulty and the solution which he found provides us with a glimpse of yet another aspect of his character. He had no means of assessing the amount of time he had undertaken to devote to his maker, particularly in a country where nights were long and dark and daylight was frequently obscured by rain and cloud. He therefore set his chaplains the task of making candles, 12 inches in length and uniform in weight, with the inches marked individually upon each of them. They were so measured and weighted, that when these were burnt continuously, one after another, they marked the passing of 24 hours. Alfred's candle clock proved vulnerable to the wind, however. He therefore gave instructions for a lantern to be designed to exclude draughts and 'to be constructed attractively out of wood and ox horn – for white ox horn, when shaved down finely with a blade, becomes as translucent as a glass vessel'. In this manner he provided himself with the means of fulfilling his undertaking, as 'far as his abilities and, of course, his health, would allow'.

Alfred was frequently distracted by ill health. We are told by Asser that one of his patron's greatest regrets was that in his youth, when he possessed the leisure and mental capacity to enjoy education, he had no teachers, but that when he was older, and had teachers and scribes to assist him, he was 'incessantly preoccupied by day and night with . . . all kinds of illness unknown to the physicians of this island, as well as by cares, both domestic and foreign'. The king himself, in the *Prose Preface* he provided to Boethius's *Consolation of Philosophy*,[32] confirmed the limitations placed upon his work by his poor health. King Alfred, he wrote,

> was the translator of this book: he turned it from Latin into English, as it now stands before you. Sometimes he translated word for word, sometimes sense for sense, so as to render it as clear and intelligible as he could, given the various and multifarious worldly distractions which frequently occupied him either in mind or in body.

It is not precisely clear what sickness he suffered but Asser, amid somewhat clouded narrations of spells, witchcraft and miraculous substitutions of illnesses, provides us with some indications of the symptoms Alfred endured. His problems appear to have commenced in adolescence when, concerned with his inability to contain his sexual impulses, he prayed to God to be relieved of such sins and, if necessary, to be granted some other form of physical infirmity. It was not long before he was afflicted by haemorrhoids, a problem that affected him for some years until, not unreasonably, he asked for the problem to be exchanged for something less troublesome. Again, his prayer was seemingly answered and for a while he appeared cured. Then, dramatically, during his wedding in Mercia to Aelswith, daughter of Aethelred, ealdorman of the Gaini,[33] and at the age of nineteen, he was suddenly struck down by a severe pain, in the presence of the entire gathering which numbered 'countless persons'. It signalled an infirmity that was to affect him periodically for the rest of his life; occurring at such a politically important moment and in such company, it was an event which must have caused widespread consternation, although its effects may have been exaggerated by his biographer for propaganda purposes.

A diagnosis of Alfred's sickness, compiled from the detail set down for us in the pages of Asser's *Life*, was published in 1991 in the *Journal of the Royal Society of Medicine*.[34] This proposes that Alfred suffered from Crohn's disease, a chronic and painful illness characterised by abdominal pains, fever and wasting, followed by remissions and relapses. That is to say Alfred was afflicted by it intermittently but still remained able to contend with the Viking wars, and to 'direct the governing of his kingdom, pursue all manner of hunting, give instructions to all his goldsmiths and craftsmen, direct his falconers, hawk trainers and dog keepers, as well as making his own design for treasures'. The author concludes that, despite the painful physical handicap that struck him periodically, the advent of which he must have dreaded, the king was able to live a very full life, far more in keeping with the young warrior who headed his troops up the hill at Ashdown, to cast himself against Halfdan's shield wall like a 'wild boar' and win the day for Wessex. Nor can we see in him the leader who, in 878, at the age of twenty-nine, presented himself to the acclaim of his troops at Egbert's Stone, before his epic defeat of Guthrum at *Ethandun*. Indeed we are compelled to question why Asser considered it necessary to introduce such a lengthy and uninhibited account of Alfred's physical ailments.

Several factors probably contribute to the answer. Firstly, there is the king's age at the time this passage of the biography was written. He was apparently forty-five, had barely five more years to live and, with the average life expectancy of the day, was already living on eleven years of borrowed time. In this sense, therefore, he may have been concerned at lost opportunities forced upon him by sickness and have felt the need to explain to posterity the handicap his ailments had forced upon him. There is, however, a second and more important factor which becomes clearer when we turn to the introductory paragraphs of King Alfred's will,[35] which explain the mutual arrangements he had earlier made with his brother Aethelred for the disposal of their joint and private properties. These touch upon a sequence of events intitially set in hand by their father Aethelwulf and concern three types of property with which the royal family was associated, namely: the folkland, the inheritance of which was regulated by the law of the land and which customarily passed with other property provided for the maintenance of the king, to the occupant of the throne; accumulated family holdings of chartered land, which they referred to as joint property and which in turn had been bequeathed to surviving brothers; and private property which each had personally acquired.

When his brother Aethelred succeeded Aethelberht to the throne, Alfred expressed a wish to receive his share of the 'joint property' which by custom had remained in the hands of the king. Aethelred declared his reluctance to release it. It was, however, agreed that the joint lands would remain with the survivor but that the private holdings of the deceased would be bequeathed to the latter's children according to his wishes. Thus, the joint properties and, by inference, the succession to the throne, would in due course pass to the children of the survivor. In this event, if Alfred had predeceased Aethelred, then the latter's sons would have rightfully succeeded to the throne of Wessex. In an age of such brief life expectancy, and in view of the younger brother's apparent sickliness, this may not have been thought an unlikely happening. In the event Alfred outlived Aethelred by many years and in the early 890s, when his biography was being prepared by Asser, he was probably already aware of the festering discontent that his nephew Aethelwold was to voice, after Alfred's death, about the inheritance arrangements he had negotiated. It is thus not improbable that Asser's verbose explanation of his patron's ailments was designed to defuse this potential timebomb.

Indeed, this use of Asser's *Life of King Alfred* as a vehicle for making propaganda points frequently tends to cloud the historical truth. Additionally, there is the influential fact that the king's biographer was not only a scholar but a devout Christian and a devoted servant and viewed his subject from all three standpoints. Thus, those characteristic qualities that Asser saw in Alfred, and which appealed to him, were not necessarily those which might have impressed themselves on a less subservient, more worldly observer. Added to this, there lies the fact that much of what we know about the king is derived from documents which were either basically his own work or were strongly influenced by him. Indeed, one historian has gone so far as to voice the iconoclastic view that we believe Alfred to have been a great and glorious king in part because he tells us that he was. Clearly for these reasons it is important in any study of Alfred's life and campaigns to heed these warnings.

Alfred ascended his throne at a time when the Viking sword was pointed at the throat of Wessex. The West Saxon people were close to total defeat. The kingdom inherited lacked resources and had no integrated defensive system with which to withstand the assault being pressed home against it. Throughout his reign, Alfred can surely have had few problems greater than this. His success at the key battle of *Ethandun* set England on the path to becoming the united kingdom his successors would ultimately attain. In this work we examine the development of the campaigns which first brought him to near defeat, and the reversal of fortune, engineered by his clarity of thought, which ultimately led to the total subjugation of his Danish enemy.

CHAPTER 2

'Devils of the Sea'

Either this is the beginning of greater tribulation, or else the sins of the inhabitants have called it upon them. Truly it has not happened by chance, but is a sign that it was well merited by someone. But now, you who are left, stand mindfully, fight bravely, defend the camp of God . . .

Alcuin, to the Bishop of Lindisfarne, 793[1]

In 845 the Danes penetrated the Elbe and burnt Hamburg. In March of the same year another Viking fleet, under the leadership of the notorious raider Ragnaar, entered the mouth of the Seine with 120 longships and ascended the broad, deep waters of the river as far as Paris. This Ragnaar is generally accepted to have been the legendary Ragnaar Lothbrok,[2] the hero of so many Norse sagas that the historic facts of his activities have become obscured by their poetical enhancement. His raid on Paris, deep into Frankish territory, was a notable event, as much for the pain and tribulation it brought to the wretched population as for the repercussions that were later to be felt in England and which, through an unusual sequence of events, were to bring about dramatic changes in the course of English history.

Ragnaar's journey up the Seine was tormentingly slow for the inhabitants through whose country he was passing. As he advanced he systematically plundered the fertile districts lying within his reach, helping himself to the treasures of religious houses and to the riches accumulated by the prosperous agricultural communities. Abandoned as they were by their peers and increasingly apprehensive as they heard each fresh rumour concerning the disaster remorsely moving in their direction, the local people had neither the military knowledge, the courage nor the wherewithal to organise any meaningful stand in their own defence. They fled to safety, taking with them such valuables as they could carry and, in some cases, the relics and exhumed bodies of their patron saints.[3] The remains of St Denis, as well as those of other saints interred in the monastery of his name, situated in the environs west of Paris, were among those removed in this manner but they were quickly replaced by order of Charles the Bald. The king had cause to have a healthy distrust of the efficiency and fortitude of his hastily assembled army, once the pride of the heroic Charlemagne. Their previously high standards had fallen and their failings were widely remarked upon. Leo the Wise, writing in scathing terms, commented that:

> they readily fall into confusion if attacked in flank or rear – a thing easy to accomplish, as they are utterly careless and neglect the use of pickets and the proper surveying of the countryside. They are impatient of hunger and thirst and after a few days of privation desert their standards. They are destitute of respect for their commanders, nor are their chiefs above the temptation of taking bribes.[4]

In the circumstances Charles wisely decided to retreat to the security offered by the monastery walls of St Denis, vowing his intention to defend them at all costs. The morale of his soldiery, however, was soon to be further shattered by the summary execution of those of their comrades who had suffered the misfortune of falling into Danish hands. The hanging of these unfortunates, staged with elaborate horror on an island in the river, in full view of the Franks, was designed to lower their morale yet further.[5]

Ragnaar saw no reason to delay his advance on Paris, despite the potential threat posed by Charles's force, situated on his flank. If it had been of better quality he might, perhaps, have been compelled to do so. As it was, he ignored it and hastened onwards with his fleet, to cast anchor in the city on Saturday 28 March 845. It was Easter and the streets, which under other circumstances might have been full of worshippers, were empty. Next morning, he occupied the deserted monastery of St Germain-des-Prés, on the south bank of the Seine, and from there sent envoys to the Frankish king expressing his readiness to quit the latter's kingdom if offered adequate tribute.

It was not an easy situation for either man. The treasure that the Danish freebooter had hoped to find in the city had been carried away into the surrounding countryside. If he were to send a force out to search for it, with an undefeated Frankish army to his rear, strongly entrenched in the monastery of St Denis, he would be both weakening his position and jeopardising his whole operation. Moreover, his men were beginning to show signs of a sickness that was soon to have a drastic effect on their numbers. Charles, for his part, had little confidence in either the loyalty of his nobles or the performance of his troops. Additionally, the wing of his army responsible for safeguarding the south bank of the Seine had earlier been routed and scattered. In the confusion created by this upset, he had been unable to assemble a force of sufficient size to guarantee the defeat of Ragnaar in battle and prevent him from extending his area of plunder and devastation yet further upstream.

Charles the Bald therefore agreed, at a meeting with the Danish chieftain and his commanders in the monastery of St Denis, to pay Danegeld in the sum of 7,000 pounds in silver and gold and to permit his enemy to depart unhindered and in peace. In order to accumulate this money, taxes had to be levied and collected. There was thus a delay of about two months before Ragnaar could be paid and could set forth on his journey home. By that time the Dane was more than ready to depart, for his ranks had in the meantime been gravely depleted by a virulent epidemic disease, probably dysentery, which had already begun to reveal itself within his army at the beginning of his negotiations. It was a disaster of such proportions that the population of Paris saw it as a miracle, an act of retribution by God delivered upon their enemy in answer to their prayers.[6] Whatever its magnitude, Ragnaar seemed not unduly concerned; nor, as he sailed out of the Seine estuary, was he deterred from wreaking yet more profitable havoc among the trading and fishing ports along the Frankish coastline. Had he been able to foresee the future, he might not have regarded his situation with such apparent equanimity.

At that time the supreme ruler of the Danish people was Horik, a moderate king who, apart from leading an earlier and not notably successful expedition up the Elbe, generally strove to live at peace with his continental neighbours. He was constantly frustrated in this purpose by a quarrelsome and independent-minded nobility, to many of whom he was personally related, and he became increasingly embarrassed and angered by the growing number and scale of their incursions into Frankish and German territories, where great riches lay ripe and ready to be garnered.

Despite the powerful appeal of Christianity and the inroads it was making elsewhere into international society, Horik had remained unconverted. He was perhaps reluctant to adopt the faith at a time when he was already beset at home with serious family and political problems which, after his death, were to throw Denmark into confusion and civil war. He was nevertheless sufficiently enlightened not to stand in the way of the spread of Christian belief among his people. Indeed the protection he extended to St Anskar permitted that great missionary to carry the Gospel into Sweden.[7] For these reasons it is not surprising that Horik reacted strongly when he learnt of the sickness being described in some circles as the judgement of God upon Ragnaar's followers. He immediately sent envoys to his neighbour, Louis the German, brother of Charles the Bald, offering to free all Christian captives and to restore stolen treasure, so far as it was in his power to do so. Then, possibly as much to placate the Christian God as to prevent the spread of pestilence within his own country, he instructed that all those raiders who had survived the disease they had carried back with them from Paris were to be summarily executed.

Ragnaar Lothbrok and his family did not number among these unfortunates. They either escaped to self-imposed exile or were banished and, according to an account by early Irish annalists,[8] sought shelter in the Orkney Islands; a megalithic tomb at Maes Howe suggests that they may have dwelt there for some time, but matters in their homeland were soon to change, enabling their banishment to be lifted.

In 854 King Horik and his royal household, almost without exception, perished in an uprising headed by his brother's son Guthrum. With the removal of the king's restraining hand, the Danish nobility were again free to lead their warriors on a new series of piratical adventures. Many nobles now returned to Denmark, almost certainly including the sons of Ragnaar Lothbrok, to seek others willing to invest shipping and men in the plans they had concocted during their enforced absence. Dreams of wealth became dreams of conquest when Viking leaders caught sight of the rich, green lands into which their longships had penetrated. It was but a short step from robbing a nation of its treasures to stealing and occupying its land. England, enriched with the agricultural wealth of the peoples of Wessex, Mercia, East Anglia and Northumbria, and with the Norwegian Vikings already beginning to establish a foothold in British Strathclyde, was ripe for plucking. Indeed the independence of its kingdoms rendered the country particularly vulnerable to assault. It now caught the attention of the Lothbrok family. Thus the palace revolution in Denmark in which Horik perished, its affects reaching far beyond the shores of Denmark and touching the whole of western Europe, was to prove one of those sea-changes so clearly identifiable in history. Frequently they are not immediately recognisable but, when they do occur, they break the mould of current events and plot a renewed course for the future.

Ragnaar Lothbrok was the father of several sons. Three of these, Ivar the Boneless, Halfdan and Ubba, now allied themselves in a sustained assault on

Anglo-Saxon England. Ivar the Boneless, probably the eldest of the brothers, is frequently identified with Imhar, who was active in Dublin in the mid-850s, and is described in the *Annals of Ulster* as King of the Norsemen of all Ireland and Britain. There is no evidence to associate any of Ragnaar's sons with the powerful Viking army which in 853 fought against the men of Kent and Surrey for possession of the Isle of Thanet, when many men on both sides 'fell or were drowned in the water'.[9] Likewise, there is nothing to show that they were linked with the 'great Viking army which stayed for the entire winter on the Isle of Sheppey' two years later, other than an unreliable twelfth-century source that suggests they may have been present. There is no doubt as to their participation in the year 865, for it was then, as leaders of the Great Army, that they landed in East Anglia and conducted an assault upon Anglo-Saxon England of such scale and organisation, of such discipline and intent, that it signalled a momentous change in the operational style of the Danish attacks. This was no piratical landing. Its purpose smacked of conquest and events will show that it could not have taken shape without considerable planning, organisation and local knowledge of land and sea.

Ivar the Boneless crossed from Ireland to lend his support to this invasion, accompanied by his Norwegian ally, Olaf, who concentrated his attention on his favoured theatre for expansion, namely the mainland of western Scotland and the 'Welsh' territory of Strathclyde.[10] Ivar, who probably brought reinforcements from Ireland with him, is generally recognised as having assumed command of the Great Army, a large composite body probably recruited from the Norwegian fjords, the western Baltic and the Frisian islands as much as from Denmark itself. Halfdan and Ubba were his able and ruthless lieutenants. The *Anglo-Saxon Chronicle* succinctly relates how it all began:

> In this year, Aethelbert's brother Aethelred succeeded to the kingdom of the West Saxons. And the same year a great heathen army came into England and took up winter quarters in East Anglia; and there were supplied with horses and the East Angles made peace with them.[11]

Asser, in his account of these events, modifies the last sentence by omitting any reference to the East Anglian 'peace' with the raiders and, when recording the provision of horses, he writes that '*almost* [my italics] the whole army was supplied with horses', by which we may assume he refers to the field army as opposed to the rear echelon of the Danish force, made up of the sailors, reserves and garrison troops discussed in the next chapter. Nevertheless in both versions it is clear that a very large number of animals were required by the Danes and that their availability in sufficient quantity formed an essential ingredient of an already prepared and carefully formulated military plan. It thus seems evident that when they came ashore they already knew that their need for horses would be met without great difficulty. Indeed the fact that the animals were found available with such apparent ease raises many interesting questions, not the least being what sort of horses were they and why did the English keep them in such large numbers? Did they also use them for riding to war? The answers can only be conjecture but it would not be unreasonable to suggest that these were possibly hunting animals and that, although the *fyrds* may have been able to boast a mounted element at this date, foot soldiers, frequently as a *levée en masse*, still provided the main plank of the Anglo-Saxon defence structure. It was not until a later date, as a result of Alfred's review of his armed forces following his decisive defeat of Guthrum at Edington, that he created a standing force of mounted infantry to counter Danish mobility.

The Great Army of the Vikings wintered in East Anglia in 866, staying well into the following year, draining the surrounding countryside of its food stocks. Then, with the approach of autumn, and fed, horsed and paid off by the East Angles in exchange for guarantees of peace, the Viking force marched northwards. We may imagine that they also carried a handsome share of the newly garnered summer harvest. Their purpose was to occupy York, the capital of the Anglo-Saxon kingdom of the Northumbrians and the seat of Archbishop Wulfhere, who, in the ensuing Danish occupation of the city, was to distinguish himself as a priest of questionable loyalty.

The first important English city to fall into Danish hands, York stands on the river Ouse, a tributary of the Humber, the mouth of which in turn widens to become a great estuary opening out to the North Sea. Trade to and from Europe had been carried along this river since ancient times, much of it conducted with Scandinavian countries, but archaeological evidence has yet to be found to suggest that its scale in ancient times was of any significance. This may be because the goods traded were not made of durable materials. Even so the quantities imported would probably have been of sufficient volume to attract the settlement of an international merchant community dealing in wines and other commodities from France and Germany, as well as trading to and from Baltic waters.[12] Thus, seen through Scandinavian eyes, with contacts already established in Ireland, York presented a desirable prize, a flourishing centre, located in rich farming land and situated midway between Dublin and the coastline of north-west Europe. More than this, excellent overland and river routes, established by the Romans during their centuries of occupation, led from York to west coast ports at Chester and the more northerly Ribble estuary. These and others afforded ready access to the Irish Sea and provided the means of avoiding two hazardous options: a 600-mile sea voyage around the north of Scotland, or the perils of an overland route, along the axis of the Forth and the Clyde, through bleak territories populated by troublesome Pictish tribesmen.[13]

For all these reasons the Vikings may be expected to have had useful links with Northumbria and considerable knowledge of local topography. They would undoubtedly have been aware of the strategic importance of the Humber, which provided flexibility of access, as events were later to demonstrate, not only to York but also along the River Trent to Nottingham, the capital city of Mercia. The movement of Viking longships to the Humber, therefore, and their seizure of York set them in a position from which they could dominate the north of England and allowed them access to the midlands and the heart of Mercia. The military role of Viking warships, it will thus be seen, was not solely seaborne but was closely linked to land operations, working in conjunction with the mounted element of the invasion force.

The Danish army entered York on All Saints' Day, 1 November, and a graphic description of the situation they discovered there, of which they must have been well aware and were happy to exploit, has been provided by Roger of Wendover:

> At that time a great discord had risen amongst the Northumbrians, and the people, driving out of the kingdom their legitimate king, Osbert, had raised to the crown of the kingdom a certain tyrant, Aella by name, not born of the royal line. But by the divine council, when the Danes came, Osbert and Aella made peace between them for the common good, and then, uniting copious forces, went to the city of York.[14]

Unfortunately for the people of York, this reconciliation did not take place without some considerable delay and the joint force commanded by the two men did not arrive in front of the city walls until Palm Sunday, 21 March, by which time the enemy were well reinforced and entrenched behind them. The Danes then sprang a carefully prepared trap and seemingly allowed the Northumbrians to burst in upon them. In the street fight that followed, both Osbert and Aella, together with eight ealdormen and 'a large multitude of their forces', were slain and then, these most abominable victors, the Danes, ravaging the whole province of Northumbria as far as the mouth of the Tyne, brought the country under their rule when they had defeated their enemies. Then, since the kings of the Northumbrians had been killed, a certain Egbert, of English race, acquired the kingdom under Danish power and ruled it for six years.

The appointment of Egbert, who 'ended his last day in 873', together with the treacherous collaboration of Archbishop Wulfhere, enabled the Danes speedily to tighten their grip on the kingdom and, after a year of reorganisation and preparation, freed their forces for work elsewhere. Leaving Northumbria under Quisling rule, their army, led by Ivar and his brother Ubba, now turned upon Mercia. Even at this stage it is possible to read the pattern of Danish intentions. The southern frontiers of Mercia extended southwards to the line of the River Thames. The Danish tide had begun to flow slowly but perceptibly towards Wessex.

The King of Mercia, Burghred, possessed strong links with the Wessex royal family. In 853 his appeal to Aethelwulf for help in subduing a Welsh rebellion under Roderic Mawr had not been unavailing. The King of Wessex had marched with a substantial force to the aid of his ally and had helped to bring north Wales, as far as Anglesey, back under Mercian dominion. The value which Aethelwulf attached to his links with Mercia is demonstrated by the fact that, in the year after this joint military venture, he gave his daughter's hand in marriage to Burghred. The wedding is said to have taken place at Chippenham and sealed a politically and militarily satisfactory alliance.[15] This was further consolidated in 868, when young Alfred, then twenty years of age, married Aelswith,

a wife from Mercia, of noble family, namely the daughter of Aethelred (who was known as Mucil, ealdorman of the Gaini). The woman's mother was called Eadburh, from the royal stock of the king of the Mercians . . . She was a notable woman, who remained for many years after the death of her husband a chaste widow, until her death.

Given this relationship with Wessex, it is unsurprising that, when the news was received of the fall of Nottingham, the first instinct of Burghred and his *witan* was to turn to his West Saxon kinsmen for help. Aethelred and Alfred responded promptly: 'they gathered an immense army from every part of their kingdom, went to Mercia and arrived at Nottingham, single-mindedly seeking battle'[16] and laid siege to the city. The Danes, outnumbered, very sensibly did not emerge to provide the men of Wessex the contest they were seeking: perhaps they knew the profitability of patience. The walls proved impregnable and the West Saxon army drifted away, back to their homesteads, to deal with the pressing business of crops and harvest. If neither side was visibly defeated, the ultimate victory could only be awarded to the Vikings for, in the parlance of the day and with barely a stroke being struck, they had held the battlefield. More than this, their army had now been transformed into an occupying force and it was not long before Burghred was compelled to acknowledge their supremacy.

The true significance of the withdrawal of the Wessex *fyrds* from Nottingham is tactfully ignored by Asser when compiling his *Life of King Alfred*. He simply records that 'since the Christians were unable to breach the wall, peace was established between the Mercians and the Vikings, and the two brothers, Aethelred and Alfred, returned home with their forces', with the inference that peace was mutually established before the men from Wessex departed. The author of the *Anglo-Saxon Chronicle*, on the other hand, comments, with a greater degree of frankness, that 'there was no serious engagement and the Mercians made peace with the host'. The terms of the peace are not stated. Almost certainly they would have been financial, but they would also have included other commitments, perhaps even an undertaking of neutrality. It is noteworthy that when Egbert, the Quisling, was turned out of his Northumbrian kingdom in 872, Burghred gave shelter both to him and to his fellow collaborator, Wulfhere, until they could be reinstated by the Danes.

In 874 the Mercian king, doubtless seeing no end to his difficulties, fled from his kingdom to seek sanctuary in Rome, where he was soon to die. Like so many others before him, he was buried in St Mary's Church of the Saxon School in Rome. From all this, we can conclude that, after the abortive attack on Nottingham in 868, Burghred lost both the political and the military initiative. For whatever reason, history is clear that from this moment onwards he did little to obstruct the Danes and within a few months appears to have been completely subject to their domination.[17] The alliance of Wessex and Mercia thus missed a vital military opportunity, and in the process came close to ceding total victory to the enemy. Neither were the East Angles blameless in this, for they appear to have followed a policy of neutrality, possibly dictated by the peace terms purchased from Ivar and his brothers when the Great Army came ashore in 865. As it turned out, their inactivity availed them little, for as a result of it the Danish forces were now free to return to Northumbria, where unrest after their occupation had continued to simmer never far from the surface, and to set in hand arrangements for the next, third, phase of their conquest – the seizure of East Anglia itself.

In modern terms East Anglia comprises Suffolk, Norfolk, Cambridgeshire and the Isle of Ely. In Alfred's time the historic kingdom was divided from Mercia in the west by the River Cam and from the forests of Essex in the south by the Stour. The country generally is low-lying and flat, the southern area containing much wild heathland. It is a place of lonely beaches, muddy estuaries, frequently stark beauty but equally charming diversity. In the winter, strong, bitingly cold, easterly winds blow straight off the sea, penetrating deep across the hinterland, freezing the fens which, even today, after so much land has been recovered, still exist in large areas. In the days of the Viking wars the fens spread much wider, extending westwards from the Wash nearly as far as Lincoln, and southwards to Cambridge. It was here that the great English hero Hereward the Wake was to defy the Normans two centuries later. Felix, in his *Life of St Guthlac*, vividly describes the area as:

> a most dismal fen of immense size, which begins at the banks of the River Granta not far from the camp which is called Cambridge and stretches from the south as far north as the sea. It is a very long tract, now consisting of marshes, now of bogs, sometimes of black waters overhung by fog, sometimes studded with wooded islands and traversed by the winding of tortuous streams.[18]

East of the fens lies Breckland, an area of rich farming land which in Anglo-Saxon times was much sought-after for cultivation, for its open terrain and good quality, well-drained soil meant that it required little work to prepare it for the plough. The capital of Breckland, and indeed of East Anglia, was Thetford, a lively centre with palaces and many religious houses. Thetford is situated where the Little Ouse, then navigable at that point, crosses the Icknield Way on its passage to join the Great Ouse, of which the Cam, from which Cambridge takes its name, was a companion tributary.

The Icknield Way runs northwards from Thetford, along its extension, Peddar's Way, until it reaches its terminus at Holme-next-the-Sea, at the southern entrance to the mouth of the Wash. In the opposite direction it travels south-westerly from Thetford, skirting the fens east of Cambridge, thence through the rich grain-producing areas of Cambridgeshire and Bedfordshire, along the western slopes of the Chilterns, until it reaches the crossing-places on the River Thames at Goring, Moulsford and Wallingford. Here, across the river, it connects with a system of ridgeway paths that not only penetrate deeply into the west country but also link, in an easterly direction, with the Pilgrim's Way, the cathedral city of Canterbury and, at that time, the sheltered waters of the Wantsum Channel. The strategic value of Thetford is at once apparent.

Cambridge had developed during the Roman period as a town of considerable military and logistical importance. The Roman general staff had quickly come to recognise it as a trading port of some consequence, not only because of its proximity to Ermine Street, the trunk road connecting London with their garrison in York, but also because of the administrative benefits it brought to their supply problems by its location on the navigable waters of the Cam, far inland from the sea, and thus, in terms of manpower, reducing the need for costly overland haulage. There were two other interconnecting factors which added to its reputation as a military base. First, the town was located on a site rarely found in fen country, where firm ground led down to the river from both banks and provided the best practicable crossing place for many miles. Secondly, the strategic value of the ford was enhanced by the fact that the line of the river defined the frontier between the kingdoms of the East Angles and the Mercians, as previously it had between the East and Middle Angles. Its possession thus carried with it not only simple trading benefits but also military control of the frontier and of movement along the Roman trunk road which in places had been constructed to overlay the Icknield Way. With its command of riverine and land communications, the possession of Cambridge was a prime military asset in the events unfolding.

The Danes launched their attack against East Anglia in the autumn of 869, with an army commanded, it is generally agreed, by Ivar the Boneless, who appears to have crossed over from Dublin especially for the purpose. He was probably, but by no means certainly, supported by his younger brother Ubba. A considerable amount of material has been written about the fighting which then ensued and the martyrdom of Edmund, the East Anglian king. A comprehensive examination of these sources and documents, with a judgement on some of the conclusions reached, was made in 1969 by the late Professor Dorothy Whitelock in a paper entitled 'Fact and Fiction in the Legend of St Edmund'.[19] The oldest source, written some time before 890, is the *Anglo-Saxon Chronicle* and, as ever, it is frustratingly brief in its presentation of the facts:

In this year the raiding party rode across Mercia into East Anglia, and took up winter quarters at Thetford. And that winter King Edmund fought against them; and the Danes had the victory and killed the king, and conquered all the land.[20]

The brevity of the chronicler conceals the military competence of the Danish commanders who, by this single operation, had achieved three valuable objectives: they had seized control of the northern Icknield Way; provided themselves with waterborne and trackway access to the Wash, to link with their support shipping; and had positioned themselves so that, after the subjugation of East Anglia, the way was open for them to advance along the Icknield Way to the completion of their final task – the conquest of Wessex.

There is some disagreement between the various annalists as to the tactics employed by the Danes in their assault upon East Anglia. The author of the *Anglo-Saxon Chronicle* records that 'the raiding party rode across Mercia'. Another account, provided by Abbo of Fleury, a continental scholar who spent some years at Ramsey Abbey, relates that Ivar left Ubba in Northumberland and then himself sailed down the east coast with a fleet, 'coming secretly to a city, which they took by surprise and burnt, slaughtering the inhabitants'. If we accept the proposition that the mounted field army and the fleet customarily worked in closely timed concert during operations of this nature, then there is no reason why both versions should not be acceptable, with one brother commanding the seaborne force and the other the mounted field army. This would have led to a neat operation based upon many of the best principles of war.

The Vikings opened their campaign against East Anglia by advancing southwards from York to Peterborough, presumably taking full advantage of the mobility offered by Ermine Street. They showed little compassion for the inhabitants they found in their path, least of all the Church, whose clergy and institutions they treated ruthlessly.

[They] destroyed all the monasteries they came to. In this same time they came to Peterborough, burnt and destroyed it, killed the abbot and the monks and all they found there, and brought it to pass that it became nought that had been mighty.[21]

There was, according to the local *Crowland Chronicle*, only one survivor, a young boy 'fair in form and face', who was seized by a Danish chief but contrived to escape.

The route taken by the field army from Peterborough to Thetford is uncertain. The commander might perhaps have been attracted by the thought of skirting the

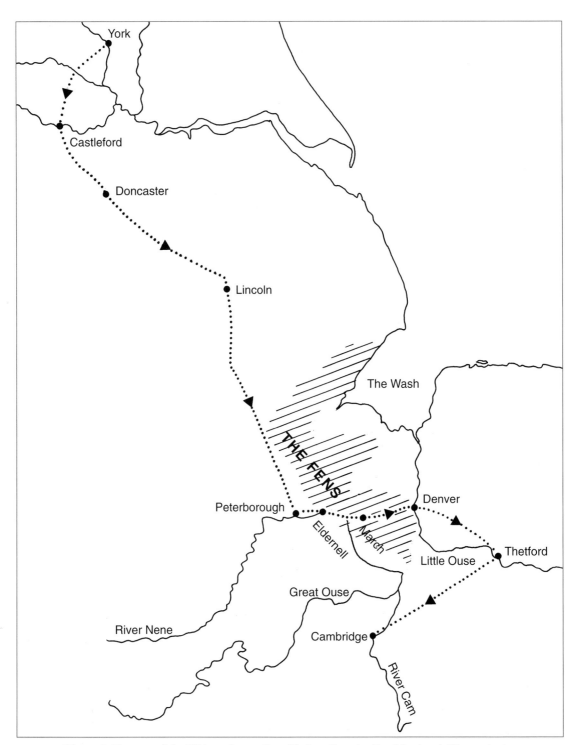

The probable route of the Viking advance from York to East Anglia. (Aardvark Illustration)

fenlands, in which the East Anglians would surely have had a tactical advantage if circumstances had allowed them to muster their army, and thence marching on to Cambridge where they would have discovered treasure in plenty. This move would have given them control of the ford over the Cam, thus discouraging any prospect of Mercian interference, and would simultaneously have placed them in a position, adjoining the Icknield Way, from whence they could advance to Thetford. Equally beneficial, their appearance on King Edmund's western frontier would have distracted his attention from his northern coastline, where the arrival of Ivar's longships was imminent.

The military probability must surely be that the mounted field force opted to ride eastwards along the causeway road constructed by the Roman army more than five hundred years earlier, the course of which is still visible. It was described by Dugdale in 1772 as 'a long causey made of gravel of about three feet in thickness, and 60 feet broad which extendeth itself from Denver over the Great Wash to Charke; thence to March, Plantwater and Eldernell, and so to Peterborough, in length about 24 miles'. This option would have brought them to the Great Ouse, close to its confluence with the Little Ouse and some 20 miles north of Thetford. Here they would have been in a position to link with their seaborne contingent which, making its way down the North Sea coast in late autumn, would without doubt have been attracted by the calmer waters of the Wash and the sheltered anchorage offered, in its most southerly corner, by the estuary of the Great Ouse. Here the whole force could have assembled before its final move to Thetford where, after the sacking of the town, they planned to spend the winter.[22]

Once again, there is a difference of opinion between various annalists as to what happened next, some reporting that a battle now took place between the East Anglians and the invading Danes and others stating that the king had not succeeded in mustering his army before he was seized and brought to Ivar. Both Asser and the author of the *Anglo-Saxon Chronicle* write ambiguously, the bishop telling us that 'Edmund had fiercely fought against that army . . . but, alas, he was killed there by a large number of his men', and the latter recounting simply that the king had 'fought against them and the Danes had the victory'. Abbo, writing some 116 years after these events had been enacted, states with clarity that Edmund had found it impossible to muster an army but gives no reason for his inability to do so. The East Anglian army would have been largely of peasant origin and, if the king had been caught unawares, as he could easily have been, it is likely that he was defeated by the time required to summon his troops together.

Abbo drew his information from the recollections of the elderly Archbishop Duncan, whom he met during his stay at Ramsey. The archbishop's account had, in its turn, been garnered in his youth from an old man who claimed to have been armour-bearer to Edmund on the day of his martyrdom.

The possibility of factual error, and the clouding of detail, will doubtless have increased in the telling but the general burden of the armour-bearer's tale need not be rejected. Similarly, Geoffery Gaimar, writing in the mid-twelfth century, describes a battle lost by Edmund, after which he was forced to flee and seek refuge in a castle. It is of course possible that the king or his followers organised some spontaneous guerrilla-style resistance to the invaders, for the earlier annalists speak of 'fighting' rather than a 'battle'. It may also be that such resistance as took place was fought out in the towns and villages. Equally, as has been said, it is conceivable that events moved so speedily that Edmund was foiled from mustering his army. It would be nice to be specific on this point but it is in any event academic, for resistance collapsed in front of the Danish assault and of this there is no doubt.

According to Abbo, Ivar now sent a messenger to Edmund, who found him in his hall. The Dane demanded that the East Anglian monarch should share with him his treasures and, more significantly, that he should agree to continue to exercise his powers as king under Danish rule. This was clearly no raid by a freebooting army. Edmund is said to have replied that he was a follower of Christ and would refrain from staining his hands with blood. He added, rather illogically perhaps, that he would only submit if Ivar would adopt the Christian faith. The Viking herald then left to deliver this response to his commander.

Edmund was in a dilemma and sought the advice of one of his bishops, Humbert, who could see only two possible courses of action, surrender or flight. Neither course appealed to the king, who was conscious that many of his subjects had already been killed in the fighting which had taken place and he had no desire to give the impression to his countrymen that he had abandoned them. There are several traditional versions of what happened next. In one, the king is said to have taken refuge in a castle from which he was forced to break cover by the Danish search for him. In another, it is fancifully related that he was found hiding under a bridge at Hoxne, 3 miles east of Diss, a Norfolk village which claims a close association with these events. His hiding-place was revealed by a pair of lovers who had seen the glint of his golden spurs. Geoffery Gaimar's account of his capture is less picturesque. He relates that Edmund is purported to have been challenged by a Viking soldier, who asked him if he knew the king's whereabouts.

Unwilling to lie, he replied: 'When I was in flight, Edmund was there and I with him; when I turned to flee, he turned also.' Unsurprisingly, he was at once recognised and seized. Abbo's version, despite his verbosity as an annalist, has yet again the ring of truth. He relates that Ivar's herald, upon instruction, returned to the hall where Edmund and he had conducted their original meeting. There, the East Anglian king was seized, bound in chains and beaten, before being dragged naked into the presence of his enemy and tied to a tree. Then, his enemy mocking his repeated calls upon Christ, he was tortured, the Danish soldiery using him for target practice until 'he bristled with arrows like a hedgehog'.

Some of the treasure from the Cuerdale Viking hoard, unearthed on the banks of the River Ribble in about 1840. (British Museum)

Ultimately, Ivar ordered him to be decapitated and, leaving the king's body where it lay, carried away the head and concealed it in a bramble thicket in Hellesdon Wood. The date was 20 November 870.[23]

After King Edmund's death, Ivar felt he could safely return to York and handed over command of operations in East Anglia to one of his younger brothers, Halfdan. *The Annals of Ulster* record that within a few months he was fighting alongside his Norwegian ally, Olaf, King of Dublin, in the storming of the 'Welsh' stronghold at Dumbarton.[24] It is unclear from the narrative whether he took any part of his army with him, although it must be likely that he returned with the Irish contingent which had accompanied him southwards in the first instance. We can only speculate on his reasons for leaving East Anglia at this juncture. He had demonstrated by his presence that the campaign to overthrow Edmund ranked high in his priorities. The reason for this is not difficult to see. The East Anglian coastline, held in Danish possession, not only offered all-weather shelter from the North Sea to longships plying northwards from the Thames estuary and the strategically important Wantsum Channel, but also, as the Romans had discovered before them, led to the mouths of the great riverways that penetrated deep into the heart of the hinterland and thus provided a key to the occupation of northern England.

Halfdan wintered in Thetford and during the following year systematically plundered the towns of eastern England, including Ely, Ramsey and Crowland, while simultaneously preparing for the fourth and final stage of the family war of conquest. In late December 870 he was ready to break camp. As was apparently customary, he planned to conceal his initiative behind the relaxed distractions of the religious festivals being celebrated by his opponents. He arrived with his army at Reading, just after the turn of the year, in midwinter.

The assault on Wessex had begun.

CHAPTER 3
The Opposing Forces

This, then, is a king's materials and his tools for ruling with, that he have his land fully manned. He must have men who pray, and soldiers and workmen. Lo, thou knowest that without these tools no king can reveal his power; also, this is his material, which he must have for those tools, sustenance for those three orders; and their sustenance consists in land to live on, and gifts, and weapons and food, and ale and clothes . . .

Alfred the Great[1]

The eruption of the Danish Vikings into Europe began at the end of the eighth century. At an early stage the brunt of their attacks fell upon Ireland, pursuing a route from Norway to the Faroes, the Orkneys and thence to the Western Isles. Simultaneously, occasional raiding parties probed the shorelines on both sides of the English Channel, in particular the estuaries of the great rivers of Frisia, France and England.

In the kingdom of the Franks, their ruler, the heroic Charlemagne, the expansion of whose empire was indirectly responsible for these events by the territorial pressures it induced, devised a military response which was typically vigorous and imaginative. He improved the quality of his fleet and set in place a system of widely deployed fortifications, linked by a chain of beacons, which gave him early warning of an impending attack and allowed time in which to prepare for it. His example was observed unenthusiastically by other European leaders and followed indifferently.

It is not our concern here to discuss in detail the scale of Viking expansion; it is sufficient to say that it was considerable and provided one of the most remarkable and exciting episodes in history, rich in adventure. On the eastern frontiers of Europe, they pushed southwards along the line of the great Russian rivers which feed the Baltic, down to Novgorod and Kiev and thence, by portage, to Byzantium, along the great waterways which carve their path to the Caspian Sea.

In the north-west, Erik the Red, outlawed for manslaughter from his native Jaeder in south-west Norway, fled to seek refuge in Iceland. Banished from there for yet more killings in about 981, he discovered Greenland, thus providing a stepping-stone that would lead ultimately to the discovery of North America. Other marauding longships penetrated the Mediterranean Sea, negotiating their way as far as Italy, and profitably visiting Moorish Spain, southern France and the western coastline of North Africa.

If evidence were required of the rapid progress and the scale of the effort made by the Vikings during this era, it is to be found in the fact that, in the fearful years 830–895, the majority of the damaging attacks mounted against England and its coastline were mounted not from Scandinavia but from bases in France and Frisia and, to a lesser degree, from Ireland.

The Vikings were a formidable foe. Their strength lay not solely in their courage, their relentless pursuit of their aims and their tough seamanship but in their professionalism. They were sailors of outstanding skill and their ships, the longships or dragonships with which they harried England and the continent, not only benefited from a considerable accumulation of military experience but were the product of great technical achievement. They were constructed both for sailing and for rowing. They were formidable in appearance and were designed to strike terror into the hearts of their victims. Their high sterns ended in a dragon's or a serpent's head; their prows were beaked and crested like a bird. Their square sails were gaily striped in bright colours and strengthened by a criss-crossed network of ropes which displayed a distinctive diamond-shaped pattern on the fabric.

A well-preserved example of a typical Viking vessel of the ninth century was discovered in a burial mound at Gokstad in 1880. It had survived because it had become embedded in thick clay. It measured 76 feet 6 inches long and 17 feet 6 inches in the beam, with an amidships depth of 6 feet 5 inches. It is estimated to have drawn 3 feet in the water, which would have been ideal for the river operations in which the Vikings specialised, but more than this, it also had a deep water requirement. To cope with this, it needed to be fitted with a strong keel, capable of taking the buffeting of high seas. The keel for this purpose, which weighed about 20 tons, had to be carved from a single length of oak to provide the necessary strength. This important requirement naturally limited the length of the ship and restricted its troop-carrying ability. The deck of the vessel, on the other hand, was made of pine and consisted of boards which rested loosely on crossbeams. An area was thus provided for storage below the deck and for the accumulation and disposal of bilge water.

The Gokstad ship as it was found in 1880. (Universitetet I Oslo)

The Gokstad ship reconstructed. (Universitetet I Oslo)

The attention paid to administration by the Vikings during the fitting-out of their war vessels is noteworthy. Each longship was provided with a capacious tent, the frames of which were made of ash wood. Several examples of frames have been recovered from a variety of archaeological sites. Each tent could be erected either on land or on the deck of the vessel when at sea. The largest frame discovered measured 17 feet 3 inches long, 14 feet 7 inches broad and 11 feet 5 inches high. Although the height of the excavated tents varied, the area of floor space appears generally to have remained constant, suggesting that each was designed to accommodate about twenty men. In addition to this facility, ships were equipped with huge bronze cauldrons and other cooking equipment, much of it not dissimilar to the items discovered in the galley of the Tudor warship *Mary Rose*. Food required for lengthy voyages was preserved in salt and ice.

Sea battles in this period of history were almost invariably fought inshore and rarely on the high seas. The action generally took the shape of a close-range exchange of missiles, customarily arrows, javelins and stones, followed, at a selected moment, by the boarding of enemy ships and fierce hand-to-hand fighting. At this stage, the soldiers, each with his battle-axe or broadsword, were the principal weapon. In order to stabilise the 'battlefield', it was the custom for vessels to be roped together in one or more lines depending upon the numbers involved. Normally such engagements were set-piece actions. Chance encounters, naturally, took a variety of different shapes. Whatever the occasion, all men aboard, oarsmen or otherwise, took part in the fighting, as was indicated by Aethelweard in his chronicle for 885:

> And in the same year . . . King Alfred sent a fleet to East Anglia and, as soon as they arrived, ships sixteen in number met them at the mouth of the Stour. They were cleared by force of arms and the officers put to the sword. The rest of the pirate fleet came on its course in their way. They plied their oars and then dropped their rowing gear. The clashing weapons shone in the sea.[2]

When at rest or approaching a beach on a raiding mission, shields were suspended along their sides, their various colours perhaps identifying with the watches aboard. In the case of the Gokstad longship they were painted alternately black and yellow. They would thus have been immediately accessible to the landing parties as their ships bellied ashore. When at sea, the shields were carried inboard. There were sixteen oarholes on either side, suggesting a total of thirty-two oarsmen. When the oars were not in use and the ship was under sail, they were affixed to a T-shaped frame amidships. Under sail the vessels were reputed to be able to achieve maximum speeds of 10 to 11 knots and to travel some 150 miles a day. They had a high rating for seaworthiness. In 1893 an exact replica of the Gokstad ship was sailed across the North Atlantic by Captain Magnus Andersen and, despite encountering very heavy seas, he completed the journey between Norway and Newfoundland in a remarkable twenty-seven days.

The numbers of men carried by a typical Viking longship has been the subject of much debate. One source has expressed the view that it would have been unlikely that 'raiding ships ever carried more than 32–35 men and the majority of them would have carried less'.[3] It is difficult to justify this statement. Indeed, it is not easy to think of any reasons why Viking raiding parties would have put to sea on any operational mission with their warships only partially manned. The inevitable outcome would have been twofold: the speed of the fleet would have been restricted to the speed of the slowest vessel and, upon landing, the security of the beached vessels and/or the effectiveness of the landing party would have been compromised by the reduced number of troops.

The eminent Dorothy Whitelock, discussing the finds on the Gokstad longship,[4] reported sixty-four shields, '32 on each side and . . . hung in such a way that each partly overlapped its neighbour, and each pair corresponded to one oarhole'. A total of sixty-four shields implies the same number of men but this would have meant a very crowded ship. An alternative answer is suggested by the capacity of the tent which, it will be recalled, provided space for some twenty men. This suggests a minimum crew of forty, divided into two watches, with one group rowing and the other resting but providing, when necessary, a full complement of thirty-two oarsmen. When examined, however, neither of these suggested solutions can be considered to provide a final answer, for much would have depended upon the duration of the voyage, its operational purpose and the quantities of stores to be embarked. It was not unknown, for example, for Vikings to bring horses with them.[5]

The importance of a full complement of oarsmen, in order to maintain headway against foul winds and to permit manoeuvres, is demonstrated by the account of a raid which occurred in 896.[6] In this instance, some longships which had sailed south from East Anglia were intercepted and brought to combat in a river estuary on the south coast of Wessex by ships of Alfred's then newly founded navy. A fierce action ensued in which the fleets of both sides became grounded on the ebb tide. The opposing sides then came to grips, fighting hand-to-hand in the accumulated silt of the river bed. The Viking longships, being stranded nearer the sea, were the first to benefit from the incoming tide and thus made good their escape. Upon entering the Channel, however, and steering towards East Anglia, they encountered a strong headwind and, owing to the many casualties they had sustained, 'they could not row past Sussex'. As a result 'the sea cast two ships upon the land, and the men were brought to Winchester to the king'. Here the unfortunate individuals were summarily hanged, paying a heavy penalty for their enforced lack of oarsmen.

Fighting sailors have always demanded three things of their ships: speed, manoeuvrability and commanding firepower. When Alfred came, in later years, to create his navy, it was his search for at least some of these qualities which persuaded him to build many of his warships of superior size to those of his opponents. He recognised that he held an advantage because he was constructing his ships primarily for defensive purposes and they would thus be fighting inshore in home waters. For this reason the king found it possible to avoid the limitations in ship size imposed by the demands of the 'one-piece' keel necessary for deep-water sailing. His vessels were thus able to carry a larger complement of fighting men than those of his opponents, with a proportionate enhancement of firepower, although admittedly at the cost of speed and some manoeuvrability.

As a general principle, it is safe to assume that a Viking longship customarily put to sea with the full number of oarsmen and soldiery for which it was designed, a reasonable and logical total lying somewhere between forty and sixty men. Indeed there is evidence that in medieval times, ship's levies were summoned on a scale of three men for each oar: one to row, one to protect the oarsman and one to fight. When we come to glance at Danish shore tactics, we shall see how appropriately these proportions would have fitted the various divisions of their land forces.

The Vikings took great pride in the quality of their weaponry and the protective clothing they wore in battle. Each man was expected to equip himself with a minimum scale of arms. This was laid down by law and was subject to inspection annually by an official of the royal court. Basically, it comprised a sword or axe, spear, shield and a helmet. In the early Viking period helmets, in the same manner as protective mail and armour, were probably worn only by the wealthy. There were also occasions when both sword and axe were carried, as Florence of Worcester records.[7] He describes vividly how Earl Godwin, in the year 1040,

gave to the king for his friendship a skilfully made galley, having a gilded prow, and furnished with the best tackle, handsomely equipped with suitable weapons and 80 picked soldiers, each of whom had on his arms two gold armlets, weighing 16 ounces, wore a triple mail-shirt, a partly gilded helmet on his head, and had a sword with a gilded hilt fastened around his loins, and a Danish battle-axe rimmed with gold and silver hanging from his left shoulder, and in his left hand a shield, whose boss and studs were gilded, and in his right hand a spear.

An additional item of armament, but rarely specified, was a bow, with two or three dozen arrows in total, carried in cylindrical quivers. Aboard ship, this weaponry was required on a scale of one to each rowing bench, probably for the use of the man whose duty it was to give protection to the oarsmen when engaged in action.

The Sutton Hoo ship burial, showing the outline of a seventh-century vessel, built with overlapping planks drawn up to stem and stern in the same boat-building tradition as the later Viking ships. (British Museum)

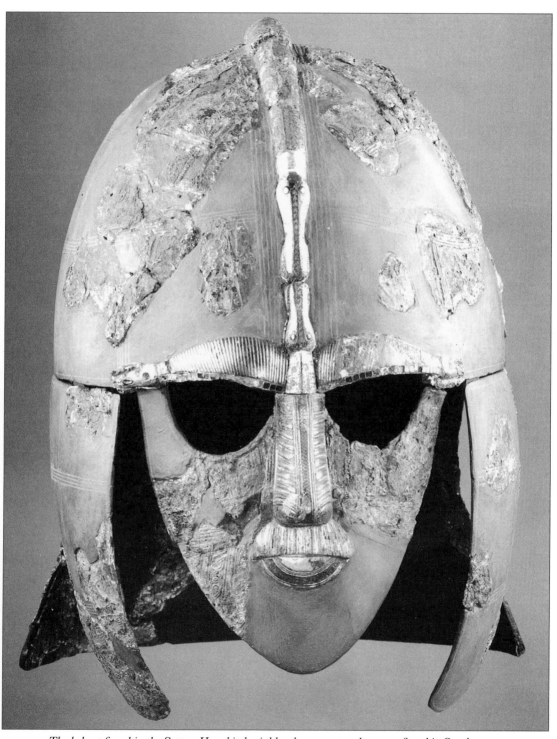

The helmet found in the Sutton Hoo ship burial has been compared to some found in Sweden, evidence of contact between England and Scandinavia before the Viking raids. (British Museum)

The Viking warrior paid close attention to the quality of his weaponry. His main means of defence was his shield, the heavy boss of which was weighted so as to be used offensively in close-quarter combat. His most important weapon was his sword, to which he tended to award a descriptive nickname, personifying its power in battle. Poems about its might and the courage of its possessor figured frequently in the nightly boasting around the camp fire and in sagas about the heroic conflicts from which they had both emerged with glory. The blade, usually double-edged and about 3 feet long, was carefully structured and balanced so that, if need be, it could be wielded with one hand only.

The spears were of two types, throwing and thrusting. Many of these, as was the case with those excavated at Lancaster in 1961 and from Esthwaite Lake in 1976,[8] were ornately designed, as much as to assist recognition and recovery from the battlefield by their rightful owner, as for any other reason. Indeed, possession of the battlefield after an engagement, as the great Hannibal appreciated after Cannae, in 216 BC,[9] was almost as desirable as victory itself, for upon it lay the debris of war, an invaluable harvest waiting to be collected by the contestant who held the ground.

In its simplest form, the general tactic of a Viking raiding party was to make the fullest use of inland waterways, either sailing, rowing or manhandling their ships upstream until they had reached their chosen objective. Almost invariably the invaders appeared to possess a vast accumulated knowledge of the topography of the area they were raiding, together with its background politics. They also had a full knowledge of existing ancient trackways, Roman roads and fortifications.[10] By this means, they enhanced their mobility and, when confronted by a stout resistance, knew of a readily accessible stronghold in which to seek refuge.

Viking tactics were systematic and largely unchanging. Either on landing or on reaching their selected objective ashore, they would dispatch foraging patrols to plunder foodstuffs from neighbouring farms and villages. At the same time they would acquire horses to provide their patrols with an increased operational range. Like the Anglo-Saxons, the Vikings did not possess organised cavalry but rather employed the animals they acquired in this albeit random manner to mount their infantry. The creation of this mounted force at a stroke provided their fighting force with three important military assets: mobility, speed of action and the ability to achieve surprise. The weakness of the plan lay in the fact that the number of infantry they could mount on horseback was limited by the total of animals available locally, initially within the range of foot-patrols from the raiders' beachhead area. The Vikings, from what we know of their general preparedness on such occasions, would almost certainly have been aware of the rough total of mounts available to them. It has been mooted that Britons, and subsequently the Saxons, had horses in plenty and that both races were 'horsey' people.[11] Certain it is that the Domesday Book in 1086 recorded a total of three thousand horses of all kinds in eastern England, in the counties of Essex, Suffolk and Norfolk.

It is evident that horses, so essential to the success of the overall operational plan but so haphazardly acquired, would have been greatly valued. They were therefore kept distant from the fighting. They were too important an asset to be risked in open combat if this could be avoided. In a much-quoted example of this, Brithnoth, in the ancient poem exalting his heroism at the battle of Maldon and allegedly commissioned by his wife,[12] 'bade each warrior leave his horse, drive it afar and trust to his hands'. But the Vikings frequently made use of their horses in a dual fashion for, whenever necessary, they also employed them as pack animals to transport foraged food and to remove plunder from the churches, abbeys, palaces, towns and villages they looted with such devastating effect.

It is easy to imagine that the need for Viking patrols to search for a large number of animals would have compromised the principles of speed and surprise that they were seeking to achieve. It is more than probable therefore that, initially at least, they would have been satisfied with the seizure of only a few hundred horses. For this reason it has been suggested that the size of Viking 'armies' landing in England has been greatly overstated. Professor Gwyn Jones, for example, has remarked that they 'should be numbered in hundreds, not thousands',[13] and that even the Great Army of 892 would hardly have exceeded a thousand men in total. He has speculated that 300 or 400 men would have comprised a very substantial Viking force and adds that medieval exaggerations in recording strengths of this nature are frequently to be found, 'sometimes to the degree of ten, thirty or even fifty fold'. He argues that ninth-century armies were recruited from limited manpower and lacked sufficient administrative backing to maintain large numbers in the field.

Likewise, P.H. Sawyer, discussing the density of Danish settlement in England, expresses a similar view. He argues that, 'apart from the difficulty of obtaining enough horses' for larger armies, there would also have been the difficulty of feeding them in winter and while on the march.[14] He then adds, controversially, that these and other practical problems, 'such as feeding and controlling a large number of men both in camp and on campaigns, make it very unlikely that the Danish armies numbered more than a few hundred men at the very most'. He will find few soldiers of experience willing to agree with such a sweeping judgement.

It is, moreover, difficult to reconcile his statement with the known fact that, some 800 years earlier, the Roman invasion force under Aulus Plautius that landed in Kent numbered some 45,000 men[15] and was accompanied by a potential 14,000 animals. They overran south-east Britain within a few weeks, without any apparent difficulties in either command or supply.[16]

How strong, then, might the Danish armies have been? The author of the *Anglo-Saxon Chronicle*, with other annalists, when giving an indication of the size of the Danish force concerned in any particular incident, generally dealt in rounded figures, whether reporting casualties, battlefield strengths or numbers on disembarkation. At the battle of Ashdown in 871, for example, 'many thousands' of Halfdan's men were said to have been slaughtered. Again, the highly educated Asser, albeit Alfred's propagandist, writing about the military situation after the battle of Wilton, commented that it was impossible to estimate 'how many thousands of Vikings had been killed'. Likewise, in 894 it is recorded that 'many hundreds' of Vikings were slain during an encounter with the *burh* garrison at Chichester.

In a similar manner, in the case of armies landing from overseas, the strength of the enemy is almost invariably recorded in terms of the total of ships involved. In 851, 350 ships 'came into the mouth of the Thames'. In 877, 120 ships on their way to reinforce Guthrum at Exeter were lost at sea. In 892 'a great Viking army came up the estuary of the Lympne with 250 ships', a total which other sources variously record as 200 or 350. This sort of variation is not unusual. Any modern-day intelligence officer will confirm that these types of statistic are the first casualties in war. It would be remarkable, to quote a particular example, if the German sentry who first sighted the Allied invasion of Normandy, at dawn on 6 June 1944, had been able, as he reached for the telephone, to put a precise figure to the number of craft emerging from the lifting sea-mist. We may be sure, however, that the first figure he mentioned, probably exaggerated and almost certainly inaccurate, would be the one etched in the memory of the recipient on the other end of the line and recorded by him in his war diary. The fact that these totals vary greatly is therefore something to be accepted. On the other hand, it is notable that when small, easily assessed raiding parties are concerned, numbers of vessels sighted are much more accurately reported, suggesting that despite a human trait for exaggeration, the practice of rounding up totals was simply employed to imply a presence of some considerable size.[17]

There are other considerations which provide guidelines to the strength of Danish raiding parties. As their visits became progressively more frequent and the English more alert, the raiders may be expected to have assumed that their approach to the coastline had been observed by look-outs on the shore, that their presence was consequently known and their movements followed. For this reason any force penetrating inland would need to have been of sufficient size to allow a group to be detached from the main body to act as a garrison for a beachhead, either at their place of disembarkation or at a selected point on the river line they were following, or perhaps even at both these places, with the prime purpose of safeguarding their shipping. The size of this base and the strength of its garrison would have depended upon a number of factors, not least being the number of boats to be safeguarded. The Gokstad longship measured 17 feet 6 inches in the beam; allowing for some 3 feet between vessels drawn up on the beach or river bank, this would have posed a width of some 7 yards per boat, or, in the case of fifty boats, a total distance of some 350 yards to be guarded. In view of the large number of ships recorded by some chroniclers, it is at once obvious that, even if their estimates were only 50 per cent accurate, many of their beachhead strongholds would have been of substantial size and would have required a considerable number of men to guard them.

Thus the necessity for such security measures would have been given prime consideration by the Vikings and would almost invariably have been premeditated. The sites they selected were broadly either administrative centres or royal palaces and *burhs*. A favourite tactic, once they had forced their way upstream, was to construct a defensive base either on an island or at the confluence of a tributary with the main stream. In this manner they provided themselves with a fortified base, guarded by natural deep water obstacles on two flanks and requiring, for completion, simply the construction of a stockaded wall on the open side. Asser portrays one such base in his description of the defensive position constructed by the Danes at Reading, prior to the battle of Ashdown in 871.[18] He tells how the enemy 'built themselves a rampart between the two Rivers Thames and Kennet, on the right-hand side of the same royal estate'. Its strength was such that Aethelred of Wessex, accompanied by his brother Alfred, found himself unable to make any headway when they assailed its walls with their combined divisions and was forced to pull back in considerable disorder when their opponents 'like wolves . . . burst out of all the gates and joined battle with all their might', thus showing themselves skilled in the art of using a fortification in an offensive role. They gave further confirmation of this in the year 867 when they invaded Northumbria and occupied York. When the Northumbrians breached the wall and poured through in an effort to retake their city, the Danes were waiting for them; they at once counter-attacked and made 'an immense slaughter' of their enemy.

Another instance of their skill in siege warfare occurred in the following year when the Danish army moved south from York to occupy Nottingham. The Mercian king, Burghred, sent a call for help to his West Saxon allies and Aethelred and Alfred, according to Asser, 'having gathered an immense army from every part of their kingdom', marched to his assistance. Asser's wording suggests that the West Saxons saw this as an opportunity to undertake a decisive joint operation against their mutual enemy and the scribe's description of the size of the combined Saxon/Mercian army which then took the field provides a deafening response to those historians who believe that the enemy they confronted numbered no more than a few hundred men. Despite their strength, the efforts of the allies were nevertheless unavailing for, having failed to breach the walls or to persuade their defenders to surrender, the Saxon host folded its tents and returned home, leaving their enemy *in situ* and the Mercians to make such peace as they were able.

Thus Alfred, at the age of eighteen, would have learnt two important military lessons, which the Danes appear already to have mastered, for they were content to remain behind the walls of their stronghold until the allied army had dispersed. First, peasant armies make reluctant soldiers unless they feel their homesteads threatened and, secondly, the problems of feeding and maintaining a host outweigh those of calling it together.

It has already been suggested that procurement of supplies of food for both animals and men would have presented both the West Saxon and the Danes with many administrative problems. A minimum daily calorific ration to sustain 1,000 men has been roughly estimated as 'two tons of unmilled flour [4 lb per man] and 1,000 gallons of fresh water'.[19] These quantities illustrate the barest form of operational ration and assume that the recipients lived on a daily ration of nothing but cold wheat gruel and drank nothing but water.[20] Every army throughout the ages has provided its soldiery with some form of hard tack for consumption in emergencies or when more palatable alternatives are not available. The Romans, for example, produced a form of hard biscuit known as *buccellatae*. The normal diet of the Roman soldier comprised corn, lard, cheese and rough wine, augmented whenever possible by foraged food from the sub-unit kettle. We may judge that the practice of the West Saxons or of the Danes would not have been much different.

The amounts above, as has already been emphasised, represent a minimum *per capita* requirement. Any additions to it would have added to the general administrative burden and, particularly during operations, would have been particularly taxing. As a simple illustration, the Normans, when forming up on the continent for their invasion of Saxon England, received a ration of 8 ounces of wine per day, a modest amount which doubtless did a lot for morale; few would have argued with its purpose. On the other hand, in strictly logistical terms and to an already stretched military transport commitment, it added a further monthly requirement of fifteen cartloads for every thousand men in Duke William's army.

Under siege conditions the horses of the mounted infantry, together with other animals, would also have presented burdensome administrative problems. The English-bred animals were neither as big as the modern cavalry horse nor of the sort which landed with the Conqueror in 1066. They were lighter weight horses, perhaps developed from those brought over by the Romans during the Claudian invasion of AD 43. The greater numbers found by the Danes in south-east England perhaps owed their presence to this fact. Each horse, in the winter, when striving to regain its fitness after the summer's operational exertions, would under normal circumstances have required a daily feed of 12 lb of grain and at least 13 lb of hay. If sufficient hay was not available, the alternative would have been to turn the animals out to graze, where they would have consumed three times as much green grass as hay, or some 40 lb per day per animal, an overall total of 9 tons for an estimated 500 animals. If it were necessary for this total to be foraged and transported, then this would have required twenty two-horse cartloads, with a lift of 1,000 lb apiece.

The difficulties for the Danes, living in walled strongholds and confronted by such administrative problems, would have been considerable. If, in the early days of their invasion, their problems had been properly understood and exploited by the Saxons, they would have been in great difficulty. If they had chosen to turn their animals out to grass, the animals would quickly have consumed a sizeable grazing area, and each day would need to find new pastures further from base. They would have been increasingly vulnerable to ambush and it would have been costly in terms of manpower to safeguard them. Additionally, in the event of an enemy attack in strength, the herd would probably have been lost. If, on the other hand, the animals were retained within the perimeter of the fort, which would suggest that the mounted force was of very limited size, this could have created grave hygienic problems.

Horses eat and drink large amounts but retain relatively little. A properly fed and watered horse each day produces 4.5 lb of faeces and over half a gallon of urine,[21] or, in relation to the contingent of the 500 Viking horses we are discussing, a ton of faeces and 280 gallons of urine. These facts present a strong argument for believing that the majority of the animals of the mounted infantry were sent back to some secure rallying position in the rear once a fort had been occupied, with only limited numbers being retained forward for reconnaissance and other such purposes.

Thus, to summarise, the Danish armies in England had a tremendous advantage over their Saxon opponents, for they were professionals who took pride in their warrior status and, as they were constantly engaged on highly profitable operations, their military performance, their skills, weapons and equipment were inevitably of superior quality and constantly maintained at the highest level. Moreover, their intelligent use of seapower, combined with their mobility ashore, allowed them to exploit that most valuable principle of war, surprise, to the fullest effect. Their weaknesses were twofold.

The first lay in the fact that they were 'playing away from home' and depended heavily upon their connections with the sea for reinforcements and, initially at least, for communications with other allied contingents. For this reason it is clear that, wherever possible, they made every effort to avoid pitched battles by retreating within fortifications whenever they met determined opposition, as at Ashdown in 871, or by providing hostages, such as those yielded to Alfred at Wareham by Guthrum six years later. There are many other such examples: casualties in the Danish ranks meant a reduction in their fighting strength, and were accepted with reluctance. Nevertheless, the Viking's professionalism and superior military qualities surely gave him a distinct edge over his opposite number in the largely peasant Saxon armies. In terms of cold battlefield efficiency, they probably rated a coefficient of 5:4 when set against their Anglo-Saxon opponents. Indeed, the ratio could well have been higher if it were not for the fact that the latter, by nature of their origins, were fighting for their families, their homesteads, their country and a way of life and Christian belief they saw gravely threatened. 'Lo', wrote Alcuin of York to Aethelred, King of Northumbria, after the devastating raid on Lindisfarne in 793:

> it is nearly 350 years that we and our fathers have inhabited this most lovely land, and never before has such terror appeared in Britain as we have now suffered from a pagan race, nor was it thought that such an inroad from the sea could be made. Behold, the church of St Cuthbert spattered with the blood of the priests of God, despoiled of all its ornaments; a place more venerable than all in Britain is given as a prey to pagan peoples.[22]

The second vulnerable area of the Danish armies lay in what at first sight was one of the strongest factors apparently working in their favour, namely their ability to live off the land. If food supplies were denied to them, their lack of outside sources upon which they could readily draw forced them to withdraw to where stocks were available.[23] It was, in many ways, a situation equal to the one that confronted Field Marshal Sir Gerald Templer in Malaya in 1952 when, in order to deny food to the terrorists operating from the jungle, he withdrew the rural population into selected villages which he then surrounded by double-apron barbed-wire fences and defended with Home Guard and armed police. Agricultural labourers went out from the villages to work in the fields during daylight but were required to return before dusk. The fruits of their labour, the rice harvest, was daily transported back to within the security of the fence, where it was closely guarded and its distribution rigorously scrutinised and controlled. In this way the terrorist enemy had the options of surrender, starvation, retreat or of emerging from the jungle to seek food at the risk of being ambushed or captured.

Templer's solution presented many similarities to that which presented itself to Alfred the Great. It was one which brought both men ultimate victory, but in neither case could its design be instantly achieved. Time was required to set it in place, together with firmly based government and the fullest cooperation and understanding of the people – a battle for hearts and minds, as Templer termed it. Alfred's plan came to be known by the name of Burghal Hidage.

Before concluding this glance at the military capability of the Danish armies in England at this time, the question of where they found their reserves of manpower cannot be ignored. However much allowance is made for exaggeration in the chroniclers' reports of casualties inflicted upon them, it cannot be denied that the accumulated wastage they must inevitably have suffered during their years of operations on both sides of the Channel, whether through battle, sickness, desertion, accident or just plain old age, must have been considerable. The *Anglo-Saxon Chronicle* for 874 provides a hint of how they might have resolved this problem, for it records, intriguingly, that when the Danes appointed Ceolwulf as King of the Mercians in place of Burghred, it was upon a condition, 'secured by oaths and hostages, that the kingdom should be at their disposal whenever they might wish to occupy it and that he should hold himself in readiness *to serve them with all who would follow them*' (my italics).[24] Danegeld, seemingly, may have yielded more than golden treasure, whether it be corn or coin. Certainly the provision of such support has taken

A silver penny from the reign of Alfred of Wessex. Enlarged. (British Museum)

place in other wars but there is little evidence in this instance to suggest that this is the way it happened.

*   *   *

The Anglo-Saxon military structure prior to the Danish invasions, and details of the selection, call-up and training of manpower for military service in the *fyrd*, the Saxon defence force, have been described as a 'treacherous bog'[25] in which to stray. The distinguished Professor Stenton, in his work on Anglo-Saxon England,[26] comments that little is known about it and that different scholars have recorded very different opinions. Nevertheless, any military study of a campaign such as that waged by King Alfred against the Danish invaders requires a broad knowledge of the military structure of the armies of both protagonists. We have discussed the professionalism of the Viking. It is now necessary to take a brief, uncomplicated glance at the shape and recruitment of the Anglo-Saxon forces of the eighth and ninth centuries. In Wessex in particular, these comprised three different types of army or *fyrd*:

- The national host or *fyrd*, which was rarely embodied but when it was came under the direct leadership of the king. In practice, and in its widest sense, the national host or *fyrd* was an array not just of the nation's able-bodied population but of representatives of all the households in the country.

- Shire *fyrds*, each led by a carefully selected ealdorman, frequently of royal blood.
- War-bands of individual thegns.

In general terms these may be regarded as a series of units, each contributing to the make-up of the main force. The command element would have been provided by ealdormen and thegns, with shire *fyrds* and war-bands maintaining their individuality; the latter may have been grouped to provide larger sub-units. There is little conclusive evidence concerning the scale of military call-out quotas demanded by English kings during the eighth and ninth centuries, other than a Mercian memorandum dated 801, in which King Coenwulf orders the holder of a 30-hide estate in Middlesex to provide him with 'only five men in the necessity of an expedition' (in other words, one warrior per six hides).[27]

On call-out, the war-bands of the thegns would have marched to the shire *fyrd* assembly point and, if required, from there to rendezvous with the national army or to take up whatever duties had been allocated to them within the overall plan. The whereabouts of rendezvous places would have been selected according to the operational circumstance. The muster of Alfred's army before the battle of Edington in 878 provides a useful illustration of this procedure. Here, the king called for the men of Somerset and of Wiltshire, together with the men of Hampshire, living on 'this side of the sea' (i.e., the west side of the Avon estuary) to meet with him at Egbert's Stone. The men of each shire would first have assembled within their own borders. Two other counties, unmentioned by the chronicler but nevertheless available at that time to turn out for the king, were assigned other duties. The men of Devon, as we are aware, were already mustered under ealdorman Odda, watching the Devon coastline.[28] The men of Dorset, although we are not told, were probably similarly employed, guarding the south coast of Wessex against a surprise seaborne attack. In the previous year Guthrum's fleet had been overcome by disaster whilst making just such an attempt.[29]

During the ninth century the national host was embodied infrequently; the shire *fyrds*, on the other hand, although it was unusual for them to serve beyond their borders, were kept well employed. For this reason shire ealdormen were granted considerable autonomy and a decision such as whether to march to the aid of a neighbour, should he be called upon to do so, was a matter delegated by the king to the commanders on the ground. Chronicles record that on at least two occasions in the year 860 ealdorman Aethelwulf and the men of Berkshire joined with ealdorman Osric and the men of Hampshire to rebuff a Danish army which had landed in southern Wessex intending to march on Winchester.[30] Clearly, such autonomy was a sensible policy, bearing in mind the size of Wessex and the time and space involved in communication with a king whose whereabouts might be uncertain.

In all these circumstances, it is to be expected that an ealdorman needed to pay considerable attention to the military training of his *fyrd*, the efficient handling of its operations and particularly to the speedy functioning of its call-out procedure. In order to assist with this, as well as with the policing of his district, he employed military retainers. It is thus unsurprising to learn that local thegns, in the first instance, tended to look to their ealdorman for leadership rather than to their king. It follows that the king, although he had himself appointed the ealdormen, would need to be careful to carry their support in all that he did, both by his leadership and by the acceptability of his policies.

It might be argued that a chain of command where underlings took their orders from a senior commander rather than their monarch was unhealthy. This, however, is recognised military practice: soldiers, while owing allegiance to the Crown, have always looked to their senior commander for direction. In the case of the West Saxon peoples the ethos was more strongly ingrained. If a lord fell foul of his king and was ordered into exile, then his followers were obliged to accompany him. If, on the other hand, the nobleman did not accept his exile and waged war on the king, his men were expected to fight at his side and would not have been blamed or punished for doing so.[31] The ealdormen thus held extraordinary powers, to such a degree that they could seek peace with the enemy without the consent of their ruler. This anomaly explains the significant lack of support for Alfred from the shires of eastern Wessex when, in 878, he was driven to seek shelter in the heart of the Somerset levels.

One fundamental weakness of the *fyrd* was to be found in its clumsy administration, which broadly rested upon the shoulders of the ceorls. A ceorl was a freeman, a responsible member of the state, whose rights were carefully secured by law. If he prospered and acquired 5 hides of land of his own, 'with a church and kitchen, bell-house and *burh*-gate', then he became entitled to the rights of a thegn, with access to the monarch. A ceorl, in short, was a homesteader and as such was granted the right to defend his household, carry weapons and be present with the national host whenever it was called upon to muster. He thus played a minor but nevertheless essentially important role in the defence of the state. This was further extended by the introduction of the 5 hides system which, on the muster of the *fyrd*, required one warrior to be provided per 5 hides, together with his essential needs. The number of hides per man are deemed to have varied according to the practice of the shire. They were sometimes increased by the king in order to restrict the size of the call-out. The cost and maintenance of the warrior's equipment, weaponry and food was paid for by charges levied against those individuals remaining on the hides upon his departure. In Berkshire the terms of service were clearly recorded, although the precise terms were not necessarily followed by other shires:

> If the king sent an army anywhere, only one soldier went from five hides, and for his provision or pay, four shillings were given from each hide for two months of service. The money, however, was not sent to the king but given to the soldiers. If anyone summoned to serve in an expedition failed to do so, he forfeited all his land to the king. If anyone for the sake of remaining behind promised to send another in his place, and nevertheless, he who should have been sent remained behind, his lord was freed of obligation by the payment of 50 shillings.[32]

It at once becomes apparent that the command of a force raised in this manner, together with its tactical handling and administration, left much to be desired, particularly if it were required to take the field for an extended period. Its structure, moreover, was totally unsuited to counter the speed and mobility of the Danes, with their systematic foraging of the countryside, their topographical knowledge of the routeways and their unhindered use by longships of the great riverways penetrating deep into the English hinterland, which some three centuries earlier had been so successfully exploited by the occupying Roman legions.

Despite the quality of the Danish forces, Wessex should have been able to extract considerable advantage from her large reserves of manpower but the shire *fyrds* were intended for localised warfare and the military organisation was totally unsuited for the widespread assaults now being mounted against it. Driven backwards by successive blows, King Alfred, with the remnants of his men, was compelled to seek refuge in the heart of the west country, losing an army with every shire surrendered. The commanders of these shires, the ealdormen of the counties lying to the east of the Hampshire Avon, many of whom had fought doughtily alongside their king in the previous year, had seemingly made their own peace with the enemy, as indeed they were quite entitled to do. Doubtless they were expected to yield considerable Danegeld to the enemy, in terms of both money and food; by doing so, they directly supported their enemy's cause, however unwillingly. Asser relates how nearly all the inhabitants of north Wiltshire 'had submitted to the authority of the Vikings' in 878, while Alfred, their king, 'was leading a restless life in great distress, amid the woody and marshy places of Somerset'.[33]

The defence structure and command organisation of Wessex, which Alfred had inherited from his predecessors, were totally inadequate to cope with the military situation which now confronted him. His army was the antithesis of its Danish opposition, for the *fyrd*, in general terms, was largely an unprofessional peasant army, which had to be called from home before it became operational. It was inevitably clumsy to handle, slow moving, poorly administered and trained. Its members were generally unwilling to serve beyond the borders of their individual shires and then only for limited periods. It was thus natural that commanders and men should tend to look at operations through a narrow perspective and be careless of national needs. Yet in practice the shires provided the great strength of the Anglo-Saxon kingdoms, for here lay their wealth, together with great reserves of organised manpower; and here also lay the reserves of foodstuffs that the Danish invaders desperately needed to sustain their armies.

After his success at the battle of Edington and the respite offered to him two years later by the withdrawal of Guthrum to East Anglia, King Alfred embarked upon a programme of military reorganisation and, by the construction of fortified towns, adopted a policy of offensive defence for Wessex. He did this, in Asser's words, despite 'the great trouble and vexations . . . he had with his own people, who voluntarily submit to little or no labour for the common needs of the kingdom'.[34] His purpose was threefold, namely:

- to deny the Danes the mobility which until now they had been able to exercise almost without let. This involved the strategic siting of fortified *burhs* or townships so that they guarded the focal points of routeways, including crossing-places over the Thames; secured control of the courses and estuaries of navigable rivers; and watched over coastal inlets which offered safe harbourage.
- to deny the enemy an ability to manoeuvre freely across country.
- to deny foodstuffs to the enemy by retaining harvest stocks and granaries within fortified townships.

Aerial picture of Portchester, a Roman fort used as a burh *stronghold. (Aerofilms)*

The network of defences planned by Alfred, and seemingly set in hand in about 880, comprised thirty-three fortified *burhs*, each located within 20 miles of another. Some were newly constructed townships; others, such as Portchester, were sited within ancient fortifications, either Iron Age or Roman in origin; and in other cases, existing townships were reconstructed for the purpose. Wallingford in Oxfordshire, situated on the Thames, provides a good example of the king's intentions. Its ancient defences may still be observed, standing astride the river, and thus able to exercise control over the flow of passing riverine traffic and to dominate the highway which at that time forded the water beneath its walls. When Alfred's plan was completed and Wessex had been regained, Wallingford formed one of a chain of four such riverine *burhs* on the Thames, reaching from Southwark, in the heart of London, to Cricklade at the western source of the river. These were the mainstay of a continuous line of defence along the river which formed the northern frontier of the kingdom of Wessex.

Aerial view of Wallingford, showing the ramparts of the Saxon fort with the river along one side. (Ashmolean Museum, Oxford)

While putting these defensive measures in place, King Alfred also turned his attention to the reorganisation of the army and the creation of a navy to defend his open coastline. He determined to provide each of his newly created *burhs* with a garrison, sufficient in numbers to be able to rebuff any Danish attack. To this end, he 'divided his army into two, so that always half of its men were at home, half on service, apart from the men who guarded the boroughs'.[34] By this means he aimed to achieve two objectives: firstly, his strike force would no longer be looking over its shoulder, worried about events at home; and, secondly, although the permanent garrison of a *burh* might be threatened with attack, no enemy force would contemplate a siege while there was any threat of intervention by the garrisons of neighbouring townships. The text of the Burghal Hidage provides a statement which demonstrates how manpower allotments for these garrisons were to be calculated:

> For the maintenance and defence of an acre's breadth of wall, sixteen hides are required. If every hide is represented by one man, then every pole [i.e. 5.5 yards] can be manned by four men. Then, for the maintenance of 20 poles of wall, 80 hides are required by the same reckoning, as I have stated above . . . For the maintenance of a circuit of 12 furlongs of wall, 1920 hides are required. If the circuit is greater, the additional amount can easily be deduced from this amount for 160 men are alway required for one furlong, then every pole of wall is always manned by four men.[35]

The average strength of a borough garrison, calculated by this formula, was rather less than 900 men. The largest garrisons were located at Wallingford and Winchester, two strategically important townships, and each mustered 2,400 men (see Appendix B). These manpower totals, which were earmarked solely for defence, must inevitably cast doubt on the views of historians who consider that the strength of the opposing Danish armies should be numbered in 'hundreds rather than thousands'.

The meticulous calculations and careful attention Alfred paid to the defensive distribution of *burhs*, and the allotment of garrisons to them, is evident even today. The coastal fort at Wareham, for example, assessed at 1,600 hides, had an implied garrison of 1,600 men. From this manpower requirement it may be deduced, at four men per 5.5 yards, that the defensive wall of the fortification, which is bounded on one side by the River Piddle, originally extended for 2,200 yards. Currently, it measures 2,180 yards.

The detail of the reorganisation of the king's land force is not much less clearly defined. We are told quite simply that the king 'divided his *fyrd* into two, so that always half of its men were at home, half on service'. We are left to speculate how the proposed new system was intended to operate within the pattern of the newly laid out *burhs* and, importantly, how the proportional relationship between numbers earmarked for field service compared with those for garrison duties. Presumably each township made its own contribution to the king's *fyrd* and thus, if the strength of the national army was to be kept within a sensible but adequate total, and the townships were not to over-subscribe to its manpower, each would be required to make a select contribution, probably of mounted noblemen and retainers. Thus the borough garrisons would tactically have been able to reinforce the field force with foot soldiers if required to do so in time of emergency, as happened at Buttington in the autumn of 893.[36]

The kingdom of Wessex, however, was large, reaching from eastern Thanet to the banks of the River Tamar, running between the county of Devon and a provenly hostile Cornwall. For this reason Alfred may well have maintained two standing armies, one located centrally in each of his eastern and western provinces. The phrase 'standing army', in its modern connotation, suggests a well-trained, disciplined fighting force, carefully administered and equipped. Alfred's military reorganisation, although moving sharply in the right direction, did not immediately qualify for this definition. An incident in 893, when some levies successfully pursued a Danish raiding party across the Thames to the River Colne, where they were compelled to seek refuge on Thorney Island, demonstrates not only poor discipline but lax administration. The *Anglo-Saxon Chronicle* relates that, with the Danes trapped and unable to move because their leader had been wounded,

> the levies surrounded them there as long as their provisions lasted; but they had completed their tour of duty and had come to an end of their food, and the king was on his way to relieve them with the division which was campaigning with him.

Despite this, and the considerable advantage they had gained over their enemy, the levies were content to surrender their positions and return home. These were the old, lamentable failings which Alfred, by his reforms, was striving to eliminate.

No clear definition of the operational organisation of Alfred's new army has been provided for us, any more than it is possible, from the information left to us, to identify a visibly recognisable pattern when considering the military composition of the earlier *fyrd*. Both structures comprised mixed forces of infantry and mounted troops. In the case of the *fyrd*, as we have seen, the foot soldiers were largely unskilled and were supported by a limited force of mounted men, almost inevitably restricted by their small numbers to a mainly reconnaissance role. In the king's new army, in the years which followed his victory at Edington, emphasis was placed upon sustained defence, with greater constancy and preparedness. In the field, in order to gain the mobility he had so far lacked, he maintained increased numbers of mounted infantry, on occasions deploying whole divisions of horsemen.

CHAPTER 4

Wessex under Siege

The Kyng and Alfred ys brother nome men ynowe
Mette hem, and a batayle smite up Assesdowne –
There was mony moder chylde, that some lay there doune –
The batayle ylaste vorte-nygt, and ther was aslawe
Vyf dukes of Dene-march, ar hii wolde withdrawe,
And mony thousende of other men, and tho' gone hii to fle;
Ac hii adde alle ybe assend gyf ye nyght n'adde y bee.

Robert of Gloucester (1260–1300)[1]

In the mid-ninth century Wessex, in the simplest terms, extended south of the Thames, from the most easterly shores of the Isle of Thanet to the River Tamar, dividing Cornwall from Devon. It was a loosely knit kingdom, not only because of the nature of its administrative, political and military structure but also because of its wide geographical spread. This latter characteristic provided a potential defensive weakness which was seemingly well appreciated by the West Saxons for, when Aethelwulf succeeded his father Egbert to the throne in 839, one of his earliest actions was to give his son Aethelstan 'the kingdom of Kent and Essex and of Surrey and of Sussex'.[2] The province allocated to Aethelstan was an area of high strategical importance and included not only Thanet, the traditional invasion highway from the continent, but, *ipso facto*, the Wantsum Channel and the vital Thames estuary, both of which gave access to the heart of England.

The rulers of Wessex saw the situation differently. Asser tells us that 'the western part of the Saxon land had always been more important than the eastern',[3] particularly, as events were to demonstrate, that area of land lying west of the Hampshire Avon, a substantial river obstacle with considerable defensive qualities. More than this, of course, the eastern area of Wessex was so splintered by its topography that it must have been extremely difficult to administer and, given the military structure of the day, which depended *in extremis* upon the speedy call-out of the national *fyrd*, almost impossible to defend in a major emergency with any sense of confidence.

A glance at the layout of the eastern area is sufficient to make clear the reasons for this. The country of the East Saxons lay isolated, north of the Thames estuary. Further south, land access to and from Kent, the traditional stepping-stone for invaders from Europe, was largely restricted to two major highways. First, there was the ancient trackway variously called the Pilgrim's Way, Hardway or Herepath, which ran along the North Downs in a sweeping arc from Canterbury, crossing the Medway at Rochester, through North Kent and Surrey to the strategic junction of ridgeways which come together on Salisbury Plain; secondly, the Roman Watling Street, which broadly followed a course along the line of the River Thames, between the river and the North Downs, from Canterbury, via Rochester to London, and thence northwards across the Thames to north-west England.

The main reason for this limited access was the hindrance offered by the heavily wooded *Andreaswald* forest. This stood between the North and South Downs, extending from East Kent to West Sussex. Within that area and, around the Romney Marshes in particular, its dark recesses provided a discouraging barrier to movement, eastwards or westwards, in south-east Wessex. It placed a firm dividing line between the men of Kent and the South Saxons. Its overall effect was to isolate yet another district of eastern Wessex, namely the militarily important and highly vulnerable coastal area of East Kent, where the Isle of Thanet, which the Roman commander Aulus Plautius had selected as a first phase bridgehead for his invasion force in AD 43, had lost none of its attractions for this purpose. The physical description given of the island by Bede (673–735) in his *History of the English Church and People* illustrates with clarity the features that gave it such importance for this role:

> To the east of Kent lies the large island of Thanet, which by English reckoning is six hundred hides in extent; it is separated from the mainland by a waterway about three furlongs broad called the Wantsum, which joins the sea at either end and is fordable only in two places.[4]

In Anglo-Saxon times a hide was the original measure of land required to support a family. Bede's six hundred hides would thus suggest a population of some 3,000 people, implying considerable use of the fords connecting the island with mainland Kent.

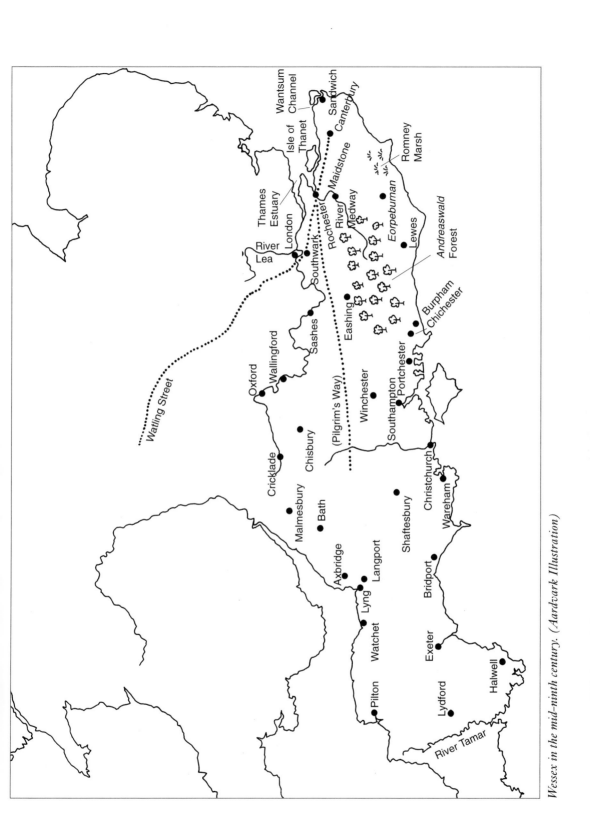

Wessex in the mid-ninth century. (Aardvark Illustration)

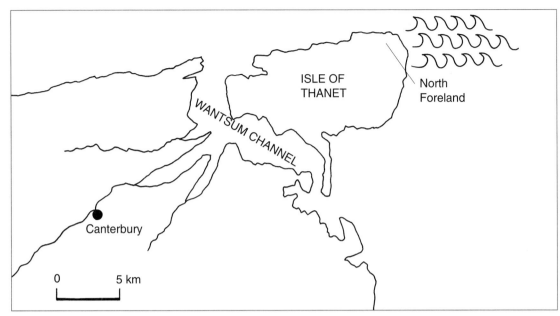

The Wantsum Channel allowed safe access to the Thames Estuary and was frequently used by continental shipping avoiding the rough seas off the North Foreland. (Aardvark Illustration)

The Wantsum possessed commercial as well as military importance. It provided a sheltered thoroughfare along which flowed sea traffic between London and the continent. Its waters enabled boatmen to avoid the troublesome currents and tides of the Thames estuary and the unpredictable weather conditions frequently to be found around the traditionally hazardous North Foreland. These attractions were enhanced by the presence of long-established markets in the busy ports that had developed at Canterbury and Sandwich, and by the secure anchorage the Wantsum could offer to large quantities of shipping. Ships would customarily enter the waterway on the incoming tide and, having arrived at Sarre, at roughly the midway point, would pause to await the arrival of the ebb tide, depending upon their point of entry, to carry them forward either to the English Channel or the Thames estuary. From Sarre, traders had several choices of destination, depending upon the size and draft of their craft. They could make their way northwards along the coasts of Essex and East Anglia; they could sail up the River Thames to London, linking with Ermine Street and the north; or they could journey beyond there to Reading, Wallingford and the Cotswolds. Alternatively, the River Medway provided waterborne access to Maidstone or, if they chose to pursue the line of the River Lea northwards, this would carry them through to Ware in Hertfordshire, close to the old Roman trading centre at Braughing. Thus the seizure of the Wantsum, apart from offering an invader a wealth of choices of direction in which to move, also provided him with a firm island base – the Isle of Thanet – from which to operate. It is small wonder that the Danish Vikings made it their first objective. For many of the same reasons the Isle of Sheppey, in the mouth of the Thames and ravaged by 'the heathen men' as early as 835, was also to prove a valuable prize.

After their descent upon Sheppey, it was to be another six years before the Danes returned to Kent. The *Anglo-Saxon Chronicle* for 841 records that 'in this year ealdorman Hereberht was killed by heathen men and many men with him in the Romney Marsh; and later in the same year many men in Lindsey, East Anglia and Kent, were killed by the enemy'. This was followed twelve months later by yet another raid, this time on London and Rochester, accompanied by the customary pillage, rape and butchery of the population. Then, in 851, the raiders overwintered the first time.

> . . . heathen men stayed through the winter on Thanet. And the same year 350 ships came into the mouth of the Thames and stormed Canterbury and London and put to flight Brihtwulf, King of the Mercians, with his army and went south across the Thames into Surrey. And King Aethelwulf and his son Aethelbald fought against them at Aclea with the army of the West Saxons, and there inflicted the greatest slaughter on a heathen army that we have ever heard of until this present day, and had the victory there. And the same year, King Aethelstan and Ealdorman Ealhhere fought in ships and slew a great army at Sandwich in Kent and captured nine ships and put the others to flight.[5]

This is a revealing extract from the *Chronicle* for, to a degree, it illustrates the pattern of Aethelwulf's defensive thinking, about which we have already commented in part.[6] Regrettably the relative timing of the various events is not provided by the chronicler. Nevertheless it is clear, from what is written, that Aethelstan's operational role in the defence of the Wessex kingdom included the security of the Wantsum Channel. His presence there, both naval and military, was in such strength that the Danes deemed it wise to pull away and head for the mouth of the Thames. Aethelstan, it should be noted, was particularly successful in the execution of his duties, for he apparently routed 'a great army . . . captured nine ships and put the others to flight'. He did not prevent them from carrying out their customary plunder of Canterbury but nevertheless such a performance could not have been achieved against a skilled, sea-going enemy without both resources and operationally experienced sailors. In actuality, it must be more than doubtful that he possessed either; thus, the suggestion that he hired Frisian mercenaries and shipping for this purpose is something to be considered seriously. Whether or not he did so, it is evident from this encounter that the strategically important waters of the Wantsum figured high on Aethelstan's list of military defence priorities.

The Vikings, pausing only to raid Canterbury, as we have seen, then made their way to London which, with Middlesex, had been Mercian territory since about 756.[7] Here they found Brihtwulf of Mercia, with his army, awaiting them. He received short shrift and was savagely put to flight. The invaders then crossed the Thames into Surrey, an action which indicates that this had probably been their initial intention had they not found a hostile Mercian force poised on their riverine line of communication and been compelled to disperse it. Meanwhile, Aethelwulf had not been idle. Aethelstan, by his action, had provided his father with time to call out his army and march east. Aethelwulf now intercepted the enemy at *Aclea* in Surrey and there dealt them a severe defeat.

Aclea is sometimes identified with the small town of Ockley, south of Dorking, and there is some evidence, in the Viking inclination to use Roman roads, to suggest that this is a reasonable suggestion. Located 15 miles from the Pilgrim's Way, itself an important ancient highway, Ockley also stands on Stane Street, an old Roman road which connected the heart of London with the ancient city port of Chichester on the south coast. From the viewpoint of road communications, therefore, Ockley would have been a logical place for the two armies to have encountered each other but we can only speculate on the Viking commander's objective in moving so far south. Upon reaching Surrey, he had arrived at the western frontiers of Aethelstan's territory and, by doing so, had successfully outflanked the latter's position. It would have been unnecessary to penetrate to such a depth if this had been his sole intention. It may be that he was aware that Aethelwulf was already in the field and felt that by bringing him to battle and defeating him, as well as Brihtwulf of Mercia, he would be enabled to despoil the countryside at will. Aethelwulf, on the other hand, if he had marched east from the ancient Wessex capital of Wilton, would have advanced with his army along the Pilgrim's Way. The military probability, therefore, is that the two opponents came face to face where the latter road crosses Stane Street, north of Dorking, in the broad vicinity of Newlands Corner. Of one thing we may be certain: the Viking commander, to have gone to such lengths, had a major objective in mind.

It would be pure conjecture to suggest that the military roles of Aethelwulf and Aethelstan, in defence of their respective regions, were integrated. It might more correctly be judged that, however tight their military liaison may have been, Aethelwulf's prime aim would have been the defence of western Wessex. In that context, in the face of a crisis of extreme proportions, West Saxon policy could have been none other than to treat eastern Wessex as being 'expendable'. The events of the next twenty years were to bring that situation to reality.

The first of these events was the death of Aethelstan not long after the battle of *Aclea*; although he is known to have attested some of his father's charters in the previous decade, he is not heard of again after 851. It is remarkable that this loyal and gallant son of Aethelwulf, who had ruled over the eastern part of Wessex with evident competence for some twelve years, should have been allowed to disappear in this manner without comment by contemporary historians. Equally strange, in the face of the constant threat under which the region was living, his successor does not seem to have been immediately appointed. Within two years the Vikings were back in Thanet and the people of Kent and Surrey, the intervening forest doubtless excluding the participation of the men of Sussex, joined together in an effort to throw them out. It was an operation of dubious success: many men were killed and drowned during the fighting and both counties lost their ealdormen, Huda of Surrey and the redoubtable Ealhhere of Kent – a clear testimony to the severity of the battle.

This occurrence, so soon after Aethelstan's death (it is notable that his presence is not recorded fighting alongside his ealdormen), must have struck a hammer-blow at regional morale. Indeed, the *Anglo-Saxon Chronicle* records no further occasion when a Kentish *fyrd*, as such, took the field although there were two opportunities when they might have done so. First, in 855, when 'the heathen men for the first time stayed in Sheppey over the winter', apparently uncontested. It will be recalled that it was in this same year that Aethelwulf set out on his oddly inappropriate journey to Rome and Francia, from where he was to return to Wessex some twelve months later with his new queen and child-bride Judith. He died two years later and was succeeded by his two sons Aethelbald and Aethelberht, the former taking the throne of Wessex and Aethelberht being granted responsibility for the eastern province of the kingdom,[8] comprising the counties of Kent, Essex, Surrey and Sussex.

The second occasion when the men of Kent might have reacted militarily against the invaders of their territory came ten years later when 'a heathen army encamped on Thanet and made peace with the people of Kent. And the people of

Kent promised them money for that peace. And under cover of that peace the army stole away inland by night and ravaged all eastern Kent.'[9]

In the year which followed, the Danish Great Army, over which Ivar the Boneless was now to assume command, landed in East Anglia. The fighting was not yet to reach Wessex but when Halfdan and his army finally launched their assault upon it, the men of Essex, Kent, Surrey and Sussex were to have no role in its defence. These counties had already played their part. They had been 'expended' and from this moment were in thrall, compelled to remain neutral bystanders. The battle, when it came to Wessex, would be for the western region.

Western Wessex was a compact kingdom compared with Aethelstan's domain. Broadly, it reached from the eastern boundaries of Hampshire and Berkshire, south of the Thames and the Bristol Avon, to Cornwall. Cornwall was the last part of Britain to be conquered by the Saxons. An attack by Ine of Wessex in 722 had been thrown back in some disorder after his troops had advanced as far as the Padstow area. Subsequently, apart from a foray in 815 by his descendant Egbert, when 'he ravaged in Cornwall, from east to west',[10] the West Saxons appear to have been too deeply involved in wars with other neighbours to undertake further military adventures in the south-west. In 838 the Cornish people were encouraged by the arrival in their midst of a great Danish naval force which joined them in an attack upon Wessex. Egbert at once struck back and administered a devastating blow to the Cornish army on Hingston Downs, near Plymouth, east of the Tamar. He followed this by meting out punishment of such a level that, even at the lowest ebb of Alfred's fortunes some two generations later, they responded with little enthusiasm to renewing an alliance with his enemies. Cornwall was not politically absorbed into Wessex until the tenth century, nor ecclesiastically until even later,[11] but in the dangerous days to come, even though apparently neutral, they quietly posed the constant threat of trouble.

Thus, to summarise the situation through the eyes of Aethelred and Alfred: in the battle about to commence for Wessex, the group of districts that formed the eastern region were expected to adopt a neutral stance rather than provoke a hostile response from the Danes. The kingdoms of Northumbria and East Anglia, together with the 'Welsh' region of Cornwall, were at best neutral. Mercia, with its districts of London and Middlesex fronting on to the River Thames and hence of considerable use to the Vikings, had to be considered hostile territory. Where then would Halfdan choose to strike and from what direction would he come? Asser provides a very abbreviated account of this:

In the year of the Lord's Incarnation 871 (the twenty-third of King Alfred's reign) the Viking army of hateful name left East Anglia, went to the kingdom of the West Saxons, and came to the royal estate called Reading (situated on the southern bank of the Thames) in the district called Berkshire).[12]

The *Anglo-Saxon Chronicle* is even more brief. It simply records that in 871 'the army came into Wessex to Reading'. In neither case is there any indication of the route Halfdan might have taken in order to arrive at his objective, although Asser makes the point that the town was situated on the southern bank of the river; thus, in order to reach it, Halfdan must have found a suitable crossing-place. Nor are we told why this particular royal estate was selected by Halfdan as his target, perhaps because the answer was so clearly obvious to the writer. One unmistakable reason, as has been discussed above,[13] must be that Reading, which lay at the confluence of the Rivers Thames and Kennet, provided an ideal site for the Vikings to establish a base adequate for both their field force and their supporting longships. In other words the selection of such a site as their objective suggests that the shipping element of their task force was as much an integral part of this operation as it had been with their previous campaigns in the north of England, the midlands and East Anglia. It is fair, therefore, to assume that, while the Danish field force was riding southwards, their fleet, with the non-mounted element of their army, was simultaneously sailing down the east coast, with the intention of linking up with them again at some agreed rendezvous on the Thames.

Geographically Halfdan had no choice other than to use the Icknield Way for the first part of his march southward. We have already discussed the benefits of this route. The first leg would have carried him as far as Royston, 13 miles south-west of Cambridge. Upon arrival there, he had two options, for at this point the trackway is crossed by Ermine Street, the great Roman trunk road connecting London with the north of England. From this focal point he could have pursued a course down Ermine Street, following the line of the Lea Valley, thence passing the eastern side of the city of London as it then existed, to reach the bridge over the Thames from where Ermine Street commenced its journey northwards. Alternatively, he could have continued along the Icknield Way to Wilbury Camp, near Hitchin, and thence by Offley and, bypassing Luton, to Dunstable, where the highway follows the edge of the Downs before descending the Chilterns, to pass through Little Kimble and Ewelme and cross the Thames at Goring. This second alternative would have brought Halfdan to within a few miles of his

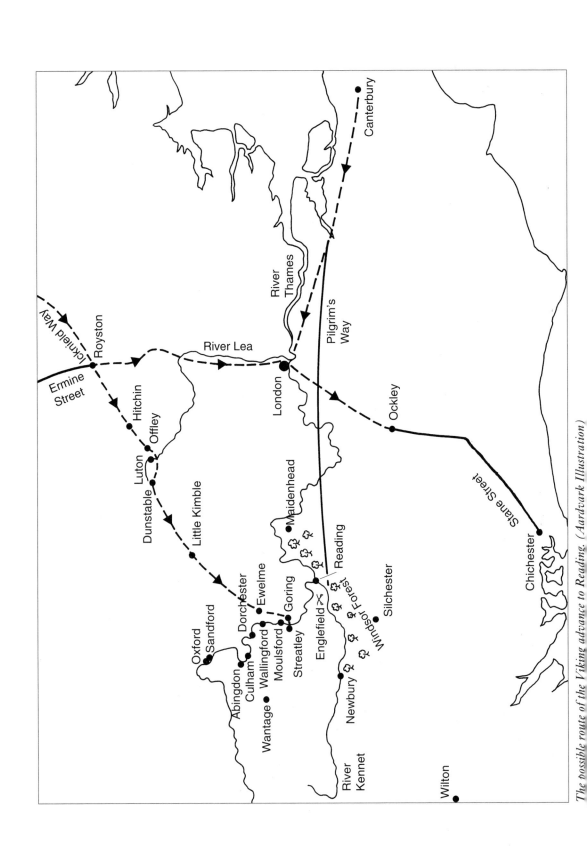

The possible route of the Viking advance to Reading. (Aardvark Illustration)

Reading objective and is the option most generally accepted. Nevertheless it would have had serious military disadvantages for, unless the two divisions of the army had synchronised their arrival meticulously, one or the other would have been placed in a very dangerous position, with the Saxons north of the Thames aroused by their arrival and, in Wessex, the men of the shires doubtless already alerted and responding to a call to arms. It would plainly have been more sensible for the two elements of the Danish task force to have reassembled in territory known to be reasonably quiescent, rather than to do so in a hostile environment of which few in either contingent can have had much direct knowledge.

In the event the Saxon tribes living astride the estuary and to the north of the Thames appear to have been paralysed in the face of this movement of enemy mounted troops which, in relation to the numbers they themselves could have mustered, cannot have been large. Burghred of Mercia, the East Saxons and the people of Kent had all undoubtedly bought peace from their molesters at some considerable political and military cost to their kingdoms. Nevertheless, aware as they must have been that Wessex would fight vigorously for its life, it is perplexing that they simply allowed the Danes to arrive, assemble and move away as an organised force, without themselves combining to exploit this particular moment of their enemy's weakness. As an extension to this line of thought, the possibility should not be overlooked that the Danish fleet did not move upriver in its entirety. Halfdan may well have felt it necessary to leave a firm base in the mouth of the Thames, to secure his line of communication should he wish to withdraw. It could also have been used as a resupply and reinforcement unit.[14]

In these probable circumstances, Halfdan would also have had to leave a rear party of sufficient size to provide it with adequate protection. This could only have been done at the cost of decreasing the strength of his field army which, in due course, would have been further weakened upon arrival in Berkshire by the need to garrison the stronghold to be established at Reading. The strange quiescence of the Saxons in the Thames Valley, and Halfdan's need to establish a rear organisation of some sort, leads us to the conclusion that there may have been another party of Vikings operational in the lower waters of the river at this time, which could have offered Halfdan the firm base arrangements he was seeking. Stenton has suggested that a Danish force may have remained in London for some years after 872[15] and comments upon the ease with which Danes raiding in East Anglia co-operated at that time with those raiding in Kent. It is not improbable that such a force was already established when Halfdan arrived and was able to offer him the security he sought.

*   *   *

If one is fully to appreciate the pattern of events that would unfold after Halfdan's arrival at Reading, it is necessary to have some brief topographical knowledge of the countryside involved. Berkshire was annexed from Mercia by the West Saxons in the 840s, the precise date being uncertain. It was clearly a part of the kingdom of Wessex when Alfred was born at Wantage in 849. Then a royal estate and obviously a town of note, Wantage lies centrally situated in the north of the county, some 12 miles equidistant between Dorchester-on-Thames and Silchester. The most northerly border of Berkshire is formed by the River Thames. On this, in the mid-ninth century, within the operational area we are considering, was situated a flourishing and influential abbey at Abingdon, together with two further royal estates at Reading and Wallingford.

The Thames was a frontier area for many centuries before and after Roman times. Many of the towns which have appeared on its banks originated because, in the first instance, they either occupied naturally defensive positions or commanded important river crossing-places. Abingdon and Dorchester, for example, were both fortified peninsula towns, located respectively at the confluences of the Ock and the Thame with the main stream. Wallingford, which in due course became a lively trading post, was initially a fortified settlement, protected on the south and west by an extensive area of marshland – the best of all natural defences. It guarded an important crossing-place over the river, with its fortifications extending to both banks and thus exercising a full and rigorous control over all road and waterborne traffic. It was a settlement with great political and military value. Its worth to the kingdom of Wessex may be assessed by the fact that it was provided with one of the earliest bridges spanning the river. A charter dated 957 speaks of the track from Wallingford to Shillingford as being the *Brcymege* or Bridgeway.[16]

There were several other such crossing-places, those of the greatest military significance being found at Streatley and Moulsford. Additionally, the fords at Culham, a mile downstream from Abingdon, and at Sandford, on the outskirts of Oxford, were considered passable but risky, for both areas flooded readily. The curve of the river, which no longer follows its original course, isolated the ground on which the first abbey was built at Abingdon in 675 and it was doubtless this defensive quality which first caught the attention of the monks. However, it did not save it from being sacked by the Danes in the heavy fighting about to take place and there can be little doubt that Halfdan was well aware of both its

The 'Abingdon' sword, found in the River Thames at Bog's Mill in about 1874. It dates from about Alfred's time. (Ashmolean Museum, Oxford)

presence and its riches, for the abbey was not only a religious site but also a commercial centre. The monks controlled all market, fishing and mill rights and, without a licence from the abbey, no man could trade.

Halfdan and his army, having escorted his accompanying vessels up the Thames, occupied Reading in the opening days of 871 and at once set about the task of building 'a rampart between the two Rivers Thames and Kennet, on the right-hand side of the same royal estate'.[17] John Man, the well-known Reading historian, writing in 1816, identified the location of this fortification:

> Here, we see, it was on the right-hand side of the town that the trench was dug, which could be no other than the eastern, supposing a person to be looking towards the north, as is customary in laying down places on maps. I conceive, therefore, the trench here mentioned, could be no other than the Plummery Ditch, as it is now called, which actually unites the two rivers and nearly insulates the Fosbury, which it is more than probable from its elevated situation, was the part the Danes fortified.[18]

From his description of the rampart as a trench which 'unites the two rivers', it would appear that the Plummery Ditch in his time was a water-filled dyke. Indeed it is shown as such in the map accompanying his history. Today it no longer exists, having disappeared beneath the railway station when the Great Western Railway came to Reading in the middle of the nineteenth century. If John Man is correct in his assumption that this dyke did in fact represent the rampart dug by the Danes, then the obstacle presented to an enemy would have been 800 yards long, surmounted by a palisade and fronted by a moat. If one applies to it the manpower formula stipulated by Alfred for the defence of a *burh* (four men to a pole), then this implies, for this length of wall, a total of some 580 defenders, taking no account of the men needed to safeguard the river banks upon which, doubtless, Halfdan's longships had been grounded.

While this construction work was progressing, 'on the third day after their arrival, two of their earls, with a great part of the force, rode out for plunder'. Whether this was actually their purpose, or whether they had emerged to conduct a reconnaissance in force, we can only conjecture. They marched westwards, almost compelled in that direction by the presence of the great Windsor Forest to their south, which extended roughly from Maidenhead in a south-westerly direction towards modern-day Newbury. They were marching along the north bank of the Kennet and had reached Englefield, some 12 miles from their base, when they encountered the men of Berkshire, commanded by their valorous ealdorman Aethelwulf. How the Berkshire *fyrd* came to be there at that time we are not told. From the course of subsequent events it is evident that both Aethelred and Alfred were also within striking distance, busily assembling the army with which they were soon to confront the Danes. In this event it is probable that Aethelwulf, the most readily available of the shire ealdorman, had been dispatched by the two brothers to locate the enemy, act as a protective screen and keep a watchful eye on their movements until the West Saxon army was fully mustered.

Aethelwulf wasted no time in bringing the enemy to battle and,

> when both sides had held out for a long time, and when one of the Viking earls had been killed and a great part of the army overthrown, the others took to flight and the Christians won the victory and were masters of the battlefield attack upon them.[19]

If nothing else, the outcome of this skirmish would have provided a great stimulus to the morale of the West Saxon army but, despite having no desire to diminish Aethelwulf's achievement, this was no time for extravagant expectations, for the Danes may simply have broken off their engagement and returned to base, deeming their mission accomplished and their enemy located. Nevertheless there must have been considerable excitement and celebration in the Saxon camp that night, as the good news was carried to the king and his young brother Alfred. The two men determined to exploit Aethelwulf's success as soon as possible and so, combining their forces under Aethelred's banner, they marched on Reading. They did not enjoy the victory they anticipated and Asser gives a graphic account of their failure, doubtless recalled from Alfred's memory:

> When they had reached the gate of the stronghold by hacking and cutting down all the Vikings they had found outside, the Vikings fought no less keenly; like wolves they burst out of all the gates and joined battle with all their might. Both sides fought there for a long time and fought fiercely, but, alas, the Christians eventually turned their backs, and the Vikings won the victory and were masters of the battlefield.[20]

According to one account the two West Saxon leaders were driven off in the direction of *Wiscelet*, identified as Whistley, east of Reading, and escaped across the Thames by means of a little-known ford at Twyford. Their army must now have been scattered and they had suffered a serious loss, and one they could ill afford, for ealdorman Aethelwulf had been cut down and killed in the assault on the Danish fortifications. The respect in which he was held is illustrated by the fact that his body was stealthily recovered from the battleground and then carried northward, across the river, so that he might be buried at Derby, in his Mercian homeland.[21]

It is plain that, when the West Saxons planned their assault, they had not anticipated such a robust display from the Danish defenders. The unexpected strength they encountered can only be accounted for by three possibilities. First, that the enemy force with which Aethelwulf had skirmished at Englefield four days earlier had not been such a 'great part of the force' as depicted by Asser and had, in fact, been a foraging party or simply a fighting patrol; secondly, that Halfdan had managed to receive reinforcements from the lower Thames, unknown to the West Saxons; thirdly, that the Saxons were simply defeated by the suddenness of the Danish sally when 'they burst out of all the gates'. The Vikings had great expertise in the defence of a stronghold. They had already demonstrated this at York, when they defeated the Northumbrian army in 867; moreover, the fact that they had provided themselves in this instance with a number of gates suggests that some of them were tactically sited to benefit a counter-attack by the defenders when under siege.

Whatever the reasons for the Saxon defeat at Reading, there is one matter about which there is no doubt for it is well documented. Within four days of the encounter the two sides confronted each other once again on a battlefield 'at a place called Ashdown'. Today we are left to speculate precisely where this may have been located. Indeed its whereabouts, and the respective areas in which the two armies may have assembled, have been widely discussed, with a variety of proposals for the sites being put forward by authoritative voices on many occasions. It is not our task here to discuss the merits of any of these, for to do so would confuse the issue: rather it is intended in the light of the known facts to examine anew the military options that were open to both sides and to discover where these may lead us.

After his dramatic victory at Reading the initiative rested with Halfdan. He had by that time been in occupation of his stronghold for more than a week and, if the party confronted by ealdorman Aethelwulf at Englefield had indeed been foraging, the chances are either that it lost its plunder in the fighting or that its quest for supplies was curtailed by the outcome of the encounter. Halfdan, with some sense of urgency, would therefore have been casting around for fresh sources of supply. Although he may have beaten off the West Saxon army from its assault on his Reading base, he had to assume it was still actively operating in the area and that, once beyond the security of his walls, his foraging parties would have been vulnerable to attack. Equally, it would have been perilous for him to march out in any great strength, for it would have left his main base thinly defended and his longships vulnerable to attack and destruction.

The Danish leader's first task, therefore, would have been to bring the West Saxon army to battle and to defeat it. In order to achieve this, he would probably have selected for attack a target of such importance that Aethelred would be compelled to intervene to safeguard it. If, at the same time, he could find a target that would not only bring Aethelred to battle, but would provide himself with both the food he was seeking and an improved tactical position, he would be in the happy position of achieving three purposes by the seizure of one objective. The militarily important Saxon stronghold at Wallingford, together with the rich and long-established abbey nearby at Abingdon, with its farms, granaries and fishponds, offered him this opportunity.

'The Christians', wrote Asser, 'had been aroused by grief and shame' at their defeat by a pagan army. Defeat on the battlefield was equated by the Saxons with chastisement by God for having failed Him in His service. This is exemplified by a letter written by Bishop Alcuin in 793 to Aethelred, King of Northumbria:

> Nothing defends a country better than the equity and godliness of princes . . . Remember that Hezekiah, that just and pious king, procured from God by a single prayer that a hundred and eighty-five thousand of the enemy were destroyed by a single angel in one night.[22]

In the same way it is possible to imagine that Abingdon Abbey and its environs could equally well have furnished food for Aethelred's shaken army after their defeat at Reading. It would also have provided sustenance for his soul, with the abbot and his monks available to intercede with the Almighty on his behalf. Additionally, and in more human terms, the stronghold at nearby Wallingford would have been an invaluable base for the West Saxon forces. Thus Aethelred, as a devout Christian and an experienced commander, had two good reasons for defending the Wallingford and Abingdon area and, in a very practical sense, it was vital for the successful defence of Wessex that it should be retained.

Halfdan would have had to move quickly to ensure that the West Saxons had as little time as possible to reorganise their forces after their rebuff at Reading. It is unlikely that he would have been able to do so secretly. Indeed we may be sure that, when his army marched out through the gates of his stronghold to open the next phase of the campaign, enemy scouts would have been watching his movements and, as soon as the direction of his march had been determined, news of it would have been quickly carried to the West Saxon king. The Dane could have had little doubt as to the best route to his objective. It is not improbable that his earlier attempts to reconnoitre the way forward had resulted in the opening skirmish at Englefield, for the encounter had taken place on a section of Roman road linking Silchester with Dorchester-on-Thames. This would have carried him directly to Moulsford and Wallingford and, on its way, would have passed through Cholsey, where Honey Lane today forms part of the original alignment.

The mention of this area instantly recalls that the Great Ridgeway enters Wessex at or near Streatley, through the gap cut by the Thames at Goring, and that the ancient Icknield Way traditionally crosses at Moulsford, as well as looping a subsidiary track through Goring and across to Streatley, before once again joining with the main trackway and the Fair Mile on the intriguingly named Kingstanding Hill. This line of advance, with its proximity to the River Thames, would have offered many attractions to the Danes, whose field operations were invariably closely linked to their longships. The presence of these ships always posed a threat, and the possibility on this occasion that Halfdan might move some of them upstream for a quick thrust at Wallingford, while the West Saxons were manoeuvring to intercept his army in the field, is one that neither Aethelred nor Alfred could have failed to recognise. Halfdan, unlike themselves, was operating upon external lines of communication. Reserves of manpower were not readily available to him. For this reason Danish military practice generally was to avoid large-scale confrontations that might result in heavy casualty figures. Thus, unless they could sense a quick victory, they would choose either to bypass a position or to fall back on an already established stronghold. We may expect Halfdan to have been equally cautious in these opening stages of his campaign.

The West Saxon leaders, for their part, were seeking a location which would enable them to counteract this tactic. It would have required three qualities.

- In particular, it would have needed to block any Danish advance down the Roman road running along the south bank of the river between Streatley and Wallingford.

- It would have to allow them the opportunity, if occasion arose, of moving laterally to deny a Danish attempt to pass around their open flank.
- It would have to be sufficiently close to Wallingford to permit the West Saxons to fall back to defend the ramparts of that town should they fail in any of these efforts.

The feature today known as Kingstanding Hill, lying on the Icknield Way just west of the ford across the Thames at Moulsford, offered the West Saxons all these qualities. Its name is significant. To the east its slopes descend towards the Thames and overlook its waters. In the mid-ninth century its heights would have commanded the Roman road as it ran northwards along the widening valley to Wallingford, situated barely 3 miles distant. To the west the Cholsey Downs and the Fair Mile led directly to a major track junction at Lowbury Hill and thus would have offered the Saxons the ability to sidestep swiftly in that direction should Halfdan have begun a move around that flank. The facts suggest that it was here, on Kingstanding Hill, that Aethelred caused his royal tent to be erected and here that he and Alfred determined to make their stand, astride the axis of the Danish advance.

Factors of time and space are relevant to the events of the day. In January, in southern Britain, dawn arrives at about 06.45 hrs and dusk at roughly 16.00 hrs. Kingstanding Hill lies some 13 miles – or four hours' march – from Reading. There is no evidence to suggest that Halfdan arrived on the scene of the coming battle earlier than the morning of the day itself. On the contrary there are good administrative and military reasons why he would not have wished to do so, for not only would he have lost the benefit of surprise but he would also have denied his men the opportunity of a good night's rest and a meal before departure. Indeed, the shortness of his approach march should have rendered any other alternative unnecessary. Thus if Halfdan had marched out of his stronghold at dawn, it is likely that he would have arrived at his battle-station on Moulsford Down, opposite the West Saxon position, at about 11.00 hrs. Then, according to Asser, the Vikings split their force into two divisions, and

organised shield walls of equal size (for they then had two kings and a large number of earls), assigning the core of the army to the two kings and the rest to all the earls. When the Christians saw this, they too split up the army into two divisions in exactly the same way, and established shield walls no less keenly. But as I have heard from truthful authorities who saw it, Alfred and his men

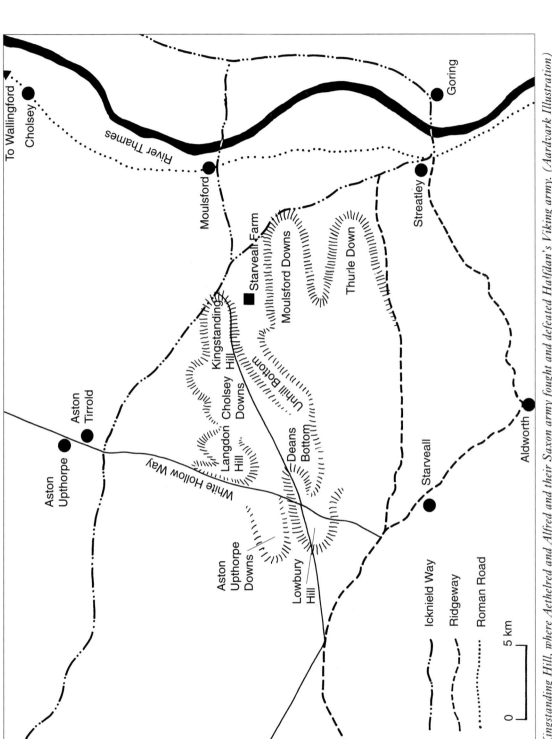

Kingstanding Hill, where Aethelred and Alfred and their Saxon army fought and defeated Halfdan's Viking army. (Aardvark Illustration)

reached the battlefield sooner and in better order: for his brother, King Aethelred, was still in his tent at prayer, hearing Mass and declaring firmly that he would not leave that place alive before the priest had finished Mass.

Now the Christians had decided that King Aethelred and his forces should engage the two Viking kings in battle, while his brother Alfred and his troops should submit to the fortunes of war against all the Viking earls. Matters were thus firmly arranged on both sides; but since the king was lingering still in prayer, and the Vikings were ready and had reached the battlefield more quickly, Alfred (then 'heir apparent') could not oppose the enemy battlelines any longer without either retreating from the battlefield or attacking the enemy forces before his brother's arrival on the scene. He finally deployed the Christian forces against the hostile armies, as he had previously intended (even though the king had not come), and acting courageously, like a wild boar . . . he moved his army without delay against the enemy.[23]

The amount of daylight available to Halfdan must have been a worrying factor for him, for he had barely five hours in which to achieve a victorious outcome. If at the end of that time he was unsuccessful, his army was then faced with a night withdrawal to Reading, with all the loss of morale, increasing with the deepening darkness, that such occasions bring with them. He had two courses open to him: to advance without delay against the Saxon army, or to start a movement around their flanks. The Saxons were already established on high ground. In order to reach them, Halfdan would have to descend from Moulsford Down, cross the valley where Starveall Farm stands today in sheltered isolation, and fight his way up the opposite slope at considerable disadvantage to his troops. Aethelred, on the other hand, was in no hurry. He was near his firm base at Wallingford and his supply lines were conveniently short. If it had been otherwise, he might not have spent so long at his devotions. As it was he saw no reason to abandon his chosen position and left it to Halfdan to make the first move.

If we interpret Asser's concealed meaning correctly, the Dane appears to have chosen the outflanking option. He split his army into two divisions and then moved his weaker right flank division along Moulsford Down in the direction of the river road. It is not clear what happened next, but it is likely that Alfred, who had been keenly watching the movements of the enemy, observed this manoeuvre and sought the authority of his brother to divide their forces in a similar manner. Permission was seemingly quickly forthcoming, which would suggest that Aethelred was not totally immersed in his prayers. Alfred now moved his division down the sloping shoulder of Kingstanding Hill as a counter to the Danish threat developing to his front. At his stage we may judge that the Danish right flank, impatient to press forward while the opportunity still presented itself, made to descend the north-eastern edge of Moulsford Down as though to thrust between Alfred and the river. The young prince delayed no further. He gave the order to charge and his men, fighting for God, for Wessex and their families, threw themselves at the Danes with unrestrained ferocity. The clash with which they met resonated around the Berkshire hills and the Danish earls, shaken by the impact, pulled backwards along the ridge, thus exposing the right flank of their main body. What had started as Alfred's spontaneous reaction to a dangerously unfolding situation had now developed into a classic flank attack on the enemy position.

At this juncture, Aethelred's division, noting the disarray in Halfdan's shield-wall as he reacted to the disastrous events on his eastern flank, charged down from their vantage point across the valley and joined the fray on Moulsford Down. Some time elapsed, amid the confusion and movement of the battle, before the Saxon domination became evident, and then,

> the Vikings . . . took to ignominious flight. One of the two Viking kings and five earls were cut down in that place, and many thousands on the Viking side were slain there too – or rather, over the whole broad expanse of Ashdown, scattered everywhere, far and wide: so King Bagseg was killed, and Earl Sidroc the Old, Earl Sidroc the Younger, Earl Osbern, Earl Fraena and King Harold; and the entire Viking army was put to flight, right on till nightfall and into the following day, until such time as they reached the stronghold from which they had come. The Christians followed them until nightfall, cutting them down on all sides.[24]

The statement that 'many thousands' of the Vikings were slain is doubtless an exaggeration but the high mortality rate among their leaders provides a sure indication of heavy fighting and suggests an unusually high casualty rate among the rank and file of both armies, probably numbering several hundreds on both sides. Moulsford Down stretches for more than a mile from east to west. It is thus not difficult to accept the description that the slain lay, scattered far and wide, 'over the whole broad expanse of Ashdown', for many would have fallen in the wake of Alfred's flank attack along the ridge as he cut his way towards the main body of the Viking army.

In view of the Viking tactical policy of avoiding large-scale military confrontation, the Danish commander clearly could not have anticipated that his army would sustain casualties of this magnitude. Only a few days previously, with apparent ease, he had repulsed the combined assault of Aethelred and Alfred on his Reading stronghold. The ferocity of the West Saxon stand at Ashdown must therefore have come as rather a painful surprise and, if his losses were as severe as seems likely, then any plans he may have had for further operations would have needed to be drastically curtailed, if not abandoned, until his numbers could be strengthened. Yet within a fortnight we find him in the field once more, this time fighting a battle against the West Saxons at Basing, suggesting strongly that he had either received reinforcements or, alternatively, that reports of his casualties at Ashdown had been greatly exaggerated. Indeed many early and medieval chroniclers are guilty of distortions of this nature, nor can Asser's *Life of King Alfred* be said to be free from them, both from his evident desire to flatter his royal patron and because it was written, in part, for wartime consumption and, in the manner of all such propaganda, unpleasant truths are frequently concealed or minimised. It is noticeable in his account of the Ashdown battle, for example, that no mention is made of West Saxon losses, despite the fact that in the bloody, hand-to-hand fighting which then took place, these must have been as numerous and comparably as severe as those inflicted on the enemy. Thus, after three weeks of fighting, the West Saxons would also have been seeking replacements for their accumulated losses; however, because of the structure of their peasant-based army, their reserves on this occasion would not have been so readily to hand as those of the Danes.

The armies that the royal brothers commanded were organised geographically by shires and each of these territorial units, commanded by its ealdorman, as already mentioned above,[25] was capable of operating as an army in itself, but the logistical support of a shire force was easiest when operating within its own borders. From the viewpoint of the king, the supreme commander, the weakness of the shire unit was twofold. First, the motivation that inspired it was the defence of its own territory; secondly, in the event of a war and a shire being overrun by enemy action, the unit was almost certainly lost for further service with the national *fyrd*. In the face of defeat, except in rare instances where professional warriors may have followed the royal standard, the peasant soldiery tended to return to their homes and families. Thus, as the shires fell like ninepins in the face of the Danish advance, the West Saxon manpower problems multiplied.

In these circumstances, and as intelligence reports began to filter through of reinforcements advancing up the Thames to join Halfdan, it would not have been long before the royal brothers began to appreciate the scale of the predicament confronting them for, as the Danes built up their strength at Reading, Halfdan could release his main force to maraud almost at will. As the West Saxons moved to counter these threats, the way would open up for a Viking thrust along the Thames Valley and the seizure both of the supply centre at Abingdon and the Saxon stronghold at Wallingford, with its vital command of road and river communications. The achievement of this aim, bearing in mind Mercia's neutrality, would have rendered the whole of the northern frontier of Wessex vulnerable to attack.

At that time, the Thames was probably navigable as far as Cricklade and certainly as far as Lechlade, and, in the manner that the Danes used the roads and riverways of Northumbria to cross northern England, the waters of the Thames, the Severn and the Bristol Avon would now become available to them, together with the vital land bridge between the latter two rivers – the traditional invasion route which linked Mercia with Wessex.

For these reasons, particularly the growing Danish strength and the increasing fragility of the West Saxon tactical situation, the military efforts of both protagonists would have been increasingly concentrated on the north-east corner of Wessex. It is thus essential to bear this consideration in mind when contemplating the manoeuvring of both sides from this point forward.

The *Anglo-Saxon Chronicle* relates that a fortnight after Ashdown, on 22 January,

> King Aethelred and his brother Alfred fought against the army at Basing, and there the Danes had the victory. And two months later, King Aethelred and his brother Alfred fought against the army at *Meretun*, and they were in two divisions; and they put both to flight and were victorious far on into the day; and there was great slaughter on both sides; and the Danes had possession of the battlefield . . . And after this battle, a great summer army came to Reading . . . And a month later, King Alfred fought with a small force against the whole army at Wilton and put it to flight far on into the day; and the Danes had possession of the battlefield.[26]

Asser, in his version of these events, omits any mention of *Meretun* and implies that the new Danish army, headed by the kings Guthrum, Oscetel and Anwend,

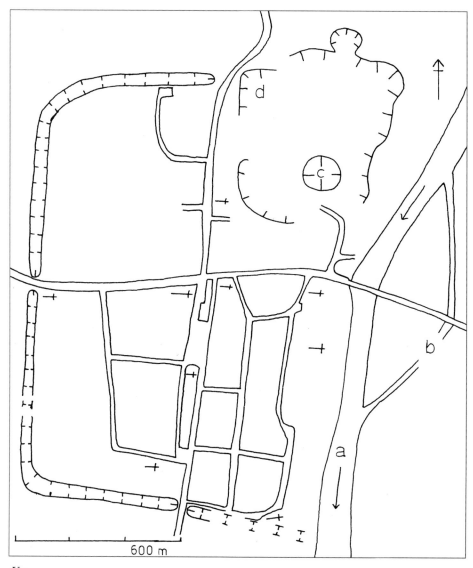

Key:

a – *River Thames*
b – *boundary ditch marking possible bridge-head defence*
c – *Norman castle*
d – *Saxon gateway and road, obliterated by thirteenth-century extension of castle.*

A plan of Wallingford, an important Saxon stronghold on the River Thames. (Author's Collection. From D.A. Hinton, Alfred's Kingdom: Wessex and the South 800–1500)

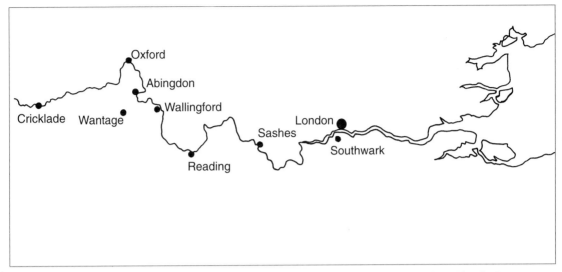

The course of the River Thames, the principal access route for the Danish invaders. They built a stronghold along the river at Reading, and the recorded burhs *at Cricklade, Oxford, Wallingford, Sashes and Southwark show its importance. (Aardvark Illustration)*

arrived after the battle at Basing. He relates, quite simply, that 'when that was over, another Viking army came from overseas and attached itself to the band'. The author of the *Anglo-Saxon Chronicle*, on the other hand, relates that the 'summer army' came to Reading after the battle at *Meretun*. By this wording it is clearly possible that Guthrum arrived in the lower Thames at a much earlier time and this possibility should not be overlooked when discussing the various factors that would have influenced the operational decisions made by Aethelred and Alfred at this moment. Indeed the threat of Guthrum's presence in the river estuary may well have brought about the weakening of West Saxon resolve which reveals itself after the Basing affair.

The site of the battlefield at Basing is traditionally said to be situated east of Basingstoke, at the north-east corner of Hackwood Park and 18 miles, or a day's march, south of Reading. It lies within easy reach both of the Hardway and the North Hampshire Ridgeway which, in its journey westwards, later becomes known as the Inkpen Ridgeway. Its route carries it past Oakley to Walbury Camp and thence onwards, through the great junction of tracks and Ridgeways at Tidcombe.[27] We can only speculate on the events which led both armies to Basing to renew their conflict yet again. It is sometimes suggested that the Danes were intercepted by the West Saxon army while marching south to plunder Winchester

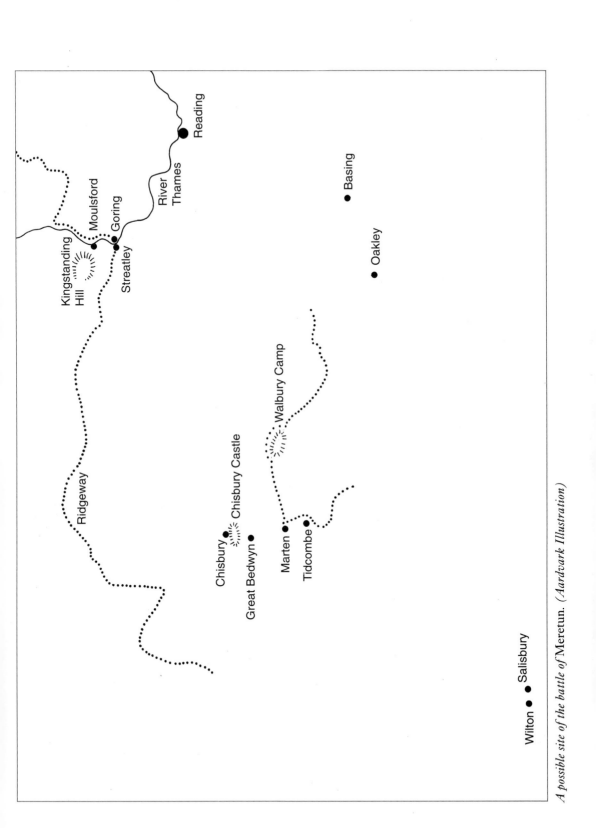

A possible site of the battle of Meretun. (Aardvark Illustration)

but it must surely be unlikely that, only a fortnight after their defeat at Ashdown and with a victorious army in the field, they would have risked plunging unnecessarily and, for them, uncharacteristically, into hostile territory in this manner, so far from their secure base. It is more probable either that they were out in strength on a foraging expedition or, alternatively, that they were once more engaged in a ploy to bring the West Saxons to battle.

The scene of the action at Wilton in 871, the final encounter with the Danes before Alfred made peace with Halfdan, has been equally clearly defined. Asser describes it as having taken place in the proximity of a hill 'situated on the southern bank of the River *Guilo* or Wylye, from which the whole district takes its name'. This locates the battlefield on the western fringes of Salisbury and this fact, together with a firm location for Basing, provides the alignment for the withdrawal of the West Saxons which now took place, either westwards from Basing or south from the Wallingford and Moulsford area.

In the interval between the confrontations at Basing and Wilton, the battle at *Meretun* was fought. The whereabouts of this place has provoked much discussion over many years, perhaps because the sites suggested for it, with one exception, bear little relationship to the general pattern of the campaign. The suggestions include Morton in Berkshire; Merton in Surrey; Merton in Oxfordshire; Marden in North Wiltshire; and Martin, some 16 miles north of Wimborne, on the Dorset border. This was at one time in South Wiltshire but in 1895 was transferred to Hampshire. The latter is the more popular suggestion, principally on the grounds that King Aethelred, either having died through exhaustion or perhaps having been mortally wounded in battle, was buried in royal state at nearby Wimborne Minster on 23 April, his funeral being attended by Alfred his brother. These are very weak grounds upon which to grant it the accolade, however, for the military probability is very slight. Moreover, it is noteworthy that the body of Heahmund, Bishop of Sherborne, who was killed at *Meretun*, was subsequently borne to Keynsham for burial and, as has already been mentioned, that of ealdorman Aethelwulf of Berkshire was taken to Derby after his death at Reading. Distance, therefore, presented no deterrent to the ceremonial burial of the mighty. The theory of the proximity of Wimborne in this context is thus probably irrelevant. The argument for Marden, in North Wiltshire, is marginally stronger but is seemingly based purely on its location beneath the northern escarpment of Salisbury Plain. Strangely, the much more robust claims of nearby Marten, situated some 13 miles to the east, appear to be ignored.

Marten[28] is located on the Inkpen Ridgeway, adjoining Tidcombe and some 20 miles north of Wilton. It is linked northwards, through Compton Down, with the ridgeway to Moulsford, Streatley and Kingstanding Hill. Eastwards, it connects with Basing, along the North Hampshire Ridgeway. Both these trackways pass beneath the precipitous slopes of Walbury Camp, the highest chalk hill in England, with commanding views over Savernake Forest and the surrounding countryside. The Inkpen Ridgeway runs through the Camp, from the north-east to the south-west corners, and originally provided the old county boundary between Berkshire and Hampshire, before the parish of Combe was given to Berkshire.[29] It would thus have been, administratively, an excellent site for the West Saxons to summon the shire components of their army, with their dependence upon the logistical support of their individual counties; nor is it difficult to imagine the various West Saxon contingents from Hampshire, Berkshire and North Wiltshire deployed in these hillforts at this dangerous moment, covering the downland gap between the Savernake and Windsor Forests which gave access deep into the heart of Wessex.

There is, however, more than purely geographical evidence in support of Marten as the site of the battle of *Meretun*. In the ninth century the land at and surrounding the neighbouring village of Great Bedwyn was held by Alfred himself and in 900 he bequeathed it to his son and heir Edward. In earlier times it had been the residence of Cissa, the powerful ealdorman of both Berkshire and Wiltshire, who gave his name to nearby Chisbury Castle. Indeed, it has been suggested by Hinton[30] that this ancient British hillfort, later enlarged by the Saxons, is identifiable with *Cissanbyrig*, one of the unknown *burhs* listed in the Burghal Hidage. The important strategic position of this hill feature would seem to strengthen this claim.

Thus, one may summarise the events of this period as follows: Halfdan arrived at Reading, probably on New Year's Day 871, and three days later one of his foraging parties was engaged and driven off by Berkshiremen under their ealdorman, Aethelwulf, at Englefield. On 8 January, heartened by this success, the combined armies of King Aethelred and Alfred laid siege to the Danish base at Reading but were savagely rebuffed. Despite this, four days later the royal brothers handsomely defeated the Danes at the battle of Ashdown and Halfdan retreated to his river stronghold for a space of some ten days. During this time it is likely that he received reinforcements from the lower Thames, either from a band already there or from Guthrum, for on or about 22 January he defeated the West Saxon army at Basing. It appears likely that both sides then returned to

Aerial picture of the hillfort at Walbury. The ancient Inkpen Ridgeway runs straight across the centre of the camp. (Aerofilms)

their respective operational bases, the Danes to be further reinforced and the West Saxons for withdrawal to a rear defensive position, probably in the Great Bedwyn and Walbury Camp area. The way was now open for Halfdan to advance to Wallingford. After its occupation, he moved south to renew contact with the West Saxon forces, who were then deployed in the Savernake gap. He encountered them at Marten on or about 22 March. The chronicler relates that 'there was great slaughter on both sides', with the Danes winning 'possession of the battlefield'. It is possible that Aethelred was wounded during the fighting, although this is nowhere recorded.[31] Afterwards, 'after Easter (15 April), King Aethelred died, and he had reigned for five years and his body is buried at Wimborne Minster . . . [and] then his brother Alfred, the son of Aethelwulf, succeeded to the kingdom of the West Saxons . . .'. The young king's darkest days still lay ahead.

CHAPTER 5

'That oft-defeated King'

They then addressed themselves to the water; and entering, Christian began to sink, and crying out to his good friend, Hopeful, he said I sink in deep waters; the billows go over my head, all his waves go over me, Selah. Then said the other, be of good cheer my brother, I feel the bottom and it is good.

John Bunyan, *The Pilgrim's Progress*

King Aethelred died shortly after Easter 871. He is said by some chroniclers, such as John of Brompton, to have been mortally wounded in the course of the fighting at *Meretun*. Others imply that he collapsed, broken down by the exertions and anxieties heaped upon him during the closing year of his reign. His body was then borne in state to Wimborne Minster and there he was buried in the presence of his brother Alfred. The church where he was laid, together with his tomb, was later destroyed by the Danes during one of their forays into Wessex. At a later date the present Minster was built upon the site of the original church and, in the mid-fourteenth century, his earlier burial was commemorated by three brass plates, mounted on a slab of Purbeck marble, let into the floor on the north side of the sanctuary.[1] Upon one of these he is described as both saint and martyr. He was in fact never formally canonised but it has been suggested that, if he had truly been mortally wounded in battle, fighting as a Christian king against a pagan army, he would have been entitled, 'according to the usage of the times . . . to be spoken of in those terms'.[2] This may therefore confirm the manner of his death.

Aethelred had, in the words of Asser, 'vigorously and honourably ruled the kingdom in good repute, amid many difficulties, for five years'. He left two young sons, the senior of whom, Aethelwold, might under normal circumstances have assumed he had the right of succession to the crown upon his father's death – but times were not normal, Wessex was under siege and the heir to the throne was a child. Alfred was therefore speedily appointed by the *witan* to assume his brother's place. It had, after all, been his father's wish and can only have been

The memorial brass of King Aethelred in Wimborne Minster, Dorset. (Author's Collection)

regarded as a sensible decision. Nevertheless, doubtless because the young princes were well advanced into adulthood by the time Asser was writing his *Life of King Alfred*, it cost the bishop some complicated lines in explanation.[3] They did not, however, prevent Aethelwold from contesting the succession with his cousin Edward after the death of his uncle in 899:

> Alfred who until that time [while his brothers were alive] had been 'heir apparent', took over the government of the whole kingdom as soon as his brother had died, with the approval of divine will and according to the unanimous wish of all the inhabitants of the kingdom. Indeed, he could easily have taken it over with the consent of all while his brother Aethelred was alive, had he considered himself worthy to do so, for he surpassed his brothers both in wisdom and in all good habits; and in particular because he was a great warrior and victorious in virtually all battles.[4]

In these words Asser asks us to believe that the promotion of Alfred to the throne, over the head of his older brother, at the age of eighteen and without the experience he was to gain politically and militarily during the five years of the latter's reign, was something the senior clergy and nobility of Wessex would have been prepared to support upon the death of Aethelbald. More than this Asser suggests that they would even have condoned Alfred's seizure of power from Aethelred, during his older brother's reign, had he chosen to exercise this extreme measure. In view of the fears of civil war generated by the earlier quarrel between Aethelwulf and Aethelbald, from which both men to their credit had done their best to extricate themselves, this would surely have been an unwarranted risk for the king's council to have undertaken without good reason. Such a situation could only have arisen if Aethelred had, in some way, failed to achieve the expectations placed upon him by his people; but we know this was not the case. A notoriously pious man, he is said by the chronicler to have ruled his kingdom in 'good repute'. It thus appears that, for whatever reason these thoughts were put into words, they can have borne little relation to actuality. Moreover, the further claim that the young king, at the time of coming to his throne, had been 'victorious in virtually all battles' appears equally extravagant.

According to Asser, the West Saxons fought eight battles in the year 871, concluding with the encounter at Wilton, but he makes no reference to *Meretun*. Aethelweard's *Chronicle*[5] on the other hand mentions nine battles but also refers to one fought while Alfred was attending his brother's funeral ceremony at

Wimborne. He omits Wilton, so there may be some error of timing here. The *Anglo-Saxon Chronicle* records that, during the course of the year, 'nine general engagements were fought against the Danish army south of the Thames'.[6] Of these nine, details of six battles are known: Englefield, Reading, Ashdown, Basing, *Meretun* and Wilton.

Alfred was not present at the opening encounter at Englefield, where the men of Berkshire under ealdorman Aethelwulf put to flight a Danish foraging party. Four days later the combined forces of Aethelred and Alfred were forced to disengage from their assault upon the Danish stronghold at Reading after being thrown back by a fierce enemy counter-attack. Another four days later the brothers gained a significant victory at Ashdown, where Alfred distinguished himself not only by his personal bravery but also by an alert military sense, which allowed him to take quick tactical advantage of a potentially threatening situation. This success was followed, firstly, by the defeat of the two princes at Basing and, then, at *Meretun*, where it is hard to recognise the language of victory in the chronicler's account of the fighting, which left the Danes in possession of the battlefield. Finally, Alfred, with the residue of the West Saxon army, depleted of the men of Berkshire and, possibly, of a large part of Hampshire, since he had now been driven back across the eastern borders of Wiltshire and Dorset, 'fought with a small force against the whole army at Wilton and put it to flight far into the day'. Even then, we are yet again told that, at the end of the day's fighting, the Danes 'held possession of the battlefield'. Asser's account of some of these confrontations is somewhat reminiscent of that of the war correspondent of the London *Times* in February 1881, when describing the outcome of the battle of Laing's Nek: 'The engagement was not a defeat. We simply failed to take the position.'

This was hardly the stuff by which it could be claimed that Alfred had been 'victorious in virtually all battles'. It has already been suggested above[7] that Aethelred and Alfred were defeated not by lack of purpose or gallantry of effort but by the antiquated military structure they had inherited, which failed to make full use of the manpower Wessex had at its disposal. It was to Alfred's credit that he was quick to identify the problem and to take action to remedy it. It is a pity that, possessed of this knowledge, he did not make the reasons for his difficulties clear to his biographer, instead of allowing him to imply that their burden arose from the 'great losses of many men while his brothers were alive'.[8]

Equally, there can be little doubt that the members of the original army with which Halfdan marched from East Anglia at the turn of the year had also suffered grievous losses during the course of their operations, although the general effectiveness of the Danish force had been successfully revitalised from time to time by injections of fresh manpower, which culminated with the arrival of Guthrum's 'summer army'. As a matter of general habit, fighting of this severity was unacceptable to the Vikings, who were in the business of raiding with the practical purpose of living to enjoy the fruits of the labours. There are signs that Halfdan's men may already have seen their continuous operations and heavy casualties carrying them away from this satisfactory objective. Consequently, after the battle at Wilton, when Alfred offered terms to the Danes on condition that they should leave Wessex in peace, it is likely that Halfdan welcomed the opportunity of talks, despite the military advantage he then clearly held. It is likely that he extracted severe concessions for doing so. Asser makes no mention of their scale, other than the coded expression that the Saxons 'made peace with the Vikings', an expression which generally signified the payment of Danegeld or some other form of tribute. It is, however, additionally noticeable that from that moment forward, until Alfred opened his counter-attack against Guthrum in 878, West Saxon operations appear to have been confined to that part of Wessex lying west of the Hampshire Avon. It is thus not inconceivable that, as part of the terms then negotiated, the territory situated east of the river was either designated a neutral area or, more probably, in the manner of Mercia, was mutually acknowledged as being contained within the Danish sphere of influence.

In the meantime Halfdan pulled back to Reading, thus allowing Alfred the opportunity of collecting, by taxation, the sum of money agreed. The winter of 872 found the Great Army in London, raising yet more Danegeld from the Mercians, and then in the following year Halfdan's attention was claimed by the uprising in Northumbria against his puppet ruler Egbert. Halfdan marched north and took up winter quarters at Torksey, neatly situated at the junction made by the River Trent with the ancient Roman canal passing through Lincoln and linking with the Witham. He thus provided himself with speedy access by water in three directions: to the Wash and East Anglia; southwards along the Trent to Nottingham; and northwards, by means of the Trent and the Humber, to Northumbrian York. In 874 he tightened his grip on Mercia. He penetrated yet further up the Trent to Repton, situated, as it is today, midway between Derby and Burton and, while there he

forced Burghred, King of the Mercians, to abandon his kingdom against his his wish, to go abroad and to set out for Rome, in the 22nd year of his reign . . .

After his expulsion, the Vikings reduced the whole kingdom of the Mercians to their authority; however, by a wretched arrangement they entrusted it to a certain foolish king's thegn, who was called Ceowulf, on their terms of custody, that whenever they should wish to have it again, he should hand it over peacefully to them. He gave hostages to them under the terms of this arrangement, and he swore that in no way would he wish to countermand their intentions, but would be obedient in all respects.[9]

While this was happening, Halfdan was already reassessing his future plans, for the death of his brother Ivar in Ireland in the previous year had not only resulted in violent clashes between Norwegian and Danish factions for possession of the latter's territories, but had already loosened the Lothbrok family's grip on the strategically important routes in northern Britain (see Appendix B) which linked Northumbria with Dublin. These included the track and riverways connecting the Dumbarton and Clyde estuaries. It will be recalled that Ivar had marched north from East Anglia in 871 to establish his influence over the Picts and the Scots. Halfdan and Ubba now decided that their own futures lay in the same direction and, seemingly at this juncture, they handed over to Guthrum their interest in the conquest of Wessex. As a consequence, the Great Army now divided, Guthrum, with Oscetel and Anwend, marching to spend the winter in Cambridge, preparatory to launching a renewed attack on Wessex, and the Lothbrok brothers setting out for Northumbria. Events were to show that they were nevertheless still intent on operating together, despite the distances involved, should a favourable opportunity arise.

Halfdan's immediate task was to reopen the Clyde route to Ireland; then, in 875, he attacked Dublin in an unsuccessful attempt to regain Ivar's lost possessions. His persistent attempt to do this untimately cost him not only the support of his soldiers, who were now more intent on farming than fighting, but also his life. He travelled in 877 on his last journey to Ireland where, among many other traditional tales, he is said to have been killed in a sea battle on Strangford Lough by his son's successor, the ruthless Norwegian Bardr, King of Dublin.

*   *   *

It is apparent from the various chronicled accounts of Guthrum's surprise attack on western Wessex in 876 that his plans had been meticulously prepared. This was no piratical raid, seeking plunder. His army moved in two divisions, the field force, mounted and thrusting across country at surprising speed, was given the task of penetrating to the south coast and seizing his chosen objective, Wareham. The main body, travelling by sea around the south-eastern coast of Wessex, was planned to reach the same objective almost simultaneously. The field force, presumably under the command of Guthrum and with the purpose of forestalling any attempt by the Mercians to send a prior warning to Alfred, marched from Cambridge under cover of darkness and in conditions of great secrecy. The success of the Danish operation depended upon their commander's ability to achieve surprise but the likelihood of this was weakened by the fact that he had a march of some 130 miles which, at best, would take the column four days to cover. It was therefore essential that he should choose the most direct and least complicated route, which would allow him to lay up by day and travel by night (assuming the light of a moon).

We are not told of Alfred's whereabouts at this moment but we do know that he had not been militarily idle since his defeat at Wilton. In 875 he had headed a successful naval battle 'against the crews of seven ships, had captured one ship and put the rest to flight'.[10] More than this, the chronicle for 876 suggests that the West Saxon army was already in the field when Guthrum entered Wessex. If this is so, Alfred had anticipated a renewal of hostilities, and we may assume that he had taken action to patrol the river barrier offered by the Thames and to watch and guard its more important crossing-places. He held under his hand, for immediate operations, the *fyrd* provided by the men of Wiltshire, strengthened by the men of his own household bodyguard and doubtless by many volunteers ready to fight for his cause. It would not have been wise for him, at this stage, to have committed his army to the defence of any particular area. His priority would have been to discern his enemy's intention at the earliest possible moment. For this purpose no position could have been more suitable than the site of his earlier encounter with the Danes at *Meretun*, from where he could have moved north to defend his frontiers with Mercia or south to the ford at Old Sarum, upon which a network of Roman and ancient roads converged from the north and the east.

It is generally judged that Guthrum's journey south would have led him straight down the Icknield Way and thence, by East Kennet, through the Vale of Pewsey and across Salisbury Plain to Old Sarum, fording the Avon at Harnham, before continuing on his road to Wareham. Such a route would, however, have been hazardous. It would have carried his field force, which by necessity would have comprised the minor part of his total army, directly into the West Saxon military heartland and consequently into a veritable hornets' nest. The Danish

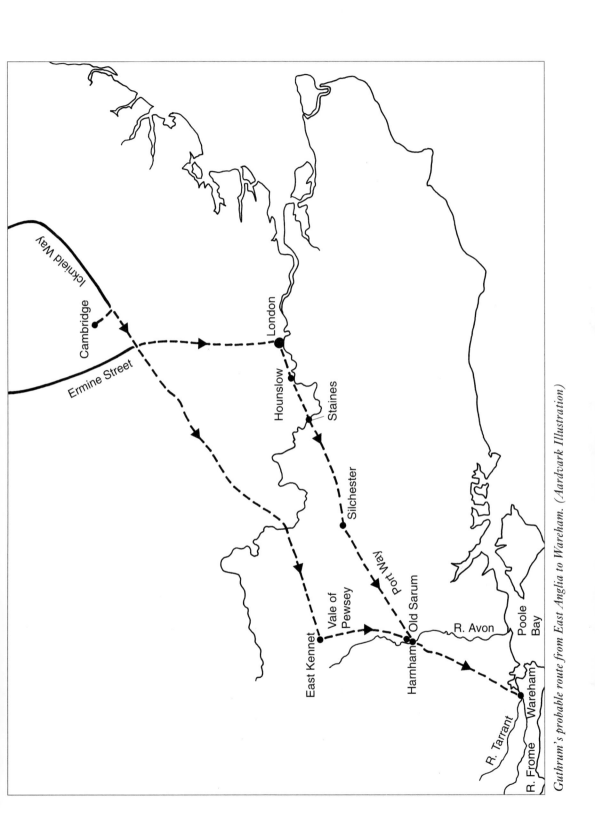

Guthrum's probable route from East Anglia to Wareham. (Aardvark Illustration)

commander's secret departure from Cambridge indicates that he was well aware of Alfred's preparedness and, since he hoped to evade combat, it is more probable that he would have opted to cross the Thames further downstream, in a less sensitive area, perhaps even disguising his real intentions by marching directly down Ermine Street to London. From there, he could have taken the Silchester road, the main Roman arterial route to the west country, heading through Brentford and Hounslow, to cross the river by the bridge at Staines. He would then have marched to the great track and road centre at Silchester, afterwards taking the line of the old Roman roads of Port Way and Ackling Dyke, a route that would have carried him away from the West Saxon frontier posts and to his chosen objective, the fortified port at Wareham.

If he did in fact cross the Avon under cover of darkness and outpace the opposition, it would fit the words of the *Anglo-Saxon Chronicle* that he had 'slipped past the army of the West Saxons into Wareham'.[11] Even so, the question remains, why did he select Wareham in the first place? Since Guthrum's ultimate intention was clearly the conquest of western Wessex, the answer can only be that he saw the port as an essential step in this direction: but to what end?

The Viking military dependence upon waterborne operations has already been emphasised. Undoubtedly Halfdan had achieved his victory at Wilton by a three-day march into Wessex but this had been an uncharacteristic movement, which stretched his lines of communication to such a dangerous degree that he not only put his river base in jeopardy but also placed at risk his own position in the field, should matters have gone against him. Consequently if Alfred had possessed the resources at that moment to fall back yet again and continue fighting, it is likely that the Danish commander would have been reluctant to pursue him further, for the West Saxon shire system of defence, inefficient as it was in many ways, had one most satisfactory feature: it provided defence in depth. Moreover, at this most vital moment in the campaign, the manpower resources of Devon, Dorset and Somerset had not yet been committed to the field: they stood intact, ready to be called upon and, as has been demonstrated, out of reach of the Danes.

Guthrum fully appreciated that he could not succeed in his aim until he had successfully brought the west country shire *fyrds* to battle and had defeated them in the field. There can be little doubt that this was a problem fully discussed between Halfdan and himself before they went their respective ways in 875. Their natural dependence upon shipping, and the lack of suitably large riverways penetrating southwards into Wessex from the Thames Valley, applied a topographical brake upon the Danish scope for manoeuvre in their endeavour to occupy what was left of the last remaining independent Saxon kingdom in Britain. In the past few years they had taken considerable steps towards attaining total conquest but, unless they drastically reappraised their military strategy, they had now reached an impasse. It is thus likely that, before departing from Repton on their respective missions, they had already agreed plans to open a second front against the West Saxons, which would enable them jointly to strike a vital blow at the hitherto secure south-west corner of the kingdom.

The ancient British inhabitants of Strathclyde, Wales and Cornwall, or the 'Welsh' as they were called at this time, had no cause to look upon their Saxon neighbours with anything other than deep animosity. Over many years they had been driven into the western extremities of the British Isles by the relentless advance of generations of Saxons. Consequently it is not surprising that they should have strenuously resisted any suggestions of further intrusion and regarded the land-hungry Saxons with a hostility that frequently erupted into open warfare. There is no shortage of examples: in 838, when a great Viking 'naval force arrived among the West Welsh in Cornwall', the latter eagerly allied themselves with these new arrivals to make war against Egbert of Wessex. They were soundly beaten for their temerity. In another instance, in 853, Burghred of Mercia enlisted the support of Aethelwulf of Wessex in subduing the tribes along his Welsh frontier. A few years later, the 'Welsh' of Strathclyde joined with Norwegian Vikings in making life uncomfortable for the inhabitants of Northumbria. In these circumstances it is not unreasonable to assume that, although the men of Cornwall had been remarkably quiescent since their defeat by Egbert, Guthrum regarded them as potential allies. Indeed one might go yet further and suggest that either he or Halfdan had already opened negotiations with Cornish leaders to this end and that the arrival at Exeter, by sea, of the main body of Guthrum's army, bolstered by the appearance in the Bristol Channel of further reinforcements under Ubba (with, it was hoped, Halfdan) could well have provided Guthrum with the spark he was seeking to ignite the flame of victory.

The first stepping-stone in this splendidly conceived idea would have been the occupation of Wareham, a fort of intrinsic strength and great antiquity, tactically sited between the Rivers Frome and Tarrant, which closely skirt its southern and northern ramparts before virtually uniting about a mile eastwards and flowing into Poole Bay. Thus between the sea and the eastern walls of the fort there lay a square mile of naturally defended grazing and agricultural land, which would have proved of great advantage to the Vikings. The military defences of the town were weakest on its open, western flank, which led to gently rising heathland.

Overall, it possessed 2,180 yards of ramparts enclosing an area of one hide, or approximately 100 acres.[12] Using Alfred's later calculations, a wall of this length would have required a force of some 1,600 men to defend it, a figure that may give some hint as to the strength of Guthrum's mounted party, which had the initial responsibility for securing the base. Wareham at this time was also the location of a nunnery[13] which, in the manner of those days, may be expected to have operated a productive farm. The stronghold would therefore have offered many attractions for the Danish army.

War, like life, is seldom predictable and Guthrum's plans for the conquest of south-western Wessex were soon to be disrupted, when Halfdan met his death in battle at much the same time that the Cambridge army was setting forth on its dash for Wareham. If we are correct in conjecturing that both men had jointly planned the operation, then we must assume that Guthrum was unaware of the disaster that had befallen his partner. If he had been, he might have contemplated postponing his departure until he could have found another battle group to fill Halfdan's essential role in their plan of campaign. Nevertheless, he did not do badly. His seizure of Wareham was uncontested. A later historian attributed this to the battle-weariness of the men of Wessex: 'the battle axes and spears of the Saxons had already on many occasions resisted the encroachments of the Danes till the unfurling of the standard had lost its charm and the call to arms was unrecognised'.[14] As a result, having taken King Alfred completely by surprise, Guthrum was successfully entrenched within the stronghold before the Saxons could react to his presence. He was soon to be joined by the fleet that was making its way towards him, southwards from the Wash, carrying the main body of his army. We may assume his longships, when they arrived, made full use of the sheltered waters offered by Poole Bay and Brownsea Island.

Alfred, in the meantime, had collected his forces and marched on Wareham. His previous experiences with Halfdan had taught him the dangers of attacking Viking armies ensconced behind well-defended positions. It was presumably for this reason that he contented himself with blockading the western approach to the fort, while simultaneously opening negotiations with Guthrum to bring about his peaceful departure. These seemingly took some months to conclude but ultimately he was successful in agreeing a treaty. The chronicler Aethelweard states that Alfred gave money to the Vikings as part of the deal; if this were so, it would imply that to Alfred's mind the initiative lay with the enemy. Then, as a gesture of good faith, Guthrum

The statue of King Alfred in Winchester. (John Crook)

The frontispiece of King Edgar's charter, dated 966, refounding New Minster, Winchester. The king is offering the charter in book form to a Christ figure. The later Saxon kings took great interest in education and learning. (British Library)

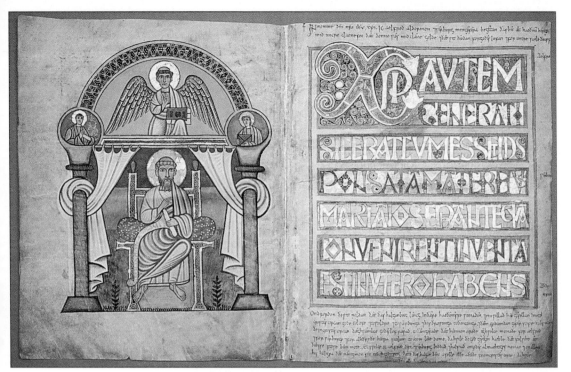

The Codex Aureus, an eighth-century copy of the four gospels made at Canterbury, was stolen by the Vikings in the ninth century. Marginal notes record how Ealdorman Alfred and his wife bought it back form the pagans for gold and presented it to Christ Church, Canterbury. (Kungliga Biblioteket, Stockholm)

The Alfred jewel. (Ashmolean Museum, Oxford)

The expulsion of the Danes from Manchester, painted by Ford Madox Brown, 1880. This mural in Manchester Town Hall is typical of the revival of interest in Viking subjects during the Victorian era. (Manchester City Art Galleries)

Vikings burying their hoard: stained glass window from Brindle public house. (David Flower/National Museums & Galleries on Merseyside)

Alfred in the Danish Camp; painting by Daniel Maclise. (Tyne & Wear Museums)

Saxon swords. (Copyright Reading Museum (Reading Borough Council). All rights reserved.)

Alfred translates Pastoral Care *by Pope Gregory the Great; painting by Harry Mileham, 1909. (Bridgeman Art Library)*

A model for Alfred's navy; painting by John Horsley, 1851. (Bridgeman Art Library / Walker Galleries, Harrogate)

Part of the town of Wallingford, Oxfordshire, developed from a Saxon burh. (Aerofilms)

Westbury white horse marks the site of Alfred's victory over the Danes at Edington. (Aerofilms)

without any dispute, gave him as many picked hostages as he alone chose, and they also took an oath, on all the relics in which the king placed the greatest trust after God Himself (and on which they had never before been willing to take an oath to any race), that they would immediately leave his kingdom. But one night, practising their usual treachery, after their own manner, and paying no heed to the hostages, the oath and the promise of faith, they broke the treaty, killed all the hostages and . . . went unexpectedly to another place called Exeter.[15]

Danish hostages, described as 'the most important men in the army next to their king',[16] had likewise been surrendered to Alfred and we can only judge that these unfortunates, abandoned by their own commander, received the same cold-blooded fate as the Saxon hostages who were ruthlessly put to death by Guthrum.

Alfred would have been deeply concerned by the break-out of the Danish mounted infantry, not only because it had been allowed to happen at all (in later years he would probably have constructed a restraining rampart across the spit of land between the Frome and the Tarrant to foil any such attempt) but also because he would at once have appreciated with dismay the full implications of Guthrum's actions. He seems immediately to have gathered a mounted party from among the troops he had with him[17] and to have set off in hot pursuit but he was 'unable to overtake them before they were in the fortress [at Exeter] where they could not be come at'. Guthrum had thus achieved his first objective and the stage was set for the main body of the Danish army to sail westwards to join their commander and open the final phase of his campaign of conquest. His ships and soldiers were almost certainly assembled in Poole Bay by this time, awaiting departure. From there, they set sail in the New Year of 877 but fate was to intervene. Alfred and the West Saxons doubtless saw it as the hand of God. A severe storm struck the fleet off Swanage; 120 ships were lost. They were carrying, at a conservative estimate of thirty soldiers per longship, a total of some 3,600 fighting men.[18]

Guthrum's position, from being one where absolute victory was clearly within his reach, was now hopeless. He gave Alfred as many hostages as the latter demanded and swore 'great oaths' to keep the peace. In exchange, seemingly over generously, he was allowed to stay until the harvest was ripe. His army then marched northwards to Mercia, doubtless closely shadowed by the West Saxons, and established a camp at Gloucester. As always with Danish planning, it was a carefully selected position which allowed him many options. Here, he was not only able to receive reinforcements either along the neutral Thames Valley or

Having left Poole Harbour, Guthrum's fleet was destroyed in a storm off Swanage. Although all is peaceful in this picture, the sea can become very rough off the headlands.(British Tourist Authority)

from Derby or Nottingham by way of the River Trent, but he was also situated on the wide waters of the River Severn and in communication with his allies and friends operating in the Bristol Channel. Moreover, he was neatly poised north of the 'land-bridge' between the sources of the River Thames and the Bristol Avon: the traditional invasion route into Wessex. He was thus positioned, when he chose to do so, to resume his attack on the West Saxons.

Alfred could not have been unaware of the Danish intentions. He moved, with his army, to Chippenham, a royal estate on the east bank of the Avon, where his sister Aethelswith had married Burghred, King of Mercia, in 853. From here, he was in a position to cover the 'land-bridge', and keep a watchful eye on Danish movements north of the Thames.

Despite the substantial manpower losses he had sustained through the calamitous destruction of his fleet off Swanage, Guthrum now acted with commendable speed. Seemingly he had ample reserves upon which to draw. Within five months he had obtained sufficient reinforcements to bring his army up to fighting strength. He then marshalled his forces once again and, taking advantage of the Saxon custom of celebrating religious holidays, attacked Chippenham on Twelfth Night in 878.[19] We do not know whether the Wiltshire *fyrd* had remained mobilised since the affair at Exeter but had now been disbanded, whether the men had simply returned home to celebrate Christmastide with their families or whether the ealdorman and thegns had decided their presence was no longer necessary. However it may have been, Guthrum found the Chippenham stronghold only lightly held, protected mainly by Alfred's personal bodyguard, and it fell freely into his hands.

At first sight, it does seem that the situation called for the defences of the royal estate to be strongly garrisoned and that Alfred's failure to do so must have dealt yet another demoralising blow to the inhabitants of Wessex. On the other hand, it is possible to find a good military argument to the contrary. If Guthrum's lightning swoop had found the men of Wiltshire behind the walls of Chippenham, it is probable that the garrison would have been pinned down, possibly outnumbered and very likely defeated by the professional army confronting them. The king would have lost an important part of the army that remained to him. There was therefore a powerful case for holding back the Wiltshire *fyrd*, even sending the men home to await recall for use on a more tactically suitable occasion, while at the same time keeping the armies of Dorset, Devon and Somerset on stand-by and employed on coastal surveillance within their shire areas. We have already discussed the vulnerability of the Wessex coastline and the Danish ease of access. In these circumstances Chippenham could have been held by a strong standing patrol to give warning of Guthrum's return. Such a task could have been performed most adequately by the king's household troops. Moreover, an arrangement of this nature would have been logistically economical and would have enabled Alfred to call his army together at another time, on a battlefield of his own choosing. In the meantime his forces would have been kept widely but safely deployed in an important defensive role.

In the event this is what actually happened but it would be rash to suggest that this was the way it was planned. Indeed the manner in which the affair is treated

The south porch of Pen Selwood Church near Wincanton (opposite) contains some characteristic Norman zigzag carving. Above the lintel is carved a lamb in a circle, with a lion and lioness to either side. At the corners are the crowned heads of two kings, believed by some people to represent King Alfred (left) and King Guthrum. (S.M. Fowle)

by contemporary chroniclers is significant. The *Anglo-Saxon Chronicle*, having already mentioned Guthrum's arrival in Mercia after the débâcle at Exeter, treats the episode with evident delicacy:

> In this year, after twelfth night, the enemy army came stealthily to Chippenham and occupied the land of the West Saxons and settled there, and drove a great part of the people across the sea, and conquered most of the others; and the people submitted to them, except King Alfred. He journeyed in difficulties through the woods and fen fastnesses with a small force.[20]

Asser on the other hand – and we need not remind ourselves that his sources originated either from the king personally or from members of his immediate entourage – totally evades the issue by omitting any reference to Guthrum's earlier withdrawal to Mercia from Exeter, and relates that:

> In the year of the Lord's Incarnation, 878, the thirtieth of King Alfred's life, the Viking army left Exeter and went to Chippenham, a royal estate situated in the left hand [northern] part of Wiltshire . . . At the same time, King Alfred, with his small band of nobles and also with certain soldiers and thegns, was leading a restless life in great distress amid the woody and marshy places of Somerset. He had nothing to live on except what he could forage by frequent raids, either secretly or openly, from the Vikings as well as from the Christians who had submitted to the Viking authority.[21]

Asser's account of the Chippenham episode provides little evidence to sustain any thought that Alfred's withdrawal from there formed part of some preconceived plan.

*   *   *

King Alfred, with his personal bodyguard, sought refuge at Athelney, in the heart of the Somerset Levels, an area perfectly suited for guerrilla warfare. The Levels comprised both woodland and fenland, criss-crossed with timber trackways leading to local settlements in the low-lying marshes. Rising out of the fenland, which was frequently flooded by the inflowing waters of the Bristol Channel, were various scattered islands of high ground. On one of these, in the early part of the fourth century, there gathered a colony of holy men, seeking solitude for the practice of their religious devotions. The church which grew up around them was reconstructed in the eighth century and provided the early religious fabric of Glastonbury Abbey, which quickly became renowned as a great centre of learning and Celtic Christianity. The Levels were not therefore a friendless, unpopulated place, but their marshes and floodlands were penetrated only with great difficulty.

To the north the Somerset Levels are flanked by the Mendip Hills, and to the south-west by the Quantocks. To the south and east lie the Blackdown Hills and the oolitic escarpment that carries the ancient Jurassic Way southwards from the crossing over the Avon at Bath. Along this same axis Roman engineers built the famous Fosse Way, connecting Exeter with Lincoln, and linking Bath, Cirencester and Leicester. Passing within 4 miles of Chippenham, the Fosse was thus readily available for Guthrum's use.

Today, on the oolitic escarpment, stands what remains of the Selwood Forest. Its thick woodlands would have been a formidable military obstacle and would almost certainly have been regarded as such by the Danes, in whose time it reached from mid-Dorset in the south, northwards to the southern edge of Salisbury Plain. The Roman commander in southern Britain, Vespasian, during their invasion years, had been careful to avoid its most densely grown areas, and significantly he laid down his tactical road between Poole and Bath well to the east of the forest bounds. He also constructed two routes westward from the Fosse Way, one across the Mendips, connecting the valuable lead mines there first with Winchester and thence to the south coast, and the other leading across the Polden Hills. This ran north-west, through Puriton, to the Parret estuary, which probably then provided a Roman harbour, and is thought to have terminated on the west bank opposite Combwich. But Selwood Forest apparently held no fears for the users of the ubiquitous Hardway. This, most ancient of all trackways, ran through the heart of the forest, leading south-west into Devon and north-east towards Old Sarum and beyond.

Against this setting, Athelney provided an excellent base for an aggressive guerrilla commander, well protected by formidable natural obstacles but with easy access to a network of tracks and routeways leading into enemy territory. Its description by William of Malmesbury (see also Appendix C) is noteworthy. It was not, he wrote,

> an island of the sea, but is so inaccessible, on account of bogs and the inundations of the lakes, that it cannot be got to but in a boat. It has a very large wood of alders, which harbours stags, wild goats and other beasts. The firm land, which is only two acres in breadth, contains a little monastery and dwellings for monks.

Today, because of improved drainage and other reasons that form no part of this discussion, the Levels are no longer flooded to this extent. Athelney lies on the Tone, a major tributary of the Parret, and stands rather more than a mile from the confluence of the two rivers, just west of Burrow Bridge. The island may not, therefore, have been one 'of the sea', as William of Malmesbury makes clear, but there can be little doubt that it could have been reached by Danish longships entering the Parret estuary from the Bristol Channel. The Reverend John Collinson, writing in the late eighteenth century about river conditions at Burrow Bridge, recorded that the river is navigable in this hamlet, and hence to Langport. . . . At high waters, when the tide is in, the river is sixty feet wide and eighteen deep, and coal barges of forty or fifty tons easily come up it. Between this hamlet and the church of Ling is the famous isle of Athelney, being a spot on rising ground on the north side of Stanmoor, bounded on the north-west by the River Tone . . .[22]

It is clear that Alfred's hiding-place would have been very vulnerable to attack had a Danish naval force been able to penetrate the estuary and find its way upstream. This manoeuvre was soon to be attempted by Ubba, and once again we are left to marvel at Viking military aptitude, ably backed by an efficient intelligence organisation and a keen awareness of the advantages of co-ordinated manoeuvre. This third Lothbrok son, who was probably present at the battle in which his brother Halfdan was slain, had then seemingly sailed onwards from northern Ireland to seek shelter and regroup on Anglesey. It may be expected that he immediately informed Guthrum of the disaster that had befallen his party, and which inevitably would have gravely disrupted their joint plans for the conquest of Wessex. This done, he appears to have moved to Dyfed, at the mouth of the Bristol Channel, to await further instructions. These may well have ordered him forward to Gloucester to a place beside Guthrum, for he was so promptly back at sea at the renewal of the campaign, that we can only surmise he was in the presence of his supreme commander when its recommencement was being prepared.

The *Anglo-Saxon Chronicle* relates that in the same winter as 'the enemy army came stealthily to Chippenham', and there can have only been a few weeks' lapse between the two events,

the brother of Ivar and Halfdeane [Halfdan] was in the kingdom of the West Saxons, with 23 ships. And he was killed there with 640 men of his army with him. And there was captured the banner which they call the Raven.[23]

Asser provides a fuller account of how this came about. The Devonshire *fyrd*, under the command of its ealdorman Odda, and aware that the Danes were probing the northern coastline, entrenched in a disused stronghold at *Cynuit*, generally believed to have been an ancient fortification today found at Countisbury.[24] In the bishop's words, the fort 'was unprepared and altogether unfortified'. It had been hurriedly occupied and not only were its defences poor but it had not been victualled to withstand a lengthy assault. Ubba, doubtless well aware of this, could see no purpose in committing his scarce manpower to the costly task of storming the position. He opted, instead, to lay siege to it, 'thinking that those men would soon give way, forced by hunger and thirst . . . since there is no water near the stronghold'. Affairs did not turn out in this fashion. The men of Devon were all too conscious of the frailty of their situation; rather than wait until this was still further diminished by time, they broke out one morning at first light. Falling upon their pagan persecutors with pent-up exasperation, rage and honest Christian fervour, they put their enemy to the sword, with only a few of their opponents surviving the onslaught to escape to their ships. Ubba, the last of the three Lothbrok brothers who had arrived at the head of the Great Army of 866, was cut down and killed during the mêlée.

Patently this was a notable victory, for it at once lifted the pressure that Guthrum was hoping to apply to Wessex along the Bristol Channel coast. More importantly it also destroyed any hopes he might have had of bringing Cornwall into the war at an early stage. If he had been successful, and if Halfdan had not been slain in a campaign irrelevant to his war against Wessex, Guthrum might have gained an early victory. Now, although it may not have been immmediately evident to him, his opportunity to conquer Wessex had gone, destroyed by the unusual carelessness of those from whom he might have expected better, the Lothbrok brothers.

An interesting debate has taken place on the precise whereabouts of *Cynuit*, and the hillfort at Cannington, at the mouth of the Parret, has been suggested as an alternative location for Countisbury.[25] This likelihood has been lent credence by the Ordnance Surveyors who, on their 6 inch map, awarded Cannington hillfort the name of *Cynuit Castle* and placed a crossed-sword symbol on the site of its ancient cemetery.

The case for identifying Cannington as the stronghold featured in this incident is based upon the similarity of name between *Cynuit* and nearby Combwich. Whatever the justification, there are strong military reasons to support the theory; Odda, based at Cannington and overlooking the Parret estuary, would have been perfectly sited not only to command the river approaches to Athelney but also to warn Alfred of impending danger and to take military action to protect the king's thinly defended island refuge. There is little actual evidence to bolster either claim but, looked at in terms of what the well-known military historian Lieutenant-Colonel Alfred Burne called 'inherent military probability', Cannington must be the more favoured choice of the two places. If Ubba's target was indeed Athelney and Alfred, it is easy to understand his reluctance to penetrate inland until the Devonian guard-post had been neutralised, for its position would have threatened his line of withdrawal. It is noteworthy, moreover, that Alfred himself held land at Cannington. This, together with his properties 'at Bedwyn, at Pewsey, at Hurstbourne, at Sutton, at Leatherhead, at Alton, and all the booklands which I have in Kent', were bequeathed to his son Edward after his death.[26]

When Alfred fled with his household troops from Chippenham, he was hotly pursued and harried by Guthrum's mounted infantry. If the Danes had captured him at this juncture, Wessex would have collapsed. As it was, many of his countrymen refused him shelter and food in his plight and, doubtless, informed against him. He and his men had to fight, beg, borrow and steal in order to eat. He was forced to take to the back ways, moving through woods and swamps for safety. It was to be several weeks before he reached the security of the Levels. It is to this period that many traditional folk stories relate, each of them variously illustrating his troubles, his resourcefulness, his soldierly qualities and his ability to mix with the people, while simultaneously underlining the scale of his achievement in overcoming the tribulations that beset him. The most popular of these tales is related in the *Annals of St Neots*, which date from the twelfth century. It is a version of the famous story of the burning of the cakes:

> It happened one day that a certain peasant woman, wife of a certain cowherd was making loaves, and this king [Alfred] was sitting by the fire, preparing his bow and arrows and other instruments of war. But when the wretched woman saw the loaves which she had put on the fire were burning, she ran up and took them off, scolding the invincible king and saying: 'Look man, you see the loaves burning but you are not turning them, though I am sure you would be charmed to eat them warm!' The miserable woman little thought that he was King Alfred who had waged so many wars against the pagans and won so many victories over them.[27]

In another tale the king penetrates Guthrum's camp, accompanied by an attendant and disguised as a travelling minstrel. While seated at his enemy's campfire he overhears their plans and is thus enabled to lead his army to victory.

Alfred's determination and courage were not dulled by his experiences as a refugee king within his own land. Indeed, to the contrary, they appear to have been strengthened, from which we may assume that at some time in his wanderings he met with the ealdormen of the shires of western Wessex and was assured by them of their unfailing loyalty and their continued ability to produce their *fyrds* in his support whenever summoned to do so. Meantime, he got on with the business of establishing a stronghold on Athelney and moving over to the offensive. Within a few months, by Easter, he had been joined by a contingent of the men of Somerset, while the men of Devon continued to guard the coastline.

From this well-concealed and secure position he soon opened a brief, vigorous and sustained guerrilla war against his enemies. Later, with the experience and intelligence thus gained, he was ready to counter-attack in strength.

CHAPTER 6

Wessex Reconquered

We got run out of Burma and it is as humiliating as hell. I think we ought to find out what caused it, go back and retake it.

General Jo Stilwell, U.S. Army (1943)

The dramatic events that followed King Alfred's flight from Chippenham, including the weeks he spent in the Somerset Levels, at first sheltering from his pursuers and then subjecting them to harassing guerrilla raids, were the most important of his life. Admittedly they led to the lowest point in his fortunes. He could, with justification, have cried out with Bunyan's Christian that he was being submerged under the waves of disaster then breaking over him, but the manner and speed with which he recovered from this position of near-defeat provides us with a revealing glimpse of his character. He was, without doubt, inspired by a deep Christian faith and fortified by the knowledge that his enemy was pagan. In truth, it is hard to recognise any other single episode in Alfred's life more worthy of winning for him the title 'Great'. Indeed, without Athelney, the plans he developed there and the fruits which they bore, Wessex would have been lost and England would have been submerged under Danish domination.

Paradoxically, although this probably constitutes the best-known period of his reign, laced about with many fanciful legends, there is much about these days that remains heavily veiled from our vision. The account provided by the *Anglo-Saxon Chronicle* of the king's downfall at Chippenham is written only in the broadest terms.[1] It relates that after his stronghold had fallen into Guthrum's hands,

the enemy army . . . occupied the land of the West Saxons, and settled there and drove a great part of the people across the sea, and conquered most of the others; and the people submitted to them, except King Alfred. He journeyed in difficulties through the woods and fen fastnesses with a small force.

The paragraph contains many uncertainties. What, for example, was the extent of Guthrum's occupation of 'the land of the West Saxons'? His military strength must have been limited, as was the duration of his incursion into Wessex, which ran briefly from Twelfth Night (6 January 878) to his final surrender at Chippenham at the end of May, some four months later. We may fairly assume that during this time he would have been fully occupied, both in consolidating his position and in his pursuit of Alfred who, so long as he was allowed to run free, posed him a constant threat. Again, how should we interpret the chronicler's words that the enemy had 'settled' in the land of the West Saxons? And if 'a great part of the people were driven across the sea', and most of the others had either been conquered by the Danes or submitted to their rule, how did it happen that, within a few weeks of his arrival in Athelney, Alfred raised an army of such high morale and evident strength that he was enabled to defeat his enemy at Edington with such apparent ease?

In the twentieth century loyalty to crown and country is the behavioural norm of most citizens, whatever their political leanings, and of all servicemen, whether professional or mercenary. 'Sahib, I have earned my salt,' breathed a young *naik* of the author's Indian regiment, as he lay dying of wounds on a hillside during the Burma campaign in the Second World War. Although his words referred to a bygone custom of the old East India Company,[2] they none the less reflected the staunch commitment with which the Indian soldier – a mercenary, it might be said – was prepared both to risk and lose his life for an avowed cause. Some of them, upon leaving the army, and by virtue of their rank and the length and quality of their service, qualified for what was officially known as *jangi inam*, a phrase which translates literally as 'a reward for war service'. Generally this took the shape of an area of farm land. It seems that matters had changed only by a small degree since Alfredian times, for in those early days young men of the nobility, brought up and educated at court, expected to receive a grant of land upon coming of age. In exchange, they were required to provide military service to their lord, sharing his fortunes and physical hardships, even if need be unto death. In about 680 St Adhelm addressed himself to those followers of Wilfrid, Bishop of York, who had failed to accompany their master into exile. He questioned them:

if laymen, wholly ignorant of divine learning, desert a gracious lord, dear to them in his days of prosperity, when he is no longer fortunate and rich but overtaken by calamity and adversity, if these men prefer the security and ease of their native land to sharing the burden of exile with their lord, will not everyone think them worthy of execration, mocking laughter, ridicule and loud jeering? What then will be said of you?[3]

Loyalty of this nature was a long-standing tradition. As early as 56 BC, when observing Celtic tribes during his conquest of Gaul, Julius Caesar had noted Aquitanian vows of personal allegiance that bound a follower to his lord, frequently to the point of dying alongside him or sacrificing his own life to avenge his master's death. It was a heroic obligation, often featured in contemporary Saxon poetry as a code of duty. In reality, due to the frailties of human nature, the practice fell far short of the ideal. King Alfred pragmatically recognised this by requiring ealdormen, reeves and his other appointed representatives to take hold-oaths of loyalty to him. These men provided the key to his problems. If they failed him, the shire *fyrds* which assembled at their call would have been unavailable to him. Their fealty was thus essential. Nevertheless, despite their vows, many of his followers during the crisis year of 878 appear either to have submitted or defected to the Danes. One of these was Wulfhere, ealdorman of Wiltshire, a territory that played a large part in Alfred's defensive strategy, not only because of its command of the vital invasion routes into Wessex, but because of its domination of the 'land-bridge' discussed earlier. Wulfhere is said to have 'deserted without permission both his lord, King Alfred, and his country in spite of the oath which he had sworn to the king and all his leading men'.[4] By his action he opened the door for Guthrum and nearly destroyed Wessex. He forfeited his land for his offence and was fortunate not to lose his life.

The accusation that Wulfhere had 'deserted without permission' is one of great interest, for the words imply that it was customary in certain circumstances (for example, in the event of an ealdorman's shire being overwhelmed by enemy action) to permit an oath of this nature to be relaxed until it could more opportunely be enforced. This seems to have been the case in Hampshire after the battle of Wilton, for the men from there appear to have played little part in subsequent operations. Seemingly they had fallen under Danish influence. Shires such as this were now to be reminded of their duties. Alfred sent for the ealdormen commanding them and gave them their instructions, probably during an operational conference at Athelney. Then,

in the seventh week after Easter he rode to Egbert's Stone east of Selwood and there came to meet him all the people of Somerset and of Wiltshire and of that part of Hampshire which was on this side of the sea, and they rejoiced to see him.[5]

It is noteworthy that the chronicler makes no mention of either Devon or Dorset in this paragraph, although we are aware, certainly in the case of Devon, with its victory over Ubba, that the *fyrds* of both these territories were not only intact but probably active in the field. It has been suggested above that they were already committed to another defensive role, securing their respective seaboards against surprise attack, particularly the southern coastline where Guthrum's fleet had made an earlier attempt to come ashore but had foundered in a storm. The Danish forces stationed in the Thames estuary and eastern Wessex would at this juncture have been ideally situated to mount and co-ordinate a similar diversionary assault in support of Guthrum. King Alfred would have been guilty of great foolhardiness had he ignored this possibility.

If we base our calculations on the potential manpower contributions listed by counties in Appendix D, the above extract from the *Anglo-Saxon Chronicle* contains enough information to enable us roughly to assess the size of the force summoned by Alfred to meet him at Egbert's Stone. Since, at the very least, it may be expected that both north Wiltshire and north Somerset lay under Guthrum's domination, it is unlikely that the former, with the exclusion of the Malmesbury and Cricklade areas, could have mustered more than 2,000 men or that Somerset could have brought more than 1,500, for Bath lay too close to Chippenham to permit otherwise. Precisely what the chronicler meant by his reference to 'that part of Hampshire lying on this side of the sea' is obscure. It is generally assumed he was alluding to that area of the county which lies west of the River Avon and its estuary. It is conceivable that Halfdan and Alfred, after the battle at Wilton, may both have used this clear, topographical demarcation line to define their future zones of influence. If this were so, the *fyrd* contributed by Hampshire would probably have comprised no more than 500 levies, bringing the total of the West Saxon army, as it now assembled, to approximately 4,000 men.

This admittedly flimsy calculation provides the only yardstick by which we may assess the Danish strength. Guthrum not only had to defend his Chippenham stronghold while patrolling in force to seek out the whereabouts of Alfred, but also had to safeguard the administrative base which he must have created on the Thames. This is likely to have been situated at Cricklade, a river port in Roman times, and which was later to feature as a Saxon *burh* of no mean importance. Given these commitments, the Danish force confronting Alfred could well have numbered some 5,000 men or more.

Guthrum did, however, possess two great advantages which he worked to his benefit. First, his mobility – until the horses of his mounted infantry were seized by the West Saxons at the gates of Chippenham, in the last throes of the battle of Edington; secondly, as the chroniclers make clear, there were many in authority within the West Saxon administration who were disloyally willing to put their local influence at their enemy's disposal. It was, moreover, the spring season, the time of the year when agriculture and crop production assumed prime importance and it would have been very much in the Danish commander's interest to ensure that the annual cycle continued uninterrupted, probably under the local supervision of his new-found allies. It is easy to believe that Guthrum would have encouraged essential work of this nature and to this extent it is possible to understand Asser's comment that the Dane 'occupied the land of the West Saxons and settled there'. But to have done more, with Alfred still free, would surely have placed an unwanted strain upon his already stretched resources.

King Alfred's march to Edington to do battle with Guthrum was a carefully considered and controlled operation. It was conducted in three stages. First, he summoned the various contingents of his army to meet with him at Egbert's Stone; then, having regrouped and assured himself of their preparedness for battle, he marched with his men to a forward rendezvous at Iley Oak. There, he rested the night and then,

> at dawn on the following day, he advanced his standard to a place which is called Ethandun and, fiercely warring against the whole army of the pagans with serried masses and courageously persevering for a long time, by divine favour at last gained the victory, overthrew the pagans with very great slaughter and put them to flight.[7]

The whereabouts of each of these key locations – the meeting-place at Egbert's Stone, the area selected for the forward rally at Iley Oak on the eve of the battle, and the *Ethandun* battlefield itself – have for long been the subject of much debate. Since 1586, when William Camden[8] first selected the location of the latter as Edington, near Westbury in Wiltshire, there have been a further five claims for the site, and possibly more. These range westerly as far as Edington on the Polden Hills in West Somerset, easterly to Eddington in Berkshire, and northerly to

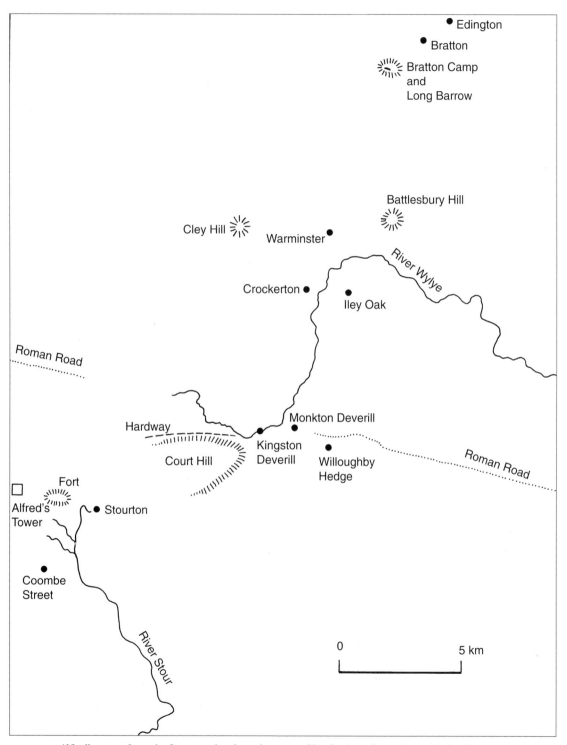

Alfred's route from the Somerset levels to the scene of his final confrontation with the Danes at Edington remains uncertain. (Aardvark Illustration)

Minchinhampton, near Stroud in Gloucestershire. Canon J. Jackson, in the
Wiltshire Archaeological Magazine in 1887, wrote:

> There are four or five claims, each of which looks so probable that, if you were
> to examine them and read the arguments you would very likely find yourself in
> the same situation as King James I once did. He was a learned man and fancied
> that he understood the laws, and the story is that, being king, he thought he
> would preside in his own King's Bench and decide a case. But the ingenious
> arguments and speeches on both sides so bewildered him that he took up his
> hat in a hurry, saying, 'Well, men, I think ye are both right and I'll have nothing
> more to do with it!'[9]

The Edington claim made by Camden has been acknowledged by many eminent
scholars, including Stenton and Hodgkin.[10] Nevertheless concrete evidence to
support any site has yet to be discovered. Equally, although the precise locations
of Alfred's first and second operational stages are broadly known, they are still
frequently subject to local dispute.

When studying the course of this historic battle, it is necessary to remember
three undisputed and documented facts, each of which relates to the ground and
is therefore of key importance when endeavouring to interpret the thinking of the
respective army commanders:

- Guthrum seized Chippenham in early January. He then appears to have
  improved its defences and to have used it as his forward operational base.
  His new stronghold possessed ready access both to the Bristol Avon and to
  the Thames, along either of which he might have expected to receive
  reinforcements. He was also well placed to control the militarily important
  West Saxon townships of Bath and Cricklade and to patrol forward into the
  surrounding countryside, using the firm ground offered by the Mendip and
  Polden Hills to penetrate the Somerset Levels, seeking information about
  Alfred's whereabouts.
- Alfred fled from Chippenham to the Isle of Athelney. We are aware that he
  did not go directly there but on arrival he constructed a stronghold from
  which he emerged, apparently frequently and without restriction, to
  conduct a damaging guerrilla war against the Danes.
- Alfred summoned his army to meet him at Egbert's Stone, *east* of the
  Selwood Forest.

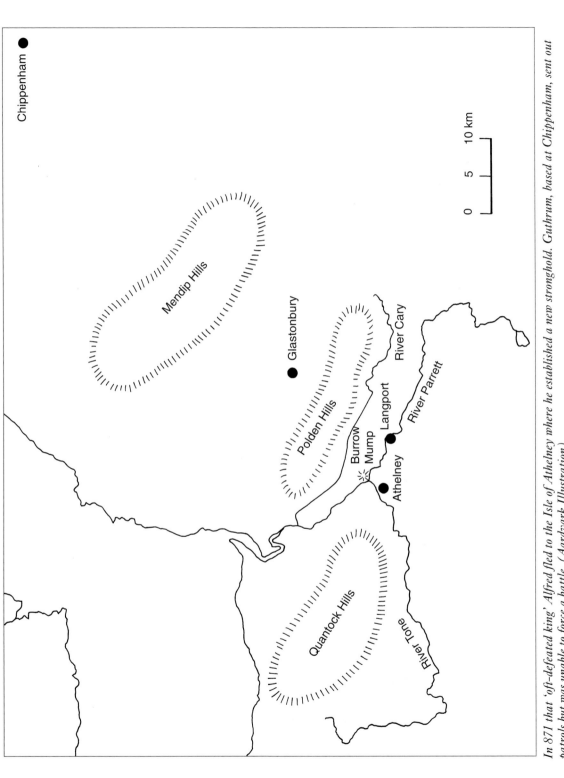

In 871 that 'oft-defeated king' Alfred fled to the Isle of Athelney where he established a new stronghold. Guthrum, based at Chippenham, sent out patrols but was unable to force a battle. (Aardvark Illustration)

A fourth and equally important military fact may now be added to this list. As the reigning King of Wessex, at the head of an army and with responsibilities for government, Alfred had been vulnerable to Danish attack by land or sea or both. The initiative had rested with the Viking leaders and the West Saxon responses to their moves were invariably conventional and set-piece. Now, from his concealed command post in the Somerset Levels and without weighty responsibilities, Alfred possessed an army, widely dispersed but ready and awaiting the recall to arms. He had, moreover, the immediate support of the men of Somerset and the ready availability of his personal bodyguard. He had discovered the art of guerrilla warfare. The initiative had passed from Guthrum and now lay with the West Saxon king.

The situation seen through Danish eyes was more complicated. Alfred, to Guthrum, must have been a shadowy figure moving with his men, almost at will, out of his marshy stronghold. Anyone with experience of this sort of irregular warfare will appreciate the uncertainties that would have plagued the Danish commander. He doubtless received accurate information of the location of Alfred's base. It is even probable that his mounted patrols on the high ground of the Langport Hills could have looked out across the low-lying marshes of the Levels and actually had the location pointed out to them, but without water transport and command of the river and the frequently submerged trackway systems, it remained inaccessible. Asser's description of the Saxon stronghold well describes the problems it presented to an enemy. Athelney, he wrote,

> is surrounded by swampy, impassable and extensive marshland and groundwater on every side. It cannot be reached in any way except by punts or by a causeway which has been built by protracted labour between two fortresses. A formidable fortress of elegant workmanship was set up by the command of the king at the western end of the causeway.[11]

This fortification in its turn was probably secured by a garrison on the nearby Burrow Mump (in ancient times known as the *Tot Eyot*, the look-out island), a hillock that rises sharply above the marshes and from its summit provides superb, dominating views of the surrounding countryside. The curve of the River Cary at one time flowed around its base. In Alfred's circumstances it would have been militarily of great importance and it would be surprising if it had not been included as part of the Athelney defensive system.[12]

Clearly, the surprise defeat of his ally Ubba, at *Cynuit*, would have had a devastating effect upon Guthrum's plans. The Dane now possessed neither the means to penetrate the marshes nor the resources to contain Alfred within them. For this reason, with the king lying frustratingly close but tantalisingly beyond his reach, the Danish commander could never be certain of Alfred's whereabouts. Equally worrying for him would have been the knowledge that, scattered throughout the unoccupied areas of western Wessex, were the surviving shire *fyrds*, impatient to be released against him. Under these pressures Guthrum's military situation deteriorated from one of seeming conquest to that of an occupying power, confronted with a resolute guerrilla campaign which threatened, at any moment, to explode into full-scale war.

For Alfred, the future had brightened. His immediate military task was the recovery of western Wessex, either by destroying the enemy army or by driving it from his kingdom. In order to achieve this, he had two courses of action open to him, dependent upon the whereabouts of the main body of the Danish force when he launched his campaign. If this were still located at Chippenham, then his choice was clear-cut. He could march on the town to repossess himself of it and destroy the enemy. Simply by laying siege to its walls and cutting the vital Danish lines of communication with the Thames, he could, as he was later to demonstrate, quickly have forced their capitulation. On the other hand, if Guthrum had moved out of Chippenham to challenge Alfred in the field, then the Saxon could either have marched to do battle with him or alternatively could have directly recaptured Chippenham, rendered vulnerable by Guthrum's absence.

Thus both commanders had a direct interest in the erstwhile royal estate: the one, with the intention of safeguarding it, but without allowing his forces to be trapped within it; the other, with the purpose of seizing it and isolating his enemy.

It is difficult to believe that Alfred, a seasoned warrior who was to demonstrate that he was also a thoughtful commander, would not have availed himself of this opportunity, at a single blow, to restore his fortunes and his prestige. Similarly, it is improbable that Guthrum would have easily let him get away with it. He would have been keenly watching for any movements which might suggest that the West Saxon army was reassembling. His patrols could not have failed to be aware of villages emptying themselves of men of fighting age nor of rumours of an army gathering at Egbert's Stone, east of Selwood. He may be expected to have at once called in his outlying troops and, leaving a holding garrison at Chippenham, to have marched to his selected battleground at *Ethandun*. This lay directly between his base and the area where Alfred was assembling east of Selwood. It would have placed him astride the axis of advance of the West Saxon army should their leader decide to march on Chippenham. It was, moreover, a position of strength, flanked by Bratton Castle, a multivallate Iron Age hillfort, perched on the western edge of the Salisbury Plain escarpment. The ancient village of Edington, which gives its name to the battle, lies about a mile north-east from it, at the foot of the downs.[13]

In its prime the defences of the Bratton hillfort would have been formidable. Today, although lacking the wooden palisades which once surmounted them, its earth ramparts are still of a size to demonstrate the deterrent they would have presented to a potential assailant. It should not be forgotten, however, that in Alfredian times the hillfort had probably already been demilitarised for some 800 years. Logistically, its position was not outstanding. Even at the height of its occupancy, water for its garrison could only have been obtainable from a spring at Stradbrook, a mile distant, well outside its defences. Moreover, this source of water would have needed to be safeguarded, and then only precariously, by detaching a substantial force from the main body. It is thus evident that Bratton Castle could not have withstood a lengthy siege. Indeed, if Guthrum could have seen any merit in sitting in a defensive position against the approach of the West Saxons, he would probably have judged it better to remain in Chippenham. We are thus forced to the conclusion that he occupied Bratton Castle because of the dominant position it offered, guarding the western flank of his shield wall and controlling the network of trackways which criss-cross Salisbury Plain at that strategically important focal point.

The method by which ninth-century *fyrds* were called out for service is uncertain. It is therefore appropriate to pause for a moment to consider the form it might have taken. Local government in those years, before the reorganisation whhich introduced the Hundred system of administration, was conducted in the presence of public assemblies known as folk-moots. These met regularly, normally at well-known and carefully selected topographical features within each administrative area, under the presidency of the king's reeve.[14] The proceedings of the folk-moot were, when it was applicable to do so, reported back to its ealdorman at the shire-moot which met twice a year, likewise at a specified assembly place.

It would be logical to assume that the procedure by which shire *fyrds* were summoned to arms was based on an identical framework of command and control. The call to assemble would have been dispatched downwards by the king, through his shire ealdorman, to villagers; village parties would then have gathered at moot assembly points and, advancing from there under the command of especially designated thegns, would have converged on their respective shire meeting places, in a steadily swelling stream. Contingents from districts and village areas, depending upon their size, were probably retained in units and sub-units under their local commanders. It may be expected that, beyond the shire rendezvous, lay yet another stage in the chain. In the event of major emergencies, when it was necessary for groupings of shire *fyrds* to be mustered for operations, either under the king or an appointed ealdorman, these would have been called to gather at some geographically suitable meeting place, prearranged and already known to all the commanders. There is evidence that, for ease of local administration, some of these rallying points were located where two or more county boundaries came together, so that *fyrds* did not leave shire logistical control until the latest possible moment.

Such meeting places may not always have been militarily suitable and we may be certain that this possibility would not have been overlooked. The task of forming up a force in an assembly area in the face of the enemy is always a highly vulnerable operation, calling for the strictest alertness and ground security. Perhaps it was for this reason that the timing of the West Saxon army's final assembly with Alfred, prior to Edington, appears to have been cut so finely. Indeed, Asser stresses that 'they made camp there for *one* night'[15] (my italics), which, by implication, indicates that, until that moment, each shire *fyrd* had been encamped nearby but remaining in its own territory. We shall see that this would have been possible when we come to consider the broad location of Egbert's Stone.

Despite the briefness of their stay, it would have been important for the assembled 4,000 men, together with their numerous animals, to be provided with a suitable area of reasonably level, sheltered, well-drained land, with an adequate supply of water. There are thus two important factors Alfred would have borne in mind when selecting his assembly point. First, its general suitability for the task and the availability of track communications to and from it. Secondly, he would have needed to examine how its location fitted with his own arrangements, for he and his party would at best have had a strenuous two-day march from Athelney to join them. He would have avoided northern trackways, so as to keep clear of the Danes, and would almost certainly have used the Hardway. Any claim therefore to the location of Egbert's Stone, almost inevitably based on conjecture because of an almost total absence of fact, would need to be considered in the light of these requirements.

There are four main contenders for the site of Egbert's Stone. Probably the longest-standing claim, and one of the most sustainable, is that made by Mr

Alfred's Tower, erected by the Hoare family in 1760 to mark the possible site of Egbert's Stone. (G. Richards)

Six Wells Bottom at Stourhead, where King Alfred is traditionally said to have prayed for water, is overlooked by Shad Hanging, a wooded hillside concealing an ancient hillfort. (G. Richards)

Hoare of Stourhead, who in 1760 erected Alfred's Tower on Kingsettle Hill to mark what he considered to be the site where the West Saxon army gathered. From the top of the tower, on a clear day, it is possible to see deep into the Somerset Levels. If he were correct in his assumption, then the nearby hillfort on Shad Hanging would doubtless also have had an important role to play.[16] It overlooks the valley that gives rise to the Dorset Stour. Here, the 'six springs' of Stourhead are said, according to local tradition, to have started from the ground when the king, thirsting for a drink, prayed for water. A few hundred yards eastwards from here, along the Hardway, which skirts the valley's northern boundary, another ancient trackway strikes off for Cley Hill and Warminster. From it, another trackway, the Redway, diverts to Crockerton, where it crosses the River Wylye to provide access to Iley Oak.

An important consideration in favour of the choice of Alfred's Tower is the proximity of the ancient Saxon village of Stourton. Colt Hoare[17] records that the Stourton family were of pre-Conquest origin and relates that 'William the Conqueror came into the West to receive its rendition there' and that the 'grandees of the Western parts waited upon the family at Stourton' at that ceremony. This was clearly a Saxon location of such importance that, two centuries after the battle of Edington, it attracted William the Conqueror to visit there for an important state occasion. The land around Alfred's Tower possesses many of the physical and military requirements to qualify as a good marshalling area but the presence of Stourton might have made it too obvious a choice if Guthrum were minded to disrupt the assembly.

A counter-claim from nearby Coombe Street cannot be overlooked, for it is held by local tradition that a large stone, standing on the banks of the River Stour,[18] was placed there by Egbert to mark the junction of the boundaries of the counties of Dorset, Somerset and Wiltshire. There is no evidence to support this claim: it might equally well be a boundary stone laid by the Romans, for it is not a marker of significant size. There is, on the other hand, a good water supply and the site would have been well concealed in a strongly populated Saxon area on the edge of Selwood Forest. The case for Coombe Street is not compellingly acceptable for three reasons. First, we know that the *fyrd* gathered *east* of Selwood, but this site lay *within* the forest as it then existed. Secondly, according to the chroniclers, Dorset made no contribution to Alfred's field army at this time and, unlike Somerset and Wiltshire, would have had little influence on the choice of rendezvous, having no administrative interest in it. Coombe Street, if selected, would have lain an unnecessary march of 4 miles south of the Hardway and distant from Iley Oak. Thirdly, the ground at Coombe Street is broken and damp and it would have proved doubtfully suitable for the encampment of a force of several thousand men, with animals.

Dr Grundy's choice of Willoughby Hedge[19] was later supported by the military historian Lieutenant-Colonel Alfred Burne.[20] Grundy reasoned that this must inevitably have been the meeting place since it was an important junction point at which so many trackways and ridgeways converge. Here the Great Ridgeway, which enters Wessex at Streatley in Berkshire, the ubiquitous Hardway and the Grovely Ridgeway, which runs westward from the Hampshire border and was an

The ancient Herepath (or Hardway) as it approaches Whitesheet Hill and Mere Down. Alfred's Tower is just visible on the skyline. (G. Richards)

ancient trackway before the Romans adopted it as part of their route to and from the lead mines in the Mendips, all meet together. For this reason, it is at first sight a logical choice but it is diminished by the fact that it is situated on high ground, in a position which, viewed through twentieth-century eyes, would have been militarily too exposed for its purpose. Moreover, the trackways that converge upon it served enemy-held territory, rather than the shires from which the *fyrds* were gathering.

Dr Grundy, however, put his finger upon an important factor when stressing the relevance of communication and trackway systems to the discussion of the whereabouts of the Egbert Stone meeting place. However, he omitted two Roman roads from his list of routeways, perhaps because in many places they now lie beneath downland turf and modern roads. The *agger* of these two roads may still be seen today as they head across the downs, one of them actually crossing the Hardway close by Willoughby Hedge, before merging at Monkton Deverill and running onwards in tandem to cross the Deverill stream at Kingston Deverill, before once more parting to pursue their individual ways. These two roads are well known: they are Vespasian's tactical road from Poole Harbour to Bath, and the Lead Road which connects Winchester with the Mendip hills. Since the Lead Road also joins with the ridgeways on their passage across the neighbouring downland, this lends importance to the nearby area of Kingston Deverill, our fourth claimant for the Egbert Stone site.

Kingston Deverill has long had an association with the Crown. Prior to the Domesday Survey it was held by Edith, Queen of Edward the Confessor, a descendant of Egbert. Subsequently it became one of the grants of the Earls of Cornwall and later formed part of the Duchy of Cornwall. It stands at the head of the beautiful Deverill valley, adjacent to Monkton Deverill, where a Saxon cemetery has recently been uncovered, suggesting the presence of a Saxon village at this time. Militarily the valley would have possessed many of the qualifications sought by Alfred: plentiful water and foodstuffs, with adequate land for encamping a sizeable force, folded away in downland hollows, out of sight of prying eyes. The *Wiltshire Archaeological Magazine* of 1877 recorded of this site that in the rectory garden, adjoining the church,

> certain large stones were examined: they are called 'Egbert's Stone' or 'King's Stone' and are spoken of by the Saxon chroniclers; they were brought by a farmer from King's Court Hill, where Egbert is traditionally said to have held court, and for some time did duty as stepping stones to a barn; subsequently they were condemned to be broken up as material for mending roads but their substance was so hard as to defy the efforts of their would-be destroyers.[21]

Originally there were three stones, with two standing upright and the third placed across the top as a capstone. In this manner they previously stood on the summit of nearby Court Hill but today only two remain. They now stand on private ground adjoining the church, dolefully leaning against each other, as if sorrowing for past glories. In 1901 the author of a carefully reasoned article in the *Antiquaries Journal*, which placed the battlefield site of *Ethandun* at Bratton, questioned their origins:

The ancient church of St Mary the Virgin at Kingston Deverill today marks the area where Alfred's Saxon host probably assembled before the battle of Edington. Two great Sarsen stones, said to be Egbert's Stone, lie in the wooded rectory paddock to the right of the church. (G. Richards)

Is it not possible, nay probable, that these two stones are the 'Petra Ecbricti' where King Alfred assembled his army before he marched to attack the Danes at Ethandune . . . The knolls [King's Hill and Court Hill] were probably associated with some royal event and possibly one or other was the site of Petra Ecbricti and therefore marks the site of King Alfred's well-known trysting place, which from a military point of view was extraordinarily well chosen.[22]

Examining the facts surrounding all these places, it is clear that both Alfred's Tower and Kingston Deverill have claims worthy of deep consideration for, applying the litmus test of available trackways, each would have been suitable as a base at which to assemble and from which to advance to the next point Alfred had selected for his army, namely Iley Oak. Stevenson, in his edited version of Asser's *Life*,[23] identified this latter place as lying in Southleigh Wood, where as late as 1439 the Courts of the two Hundreds of Heytesbury and Warminster are documented as holding their meetings; nor is it irrelevant that the same site was employed in the mid-seventeenth century as a secret rendezvous for gatherings of the popular but illegal non-conformist religious movement then spreading throughout Wiltshire.[24] Despite a rival claim for Cley Hill, lying some 3 miles north-west of this point, the selection of Iley Oak as a forming-up area on the eve of battle makes sound military sense when considered in the light of both the tactics of the day and its location.

Guthrum's move to the high ground at *Ethandun* would have left King Alfred no choice but to bring the Dane to battle. Chippenham could not now be regained until his enemy had been defeated and there was only one manner in which he could achieve this. The West Saxons possessed no formed cavalry units and, when massed for battle, were armed with few weapons of greater sophistication than the battle-axe and the throwing spear. Alfred's options were therefore restricted. There could have been no thought in his mind of scaling the sharp western escarpment at Bratton, an operation that would have brought his army into battle breathless and in dishevelled formation. His only option was to place his force on the level ridgeway, first seizing the high ground at Battlesbury and dispersing the Danish vedettes, and then to drive forward in resolute formation. The Danes would have been drawn up across the ridge to block his advance, awaiting his arrival. Both sides would have employed the shield-wall formation. It would have been for the Saxons an exercise in muscle and mobility, the soldiery moving in serried ranks, as Asser described them, their shields overlapping. As the two sides confronted each other, it was the practice for shields to be drummed to intimidate the opposition: taunts and ruderies would have been hurled backward and forward and there would have been many challenges to combat with individual boasts of courage and prowess. The clash of armour and weaponry and the sound of combat as the two forces joined battle would have reverberated across the downs.

Alfred Burne, in his essay on the battle of *Ethandun*,[25] mentions that Alfred's march from Egbert's Stone gave the Danes at least two days in which to dig defences against an unexpected attack from the south. In modern times, when armies have learnt to dig downwards to avoid missiles of varying descriptions, it is easy to think in terms of the value of entrenchments. In the days about which we write static defences of this nature, apart from being a hindrance, unless they were for long-term occupation, would have lost for their defenders the virtue of mobility. It is more likely that the 'defence works' identified by Burne were ancient boundary marks cut out at an earlier date by the abandoned Romano-Celtic village that lies nearby. Alfred, in any event, in view of the length of the ridge confronting him, would have found little difficulty in outflanking his opponent, thus obviating any obstacles of this nature.

Asser's *Life* describes in some detail the events which now followed. It was not an easy victory:

> When the next morning dawned, Alfred moved his forces forward and came to a place called Edington, and fighting fiercely with a compact shield-wall against the entire Viking army, he persevered resolutely for a long time; at length he gained the victory through God's will. He destroyed the Vikings with great slaughter and pursued those who had fled as far as the stronghold, hacking them down; he seized everything which he found outside the stronghold – men (whom he killed immediately) horses and cattle – and boldly made camp in front of the gates of the Viking stronghold with all his army.

The stronghold mentioned by Asser, the whereabouts of which are sometimes questioned, would almost certainly have been Chippenham, situated just 14 miles north of Bratton hillfort. We may safely assume that the Danish commander had not left his base devoid of any garrison and that its ramparts had been further strengthened since its abandonment by Alfred. It doubtless contained the enemy's reserves of foodstuffs and it lay on the River Avon, with a readily available water supply. Thus, Guthrum's first thought, after his line had been broken at *Ethandun*, would have been to regain the security of his firm base. Apart from the obvious military and logistical reasons for doing this, he would doubtless always have harboured the hope that the Saxon *fyrd*, having cornered him, might once again, as they had done at Nottingham, weary of the siege operation and disperse to their homes. This was not to be the case and, after a fortnight, according to Asser's colourful account of these events,[27]

> the Vikings, thoroughly terrified by hunger, cold and fear, and in the end by despair, sought peace on this condition: the king should take as many chosen hostages as he wanted from them and give none to them; never before, indeed, had they made peace with anyone on such terms. When he had heard their embassy, the king (as was his wont) was moved to compassion[28] and took as many chosen hostages from them as he wanted. When they had been handed over, the Vikings swore in addition that they would leave his kingdom immediately, and Guthrum, their king, promised to accept Christianity . . .

The *Anglo-Saxon Chronicle* provides a less flamboyant account of these events, simply recording that, after Edington, Alfred pursued the Danes

> as far as the fortress and stayed there a fortnight. And then the enemy gave him preliminary hostages and great oaths that they would leave his kingdom, and promised also that their king should receive baptism and they kept their promise.

Before discussing the implications of these two versions of the aftermath of the battle, it is necessary first to glance at the outcome of the peace negotiations. The first result became apparent within three weeks. Guthrum, clothed in white, and thirty of his most distinguished followers were baptised at Aller,[29] near Alfred's stronghold at Athelney. It was here that the king 'raised him from the holy font of baptism, receiving him as his adoptive son'. An ancient font, unearthed in the rectory garden in 1862, is today to be found in the Church of St Andrew at Aller. It is claimed by popular tradition to have been the one used by Alfred for this ceremony.[30] These were dark uncertain days in the history of Glastonbury and it may have been that the great religious centre had suffered from the attacks of Vikings. If this were so, it is surprising that the royal *vill* at Wedmore had seemingly survived Viking depradations, for it was there, after a lapse of eight days, that the rite of 'chrism loosing' was held.[31] This was followed by several days of celebration, during which the Danish party, hosted by the king, remained with him while he 'freely bestowed many treasures upon them'.

In this manner the first part of the Chippenham peace terms were honoured but the Danish army did not immediately leave Wessex as promised, instead remaining encamped within the stronghold throughout the summer of 878, before marching to Cirencester in the early autumn. It may be that there was a logistical reason for this delay, in which the availability of foodstuffs may perhaps have played some part. The army stayed in Cirencester a further year before Guthrum returned to East Anglia, now as a Christian monarch, with the adopted name Aethelstan. Within a generation, those Danes whose forefathers had murdered Edmund, King of the East Anglians, had come to venerate him as a martyred saint.

Several questions remain to be answered, most of them arising from the account of these events presented to us by Asser. Why is there such a marked difference in the scale of his reporting and that of the *Anglo-Saxon Chronicle*? If there really were such great slaughter at *Ethandun*, why has no trace of it ever been discovered, either at Bratton or at any of the other sites mooted by historians? Moreover, in the circumstances of the outcome depicted by Asser and, of course, his patron, why was Guthrum's army allowed to occupy the psychologically important fortress at Chippenham for so long after its defeat? Added to this, Asser's statement that the tough battle-experienced Viking army, well provisioned and ensconced behind well-defended walls, surrendered because they were 'thoroughly terrified by hunger, cold and fear' smacks of exaggeration. The English climate suffers many vagaries but springtime in southern England, at the end of May, is not notorious for its low temperatures. What, then, truly happened? We must return to the battlefield itself to discover some of the answers.

The Vikings, as we have emphasised elsewhere, accepted battle casualties with great reluctance. It is likely that their attitude at *Ethandun* would have been no different. They were hoping to meet a half-hearted enemy, demoralised by earlier reverses. They were quickly proved to be wrong. The West Saxons attacked with a ferocity born of years of accumulated anger. The possibility of heavy losses, resulting in battlefield defeat, was at once revealed to Guthrum, who speedily fell back to the security of Chippenham. His army had not suffered the great slaughter suggested by Asser. He still possessed a formidable strength but, with Alfred's resurgence, the Viking dream of the conquest of Wessex was no longer attainable. Alfred had convinced him that it would be a contest to the finish; more than this, his own men were weary of fighting and, as Halfdan's men before them, were looking forward to settling down with their families and farming their conquered lands. Western Wessex no longer offered them this prize.

The Saxons, for their part, had no great experience of siege warfare. Indeed their earlier performances at Nottingham and Reading had shown a marked lack of success. Further, however gallant on the battlefield, it was still likely that the largely peasant West Saxon army would regard a lengthy, demanding siege with little enthusiasm. The annual cycle of animal and crop production had already commenced. We can have no doubt that Alfred, through experience, would have been only too well aware of this inherent weakness in his army. Indeed, if the frontiers of Wessex were to be secure in the future, the whole defensive system of the kingdom would have to be reshaped and its laws redesigned to cope with the plans he had in mind: and for this he needed time. It follows that both men had good reasons to seek a negotiated and reasonably lasting peace, if this could be mutually achieved without loss of face. Thus we may judge that Guthrum's acceptance of the Christian faith, as a preliminary to his withdrawal to settle with his army on his East Anglian lands, was a gesture designed to create a new, more desirable atmosphere between himself and the powerful neighbour now arising, once again, south of the Thames. For these reasons, glancing into the future, Alfred may have 'compassionately'[32] allowed his enemy time for a somewhat lengthy, honourable withdrawal but we may be sure that both he and his advisers regarded Guthrum's force with watchful eyes until it had returned eastwards and raised the threat to the western province of his kingdom.

In the knowledge of all that had gone before – Guthrum's deceptions and treachery, his persistent attacks on West Saxon soil, the physical and political damage he had created there, his blatant breaking of sacred oaths, his ruthless willingness to abandon hostages to gain a quick tactical advantage, and his determined pursuit of the king and his followers – in the face of all this, the end of this phase of Alfred's campaign against the Danes savours of anti-climax. We know little of the personal discussions held by the two men at this crucial moment nor of the agreements they may have reached. It was to be nearly a decade before a formal treaty was signed between Alfred and Guthrum but this was to be an agreement which defined the boundaries between 'English' England and the southern Danelaw.

However, the impact of *Ethandun* should not be underestimated. Guthrum's purpose had been denied. Wessex was soon to be recovered and Alfred was now the sole surviving English king. Importantly, the reverberations of his success were almost immediately felt in the lower reaches of the Thames. The Danish war-bands, battening on Fulham and eastern Wessex, did not like the news which reached them. They were prompted to move to seek easier pickings elsewhere. In 879, according to the *Annals of St Vaast*, 'they crossed the Channel with an infinite multitude and in mid-July devastated Thérouanne, while no one offered any resistance'.

Alfred had gained the time he needed. He now had to put it to good use and reorganise his defences.

CHAPTER 7

Fortress Wessex

Qui desiderat pacem, praeparet bellum –
Let him who desires peace, prepare for war.

Flavius Vegetius (fourth century AD)

Contemporary sources are strangely vague about the practical gains that stemmed from Alfred's *Ethandun* victory. Asser, from whom of all people we might have expected a detailed list of the king's military and political profits and losses, is content to provide us with a description of the events connected with the ceremony surrounding Guthrum's baptism and then, for the rest, he considers it sufficient to record that:

> In the year of the Lord's Incarnation, 879 (the 31st of King Alfred's Life) the Viking army left Chippenham, and went to Cirencester (called Caiceri in Welsh) . . . and remained there for one year.[1]

He makes no effort to explain either the reason for Guthrum's delay in withdrawing his army from the stronghold he had surrendered to Alfred, or the circumstances which had persuaded the latter to find such a passage of time permissible. The departure of the Danish army from Cirencester to East Anglia in the spring of 880, when 'they divided up the province and began to settle there', is similarly covered by Asser in a few, scant words and without elaboration. The *Anglo-Saxon Chronicle* is no more helpful. The annalist simply relates that in 878 the Danish army 'went from Chippenham to Cirencester and stayed there for one year'; he then adds succinctly that in the following year, it 'went from Cirencester into East Anglia and settled there and shared out the land'.

Without doubt Alfred and Guthrum would have had much to discuss at this time. They were entering a new phase in their relationship and it would have been important for all decisions they reached during these early negotiations, which appear to have been far-reaching, to be sound, feasible and enduring. It is significant that the treaty that established the boundary separating Wessex and English Mercia from the Danelaw, and which both men might have wanted to see in place much earlier, had to wait a further seven or eight years before it could be completed. By that time, in the words of the *Chronicle*, 'all the English people [had] submitted to Alfred, except those under the power of the Danes'. He was consequently able to put his signature to the treaty in the knowledge that he was acting for truly one nation. Until then there was much work to be done, many obstacles to be cleared from his path and many uncertainties to be clarified.

The king can barely have started on this concentrated programme of activity when in 879 an event occurred which, when he heard of it, must have filled him with alarm and dismay. A great Viking army suddenly arrived in the lower Thames from 'foreign parts'. We may imagine they were soldiers seeking employment with Guthrum. They spent the winter at Fulham and, according to Asser, made contact with the Danish leader. It is sometimes suggested that the two armies joined together for a fleeting moment. The *Chronicle*, however, makes no mention of any such happening and, if it did take place, Guthrum can hardly have greeted it with enthusiasm, for an encounter of this nature would have put his negotiations with Alfred in serious jeopardy. More than this, given his desire for peace, which we must now accept, the intimidating arrival of yet another war-band at this particular moment could have set Wessex at war again. It is thus not improbable that Guthrum delayed his departure from Cirencester so as to hold the strategically important ground of the upper Thames area, until the newcomers had found for themselves another hunting ground. He did not have too long to wait. In the following spring, perhaps persuaded by Guthrum that there were easier pickings elsewhere, they departed from England to try their luck elsewhere. They crossed the Channel to Francia where, after sacking Thérouanne and the monastery of St Bertin at St Omer, they established a winter stronghold at Ghent, on the banks of the River Scheldt. This was destined to be their main base for the next four or five years.

Alfred watched them go, conscious that in the not too distant future they would return. He kept himself fully informed of their whereabouts and the attention he now gave to the collection of military intelligence is reflected in the unusually full account of their movements provided by the *Anglo-Saxon Chronicle* for the years 880–5. Their marauding forays from the Scheldt are carefully logged: the thrust up the River Meuse into the heart of Francia in 881; the raid on the nunnery at Conde in 883, when Pope Marinus sent a relic of the convent

Cross to King Alfred; the penetration of the Somme as far as Amiens in 883; and finally the division of the force into two bands in 885, when one party went to Louvain and the other crossed the Channel to lay siege to Rochester in Kent. It was in anticipation of such events that, after *Ethandun*, Alfred energetically set about the task of tightening the frontiers of his kingdom by entering into alliances with neighbouring and continental kingdoms, strengthening the land defences of Wessex and creating a navy with which to defend its seaboards.

The most important, and the most immediate, task confronting Alfred was to re-establish his control over the kingdom of Wessex. For him, the position was clear-cut and he was well aware of the dimensions of the problem. We in the twentieth century, with the few records which have been left to us, can only guess at its scale. Oddly, the extent of the occupation of Wessex by Viking armies during these years, in particular after Guthrum's capitulation, is never clearly mentioned by any annalist or chronicler. Professor Dorothy Whitelock has written that 'the victory at Edington in 878 caused Guthrum's army to retire and share out East Anglia in 879, leaving the lands south of the Thames, as well as south-west Mercia, in English hands'.[2] This implies that all this territory was returned to West Saxon hands immediately following the Danish surrender at Chippenham. One hesitates to disagree with such an eminent authority but are we then to judge that Guthrum commanded an army of such a size that it was capable in 878 not only of launching a large-scale attack on western Wessex, with all the logistical support that would have required, but also of holding down the shires of the eastern province? There is no evidence, nor even any implication, that it happened in this way.

Thus we come to the second alternative, namely the probability that while Guthrum's forces were campaigning in the upper reaches of the Thames, other unrelated war-bands were located not only in London but conceivably also in and around the Thames estuary. This is a viewpoint partly supported by Stenton[3] who opines that the city had contained a Viking garrison ever since Halfdan left it in the autumn of 872. We may therefore conclude that after his Chippenham victory Alfred had regained full possession of western Wessex, but since large areas of the remaining part of his kingdom were still under enemy domination, the recovery of his eastern province could not be achieved until he was better equipped and organised.

In the years before 878 Viking successes against Wessex were largely due to their intelligent and almost unrestricted use of the River Thames. In addition their constant pressure against Mercia had brought about, in 873, the abdication of its king, Burghred, who fled to spend the few remaining years of his life in Rome. With him went his wife and Alfred's elder sister Aethelswith. In place of Burghred, the Danes appointed a man whom the *Chronicle* for 874 defined as 'a foolish king's thegn', one Ceolwulf II. It was a condition of his appointment, secured by oaths and hostages, that his Danish masters should be allowed the use of his kingdom 'whenever they might require it, and that he should hold himself in readiness to serve the needs of the host with all who would follow him'.[4] Three years later the Danes invoked this provision and divided Mercia, giving the western portion to their nominee and sharing out the balance among their numbers, although it was not until 877 that the actual partitioning of the land took place.[5]

The Danes, who already had the advantage of the initiative, now had the unfettered use of both the River Thames and Mercia for the deployment of their armies in their operations against West Saxon territory. Alfred could thus have had no doubt, when planning his next moves, that he risked being outflanked and totally defeated if he were to advance eastward before he had secured western Wessex against assault from the north. Such a risk he could not accept, and in order to safeguard against it he had to gain influence over English Mercia at an early date, establish firm military control over the movement of shipping in the upper reaches of the Thames and set in hand the provision of his new-style *burh* strongholds for the defence of western Wessex. These were all essential requirements. The provision of strong fortifications, particularly on the Thames at Cricklade and Wallingford, would certainly have featured high on his list of priorities. It is noteworthy that ancient earthworks at both these two places have been identified as the remains of rectangular-style West Saxon fortified *burhs*,[6] dated to the second half of the ninth century. Later, as part of his urgent thrust to extend his influence towards London and recover his lost territory, the king strengthened his grip on the Thames by constructing two double-*burh* strongholds, one astride the Thames at Sashes, midway between Reading and Windsor, and another at Southwark.[7] These not only protected his northern frontier with Mercia against land attack but also blocked the logistically important riverway to Danish longships. This is a matter to which we will return.

Ceolwulf disappears out of history at some time during the eventful years 877–8. It may be that he was removed by either Guthrum or Alfred, as a result of the peace talks held in the wake of *Ethandun*. With whatever degree of success Ceolwulf ruled the Mercians during his brief reign, and there are signs that he did not do badly, we may be sure that the West Saxon king would not have wished

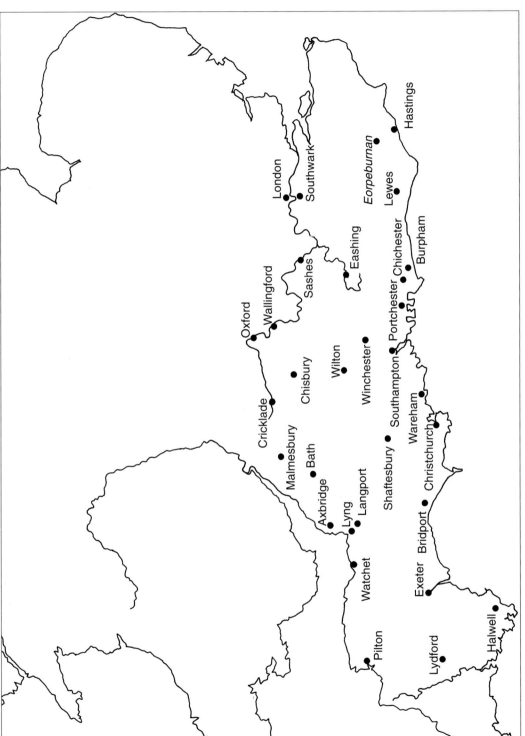

Places fortified as part of Alfred's defences against the Danes. Apart from London, all are listed in one or other of the two versions of the text now called the Burghal Hidage. Some of the locations, for example Eorpeburnan, are uncertain. (Aardcark Illustration)

such an uncertain and provenly treacherous ruler to remain on the throne of this strategically important kingdom.

Little is known of the governance of Mercia after the disappearance of Ceolwulf until an ealdorman named Aethelred emerged as its ruler in 883. His origins are obscure and he is sometimes said to have been an ealdorman under King Burghred. There is, however, little evidence of this. Stenton points out that, from the moment he came to be ruler, he regarded Alfred as his lord without question.[7] He next received the gift of London from Alfred, after the latter had reoccupied the city and, 'before the end of 889 he had married Aethelflaed, Alfred's eldest daughter', who was later to gain lasting fame as the Lady of the Mercians. Aethelred presided over the Mercian Council and led the Mercian armies with an authority that was never challenged and, as Stenton points out, his attitude and his loyalty to the Wessex king were such that he virtually made English Mercia a province of Wessex. In the circumstances he appears to have played an essential role in King Alfred's plans for the reconstruction of his kingdom.

The attitude adopted by 'free' Mercia in the years before the arrival of Aethelred is of interesting significance, for 878 – the year of *Ethandun* – found them engaged in a fierce war against their traditional enemy, the northern Welsh, who at that time were declaredly hostile to the English. The Mercians gained a decisive victory in which the Welsh king, the powerful Rhodri the Great of Gwynedd, was slain. The inevitable and bloody response to this came two years later when Rhodri's sons, Anarawd and his brothers, retaliated by delivering a resounding defeat upon the Mercians and then switched their attention to their fellow Britons in South Wales. As a consequence of these events, which may be dated to the mid-880s,

> Hyfaidd, with all the inhabitants of the kingdom of Dyfed, driven by the might of the sons of Rhodri, . . . submitted himself to King Alfred's royal overlordship. Likewise, Hywel ap Rhys, the king of Glywysing, and Brochfael and Fernfael, sons of Meuring and kings of Gwent, driven by the might and tyrannical behaviour of Ealdorman Aethelred of Mercia and the Mercians, petitioned King Alfred of their own accord, in order to obtain lordship and protection from him.[8]

An alliance of this nature with the kingdoms of south and west Wales was invaluable to Wessex. It enabled a watchful eye to be kept on the movement of Danish warships in the waters of the Bristol Channel, denied land bases in South

Wales to Viking marauders approaching from the direction of the Irish Sea and commanded the waters of the River Severn. It was a political success, ruthlessly accelerated by Aethelred of Mercia, and it must have delighted the West Saxon king. It was well in step with his ambition of setting in place, alongside his agreement with Guthrum, friendly relationships with all the nations bordering his frontiers, including Flanders and Francia. The Rhodri brothers, perturbed at the growing threat presented by the combination of Wessex, Mercia and the kingdoms of South Wales, now sought an ally of their own.

The Rhodris of Gwynedd now turned to the Northumbrians and were warmly welcomed by their king, Guthred. The alliance they proffered him provided an important strategic benefit, for it brought with it an alternative and secure means of communication, across North Wales, between York and the Scandinavian faction in Dublin and elsewhere in Ireland. It was a short-lived association but the date at which it finally foundered remains uncertain. It may be that it endured until about 894, when Alfred's forces began the business of reoccupying and fortifying northern Mercia. It may be that, at an earlier date, Anarawd had discerned the inherent dangers of his alliance. More probably, he was attracted by Alfred's growing strength, which was increasingly identifying the West Saxon as the sole Christian leader capable of taking on and defeating the Danes. This awareness at length impressed upon Anarawd that his place was within the West Saxon alliance and not outside it. He went in person to Wessex to treat for admission. He was received by Alfred with honour and accepted by him as his son at a ceremony in which the Welshman was confirmed in the Christian faith by a bishop. Anarawd then, having been 'showered with extravagant gifts, . . . subjected himself with all his people to King Alfred's lordship on the same condition as Aethelred and the Mercians, namely, that in every respect he would be obedient to the royal will'.[9] As happened in the case of Guthrum and others, Christianity formed the major part of the treaty package, for its adoption symbolised entry into the political world which the converts wished to join and the vows taken encouraged them to remain within it, for fear of being accused of apostasy.

As much as Alfred hoped to create stable, worthwhile alliances with his near neighbours in England, he was equally concerned that there should be no deterioration in the close links which already existed between Wessex and her continental neighbours. These had developed over many years through their shared Christian experience and their mutual association with Rome. Paradoxically, these were to prove to have been strengthened, perhaps more than anything else, by the introduction of Judith into the West Saxon scene – the lively young daughter of Charles the Bald, whose marriage to Alfred's father and subsequently, as a widow, to the latter's son Aethelbald, had almost caused serious divisions among the shires.

Judith returned to Francia after the death of her second husband in 860. From there, two years later, and still barely eighteen years of age, she eloped with Baldwin, Count of Flanders. Their son Baldwin II, as might perhaps be expected given his mother's character, was an energetic ruler but is also said to have been a violent and greedy man. He is frequently recognised as the architect of the innovative Flemish defences erected and redesigned in the 880s against Viking incursions. His work in this regard is sometimes said to have influenced the design of West Saxon fortifications. In addition to this common interest, both Baldwin II and Alfred were anxious to prevent the foundation of Danish settlements on the Flemish coast which, from the Wessex viewpoint, would have placed east Kent under renewed threat. The suggestion that the two men maintained close contact throughout these troubled years, exchanging information, ideas and details about new military techniques, is easy to accept. It is reinforced by the knowledge of Alfred's friendship with Grimbald, a former monk of St Bertin, the Flemish monastery that was the subject of Viking raid in 880.

Grimbald entered the community during the abbacy of Hugh I (834–44),[10] and his presence there is recorded by his signature on documents prepared by him in the years 867 and 868, and again in 885. It would thus appear that he was present at St Bertin in the year when the monastery was attacked. He came to England in 886 to join Alfred's team of 'scholarly assistants'. He is sometimes said to have been involved with the compilation of the *Anglo-Saxon Chronicle*. If this were true, it might not only explain the very full account, contained within its pages, of Danish military activity in that area at that time, but would also suggest that Grimbald had a valuable knowledge and experience of Danish tactics and behaviour which Alfred could have put to good use.

It was doubtless not entirely philanthropy which persuaded the king to pay out a substantial portion of his income 'to foreigners of all races who came to him from places near and far and asked money from him (or even if they did not ask), to each one according to his station'.[11] It would thus be no surprise to discover that a goodly part of the monk's duties were concerned with the accumulation and collation of intelligence information derived from these various sources. Indeed it is reasonable to expect that King Alfred would have possessed some organisation of this nature to enable him to anticipate enemy intentions and thus deploy his forces, particularly his overstretched navy, to best effect.

Before we move on from this glance at the values the king attached to his foreign relationships and the benefits he received from them, the telling roles played by his two daughters Aethelflaed and Aelfthryth cannot be overlooked. They both, in their own way, left a deep mark in English history. The marriage of the king's younger daughter Aelfthryth to Judith's son Baldwin II in about 893 – significantly, at a time when the Vikings were renewing their attacks upon England – opened a relationship between the kings of England and the counts of Flanders which was still firmly established in the mid-eleventh century.[12] Indeed it is intriguing to think that one of the main planks of British defensive policy throughout the centuries, which historically has always sought the friendliness (or at least the neutrality) of the Low Countries, was considered of such import at such an early date. But England had to wait many years before the full story of Judith and Aelfthryth was complete, for a direct descendant of their two marriages, Matilda, the daughter of Baldwin V of Flanders, was to become the wife of William the Conqueror, whose own origins sprang from the Norsemen who had settled in Francia.

Aethelflaed, the elder daughter and first-born child of Alfred the Great, was wedded three or four years earlier than Aelfthryth to ealdorman Aethelred of Mercia. Her marriage was politically important. It was intended to cement the friendship between Aethelred and Alfred and to restore the union between Wessex and Mercia which had existed in the happier, more ordered days before Burghred abandoned his throne and fled to Rome. Both she and her husband, throughout their lives, worked devotedly to achieve this end. Aethelflaed in particular played a vital role during the early part of the tenth century. When her husband declined into a prolonged and serious illness some two or three years before the end of his rule, she assumed from him much of the responsibility of government. She proved greatly popular with his people and after his death in 911 they appointed her ruler, awarding her the title Lady of the Mercians, in the same manner as her husband before her had been their Lord. She unflinchingly assumed every aspect of her duties. She not only led her army against the Danes to defend her northern frontiers but also set herself the task of securing West Mercia against further assault by constructing a chain of fortresses astride the invasion routes entering her territory.

Even more importantly, in concert with her brother Edward, who by that time had succeeded their father to the throne of Wessex, she campaigned vigorously and successfully to push back the frontiers of Danish-occupied England. Aethelflaed died at Tamworth in June 918 and was buried in Gloucester. She had ruled with remarkable dexterity, tact and fortitude. Like Alfred before her, she had a vision of a united England and played a major part in laying its foundation. It is a matter of sadness that what has been termed 'a conspiracy of silence amongst her West Saxon contemporaries'[13] has prevented us from knowing more about her, for she was patently a lady of remarkable character.

*   *   *

It is evident that some 500 years earlier the Saxon peoples had possessed no mean ability as sailors. Indeed the frequency and increasing scale of Saxon and Frankish raids on the eastern coast of Britain at that time had posed such a problem to the Roman commanders then in occupation that they were compelled both to expand their naval forces and to redeploy them from their main base in Boulogne. They also increased their coastal fortifications, manning these with auxiliary garrisons, to deal with those marauders who had slipped past their sea patrols. In command of this defensive system they appointed an officer with the grand title Count of the Saxon Shore. It is thus evident that the maritime skills of the Saxons in those day were not inconsiderable, although the shipping available to them in the fifth and sixth centuries is said 'to have lacked true keels, capable of supporting masts and sails'.[14]

In the years which followed, Saxon efforts were directed more towards the construction of ships for the expansion of trade rather than for the defence of their shoreline, but even here their interest appears to have been so lacking that Offa, King of Mercia (757–796), in order to end their reliance on foreign transport, found it necessary to encourage his people to construct shipping for the transportation of their own goods. The swelling number of Viking raids across the Wessex coastline during the first half of the ninth century does not appear to have stimulated any evident Saxon naval response. We have to wait until 851 before we are told by the *Anglo-Saxon Chronicle* that Alfred's eldest brother Athelstan, with ealdorman Ealhhere, 'fought in ships and slew a great army at Sandwich in Kent, and captured nine ships and put the others to flight'. Athelstan, then ruler of eastern Wessex, was fighting to safeguard the Wantsum Channel against Danish encroachment. Then in 875 we hear for the first time of a king of Wessex leading a squadron into battle when Alfred, encountering a Danish fleet of 'seven tall swift ships', captured one and put the rest to flight. Again in 882, at sea with his navy, Alfred met with four longships:

he captured two of the ships, having killed everyone on board. The two commanders of the other two ships who, with all their crews, were very much exhausted by the fight and by their wounds, laid down their arms and on bended knee with submissive pleas gave themselves to the king.[16]

Three years after this incident, the context of which is not provided, Alfred is reported to have dispatched his fleet from his Kentish base to punish Guthrum's East Anglian settlers for breaking their peace with him. This raid was initially successful and sixteen Danish longships were captured in a savage battle in the Stour estuary. However, the West Saxon ships appear to have delayed their withdrawal and to have suffered as a consequence, for 'as the royal fleet was about to go home, the Vikings, who lived in East Anglia, assembled ships from everywhere and met it in the mouth of the same river, there was a naval encounter and the Vikings had the victory'.

It is clear from the brief accounts of these skirmishes that a West Saxon navy existed during the second half of the ninth century, but there is little evidence of the intensity of its operations. We are provided only with details of the engagements in which King Alfred personally participated or which were conducted under his direct authority. There may have been – and probably were – other encounters which took place without his involvement and which went unreported. We are thus granted little opportunity fully to judge the navy's capability, except to be aware that by 885 it had reached a sufficient standard of battle-worthiness to be able to confront a Viking fleet in its home lair and capture sixteen of its warships. Its subsequent performance, especially in allowing itself to be trapped after such an initially successful outcome, would have been something which could not have satisfied the king.

It was not until the closing years of his life that Alfred issued his famous instruction for the reconstruction of his navy. The improvements in scale, design and manning levels which he then initiated are given in a paragraph of the *Chronicle* for the year 897:

The king, Alfred, commanded to be built against the Danish warships, long ships which were well nigh twice as long as the others. Some had sixty oars, some more. They were both swifter and steadier, and also higher than the others. They were shaped neither as the Frisians nor as the Danish, but as it seemed to himself they might be most useful.

The king's personal experience of war at sea would have helped him in his planning. He can have had little doubt that the Vikings would continue to possess the naval initiative, owing to their maritime skills, their vast pool of experienced manpower and their seemingly unending supply of shipping resources, which enabled them to exploit to the full the military principle of surprise. Armed with this knowledge, and aware of the potential drain on his fleet imposed by his lengthy coastline, he doubtless understood that the English would find it difficult to compete with the Vikings in terms of numbers of ships. He realised, as we have already discussed, that a vital ingredient for success was the careful collection and collation of military intelligence.

With these principles in mind, his aim was to pursue a policy of offensive defence and, wherever possible, to seek out his enemies at sea before they could launch their attack. In order to satisfy this tactical requirement, it was necessary to build ships of a size, speed and superior design which would bring them promptly to potential trouble-spots and give the edge to his fighting men. For this reason his new ships were larger and higher than their Danish counterparts and were provided with more oars. In close engagements at sea the English now had the advantage of fighting from ships with higher platforms and numerically greater crews than those of their opponents, an advantage that would have given them a preference for fighting at sea rather than ashore.

The king's method of financing the construction work is obscure but the later system of naval districts or ship-sokes of 300 hides were created, each responsible for the provision of one warship, was probably founded upon it.[16] The manpower requirement was twofold: namely, fighting men and skilled seamen. The former were provided by *scypfyrds*, in much the same manner that shire *fyrds* were raised. The limited numbers of trained seamen available, particularly in the early days of expansion, might have inhibited Alfred's ambitions at this time, but there are indications that they were bolstered in the mid-880s by an influx of refugee Frisian seamen who had fled to Wessex, driven overseas by continuing Viking raids upon their homeland.

In step with the reconstruction of his navy, the king engaged in another major and costly project, in terms of both manpower and additional taxation. This was the financing of his eastward advance, and subsequently the construction of the *burh* strongholds which were to consolidate his gains. It is perhaps surprising that his efforts at reform had met lethargy and sometimes outright opposition to the changes he proposed. Some of the eastern shires had remained under Danish domination for many years and probably now regarded with disfavour the king's new military measures and the disturbance of their settled way of life. According to Asser, the king responded by

> gently instructing, cajoling, urging, commanding and (in the end when his patience was exhausted) by sharply chastising those who were disobedient and by despising popular stupidity and stubbornness in every way, he carefully and cleverly exploited and converted his bishops and ealdormen and nobles, and his thegns most dear to him, and his reeves as well . . .[17]

It thus appears that even where Alfred's aims were not being openly obstructed, his orders were all too often received unenthusiastically and with a lack of urgency which smacked of low morale. Asser writes of instances where fortifications ordered by the king 'had not been begun, or else, having been begun late in the day, had not been brought to completion', with the result that when the Viking assaults upon Wessex were renewed in the late autumn of 892 some construction work was still unfinished, people were unprepared and those responsible were reduced to 'meaningless repentance'. The very phrase itself, 'meaningless repentance', savours of lack of supervision at the highest level.

In a sense the reluctance of the land-holding class to comply with the king's demands is understandable, albeit totally unacceptable. Their resources had probably already been severely drained, year after year, to provide tribute to the enemy war-bands which had descended upon the shires of eastern Wessex ever since Aethelwulf's death. They were now being asked to carry the considerable costs of reconstructing the navy, building or repairing some thirty *burh* strongholds, maintaining within them garrisons of several thousand men and providing a field army radically different and greatly more expensive than the old-fashioned system of levies.

Two opposing cases are noteworthy for their timing and for their outcome. The Danish assault on Rochester failed in 885 because the robust defence of the city by its inhabitants gave Alfred time in which to arrive with a large relieving army. It was a classic example of the style of offensive defence he was striving to achieve. On the other hand a fort constructed near Appledore, on the edge of the Romney Marshes in south Kent, fell into Danish hands in 892, before it had been completed and when it was manned by only a 'few commoners'.[18] This was a circumstance which presented Alfred with a situation both dangerous and intolerable. It demanded better communications between himself and his shires, so that 'his bishops and ealdormen and nobles, and his thegns most dear to him, and reeves as well' should be in no doubt as to his wishes. An indication of his realisation of this fact is contained in the *Preface to the Pastoral Care* which he translated at about this time, when the possibility of renewed war was becoming increasingly likely with each passing year:

> It has very often come into my mind what wise men there were in former times throughout England, both of spiritual and lay orders, and how happy times there were throughout England; and how kings who had ruled over people were obedient to God and his messengers; and how they both upheld peace and morals at home and also extended their territory abroad, and how they prospered both in warfare and in wisdom.[19]

His insistence that his underlings should be able to read and write or else surrender their 'their offices of worldly power' did not arise from a simple desire for the revival of learning. He could not be everywhere and personally control everything. It was important therefore that his officers should be able to read his written word in order to be informed in detail, and with accuracy, of his instructions. In other words he was seeking a medium by which his precise aims could be conveyed to his people and the reasons for his actions explained. He appears to have seen the Church playing a vital role in this process with, from about the year 892, responsibilities for the publication and dissemination of the *Anglo-Saxon Chronicle*.

The events of the year 885, when a contingent of the Danish party which had earlier been at Fulham recrossed the Channel and laid siege to Rochester, provided a catalyst for many important decisions. The raiders had brought with them a number of horses and they threw up their own walled fortifications in front of the gates of the city – presumably a contravallation to protect themselves from attack by a relieving force. The new Saxon defensive arrangements worked excellently. King Alfred was quickly on the scene with an army, catching the Vikings unprepared and forcing them to flee to their ships. In their confusion the Danes left behind their animals and abandoned the great majority of the prisoners they were holding within their stronghold. They at once returned to France. It seems possible that at some stage of its operation the war-band received support from Guthrum's settlers in East Anglia, for Alfred followed up his decisive victory by dispatching a naval force across the estuary to extract retribution from the Danish settlements along the Stour. It was a retaliatory blow which not only fully demonstrated the growing strength and confidence of the West Saxons but also carried a clear warning for the future.

Alfred was now driven to make three important decisions. First, he determined that the continued occupation of London by the Danes, which posed a constant threat to Wessex, could no longer be tolerated. He therefore took control of the city. Having restored the damage which it had sustained during its years of occupation, and strengthened its garrison, he handed it over to ealdorman Aethelred of Mercia for safekeeping. Secondly, it immediately became apparent that the security of London could never be assured until the frontiers of the southern Danelaw had been clearly defined. A treaty between Alfred and Guthrum was therefore drawn up at about this time defining the boundary between the two kingdoms and which regulated the relationships of both populations. Thirdly, the Danish raid on Rochester had emphasised only too clearly the increasing likelihood of the return of the Vikings in strength. It was essential that the population should be alerted to this danger and that every citizen should be involved in preparing for that day.

It was probably from a desire to accelerate this work that the king took the decision to bolster his staff with the addition of two learned men, handpicked for their specialist knowledge and expertise, Asser and Grimbald. In the case of the latter, he wrote to Fulco, Archbishop of Rheims, asking for the monk from St Bertin to be appointed to him, although we are given no indication for his reason for doing this. As a sweetener, he sent the archbishop a gift of hunting dogs. Fulco's response makes reference to this but is tantalisingly ambiguous. It is nevertheless possible to read into the following extract from his letter such a role for Grimbald as we have depicted:

> You seek from me not corporeal but spiritual dogs, not those which the prophet reproaches, saying 'Dumb dogs, unable to bark' [Isaiah, lvi, 10], but those which the psalmist says, 'The tongue of your dogs may be red with the blood of your enemies' [Psalms, lxvii, 24] – dogs which undoubtedly would know how and be suitable to bark out mighty growls on their master's behalf, and continually guard his flock with extremely vigilant and attentive watches, and keep far hence the savage wolves of the impure spirits who threaten and devour our souls.[20]

Asser on the other hand was employed for entirely different purposes. He appears to have been first summoned to the royal court a year or two earlier than Grimbald, possibly in the closing months of 883. He then undertook to return in six months' time but on his way home fell ill and was laid up in the monastery at Caerwent for a period of 'twelve months and one week'. By that time Alfred was sending him anxious messages, seeking the reason for his delay and urging him to come quickly. The king's desire for haste is understandable for it would now have been early 885 and the growing uncertainties of the political and military situation were demanding immediate action. He would also have been aware that a potentially volatile problem was brewing in Wales, where ealdorman Aethelred of Mercia was campaigning against Hywel ap Rhys, King of Glywysing, and the kings of Gwent. At the same time, as we have seen, Anarawd ap Rhodri and his brothers were making threatening moves against Brycheinog and Hyfaiid ap Bleddri, King of Dyfed, while simultaneously displaying unwelcome signs of friendship with the Viking Guthred, King of York and neighbouring Northumbria.

The implication of this latter alliance was clear. If at any time it should prove necessary for Mercia to go to war with the Danes of East Anglia to safeguard the interests of Wessex, the possibility that their Northumbrian kinsmen should come to their assistance was very real. If at the same time Guthred carried the Rhodri family along with him, Alfred would then have been confronted with a war on two fronts, with a smouldering situation of unrest in Wales. It was essential for his security therefore that he should break the unity of his adversaries. In order to work to this end, there was a clear need for a senior and influential Welsh representative at the West Saxon court, to advise the king on Welsh affairs and guide him towards a unifying understanding with the Welsh people, in particular with the kingdoms of southern and eastern Wales. His eye fell upon Asser, a native Welshman who, according to some documentary evidence, had already been ordained Bishop of St David's by the time he met the King of Wessex.

St David's was one of the great religious establishments in south Wales and was an important centre of learning. It follows that its community, for this reason and through the medium of its widespread Christian teaching, had considerable political influence. The establishment of St David's agreed with reluctance to the secondment of Asser to the Wessex royal court but finally sanctioned it because they could see an advantage to themselves. Their Church had been suffering from harassment by Hyfaidd of Dyfed and Asser was instructed to obtain Alfred's protection against these attacks. It at once provided the diplomatic opening that the king was seeking. Hyfaidd, when confronted on this matter, undertook to leave St David's alone if he in turn could receive Alfred's protection against Anarawd ap Rhodri.

This simple beginning paved the way for the important West Saxon alliances with the kingdoms of Wales which were to lead to the political and military triumphs of 893-5 and which, to a large degree, secured the western flank of Wessex against attack during those troublesome years.

CHAPTER 8

The Final Campaign

This is the war that we have known
And fought in every hundred years,
Our sword, upon the last, steep path,
Forged by the hammer of our wrath,
On the Anvil of our fears.

Dorothy L. Sayers

In order fully to understand the military situation in England in the years leading up to the return of the Vikings in 892, and the campaigns which followed, it is necessary to look once again at the events of the years 885–6, through the eyes of the various chroniclers. The authors of the *Anglo-Saxon Chronicle*, without embellishment and with typical brevity, tell of the arrival in 885 of a marauding force of Danes from overseas, who besieged the city of Rochester. They also tell how Alfred arrived with his army, compelling the enemy to return to their ships, in their haste abandoning their horses together with the entrenchments, a contravallation, which they had constructed to protect themselves from outside interference while concentrating upon their attack on the city. The authors also provide brief details of an encounter in the Stour estuary in Essex between a West Saxon naval force from Kent and sixteen Viking longships from East Anglia. The Saxon navy appears to have gained a considerable initial success but the Danes were able to summon up fleet reinforcements before the West Saxons turned for home and in the end the Vikings won the day.

The chronicler's entry for the following year baldly states that 'King Alfred occupied London and all the English people that were not under subjection to the Danes submitted to him. And he then entrusted the borough to ealdorman Aethelred' of Mercia.[1]

The tenth-century chronicler Aethelweard has but little to add to this picture of events. Alfred, he tells us, upon his arrival at Rochester, gave 'his orders to the leader of the men of Saruara', a district that has not been firmly identified but possibly relates to the Latin name for 'Sarum' or Salisbury,[2] indicating that at least some of his levies came from Wiltshire. The raid into the Stour estuary by the West Saxon fleet may be judged to have been a follow-up punitive expedition. The king can have been happy neither with its outcome nor with the knowledge that Guthrum's settlers had been reinforced by such a troublesome faction, even though the latter soon quarrelled with the settlers and sailed away to find easier pickings.

Asser provides a rather more verbose account than either Aethelweard or the authors of the *Anglo-Saxon Chronicle* but he has little to add that is substantially informative except to relate that, after taking it over, the king

restored the city of London splendidly – after so many towns had been burned and so many people slaughtered – and made it habitable again; he entrusted it to the care of Aethelred, ealdorman of the Mercians. All the Angles and Saxons, those who had formerly been scattered everywhere and were not in captivity with the Vikings, turned willingly to King Alfred and submitted themselves willingly to his lordship.[3]

Not one of these three versions of events by itself does much to clarify for us the situation which confronted Alfred in eastern Wessex at this moment, but of one thing there appears to be little doubt. The Rochester raid urgently concentrated the king's mind on those matters which had to be dealt with if the future of Wessex and her allies was to be safeguarded. In essence there were two requirements: first, a treaty with Guthrum to define the boundary between 'English' England and the southern Danelaw, and secondly, an eastward extension of his system of *burh* strongholds for the defence of Wessex, so that he might continue his rolling advance from a firm base. There was an obstacle to the furtherment of both these tasks. The Danish occupation of London not only constituted a continuing threat to West Saxon and Mercian territories but stood as an obstruction across the path of Alfred's progress towards the complete recovery of his kingdom. The capture of London therefore became his first priority and without further delay he laid hold of the city in 886. We are provided with little indication of the manner in which he achieved this but Asser's comment that towns were burned and people slaughtered, when taken in the context of Aethelweard's strong words about the 'foul people of East Anglia', suggests that it may not have fallen into his hands without a struggle.

Whether or not this is the way it happened is immaterial: what was important to the king was that his possession of the city now enabled him to put in place a vital component of his river defence system, namely a double-*burh* astride the river at Southwark. This would enable him to block enemy access to the upper reaches of the Thames. He had already constructed three other similar strongholds, the presence of which have been identified, one at Wallingford, another at Sashes and a third on the River Wey at Eashing. This latter defence lay surprisingly far upstream, beyond Guildford, but was perhaps sited with the aim of preventing or hindering an advance on Winchester. It would seem to make more sense if it had been situated further north, near the River Wey's confluence with the main stream, but its position was perhaps determined by the availability of manpower for its garrison. There were other such defences, two of them later to be provided in Buckingham and Hertford, equally oddly sited but perhaps for the same reason.[4]

Before the provision of the double-*burh* at Southwark, Alfred appears to have depended upon the presence of his newly designed fleet to deter raiders from forcing their way upstream. The *Chronicle* for 885, quoted above, records that the king despatched his fleet 'from Kent' on its expedition against the East Anglians. It is improbable, at this stage of his advance, with the eastern extremity of Kent still isolated and a patently hostile navy based on the north banks of the Thames estuary, that he would have stationed his ships in the Wantsum without adequate land support. He might, more sensibly, have located them at Rochester but if so they were clearly not present when the Danish host of 885 arrived.

After occupying London, Alfred appears to have moved with commendable speed to sign the Danelaw boundary treaty with Guthrum. There is little room for doubt about its timing. He gave the city to ealdorman Aethelred in 886, after he had taken it from the Danes, and 'made it habitable' and, since the treaty document shows the city lying on the English side of the boundary, it follows that it can only have been signed in that year or later. The timing of the treaty can be further defined, for Guthrum died in 890. Thus, the agreement was most certainly effected at some time during the years 886–890, more probably in 886 or early 887, after the rebuff of the Danish host at Rochester and when Alfred was consolidating his success. He is unlikely to have delayed longer. The boundary was agreed in the following terms: it commenced from the Thames estuary and thence turned north, east of London and up the River Lea to its source. From the source of the Lea, it ran in a straight line to Bedford and thence up the River Ouse to Watling Street. It is notable that Alfred applied his signature on behalf of

The document recording the treaty between Alfred and Guthrum. (The Master and Fellows of Corpus Christi College, Cambridge)

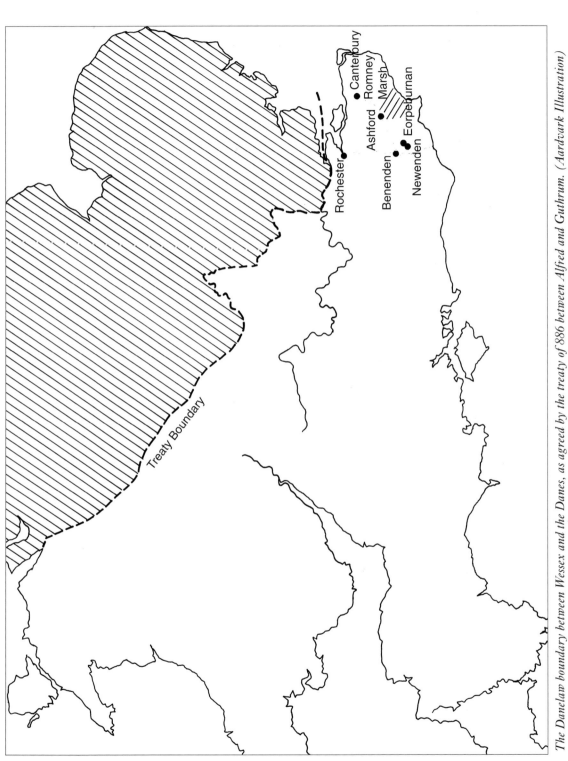

Canterbury
Romney
Marsh
Ashford
Eorpeburnan
Benenden
Newenden
Rochester
Treaty Boundary

The Danelaw boundary between Wessex and the Danes, as agreed by the treaty of 886 between Alfred and Guthrum. (Aardvark Illustration)

Mercia but no mention is made of the Mercian boundary beyond the Ouse/Watling Street junction. This is a matter to which we will return but it is sufficient to note here that Watling Street terminated in the Wirral at Chester.

A material feature of the boundary treaty was that it allowed Guthrum occupation of all land lying east of the Lea. This granted the north bank of the Thames estuary to the Danes of East Anglia, thus enabling them, menacingly for Wessex, to share and exercise an influence over the busy shipping lanes flowing to and from the North Sea and the waters of the Wantsum Channel. This, as we have previously described but which bears repeating, formed part of a larger, sheltered waterway system then running from Ribe in Denmark to Quentovic in northern France.[5] South of Quentovic, the Wantsum offered a route to traffic from the estuaries of the Seine, the Somme and the Canche rivers, all of which were heavily infested with Viking raiders in the years under discussion. These shipping lanes avoided the dangers of the treacherous North Foreland and led swiftly into the heart of southern England. The Wantsum not only provided a valuable sheltered harbour for shipping, it also possessed an additional characteristic of some significance. Vessels entering the Channel at Sandwich were carried upstream on the incoming tide until they reached Sarre on the Isle of Thanet. Once there, they had to pause to await the ebb tide which then carried them northwards into the Thames. In view of the frequent Viking presence, this was not a routine which brought much comfort either to the people of Canterbury, lying on the Stour, a few miles from where it joined the waterway opposite Sarre, or to the population of East Kent.

Finally, in this review of Alfred's military preparedness on the eve of the return of the Danes in 892, we need to examine the state of completion of his system of *burh* strongholds. This is frequently referred to as the Burghal Hidage plan, because the military and logistical detail of Alfred's plan is paralleled in a document of that name compiled for administrative purposes in about 911, during the reign of his son Edward the Elder. The purpose of the later document was to overhaul the existing system and refresh the responsibilities allocated to shires and districts on a hidage basis.[6] Our interest lies in the fact that the Burghal Hidage document lists thirty-three *burhs*, of which thirty were situated in Wessex. The remainder were provided in Mercia at a later date, outside the period we are discussing. The list makes a circuit of Wessex and is set down in a sequence which may have some tactical relevance; if so, however, this is not immediately clear. It is notable, however, that there are three important omissions for which various reasons have been suggested: no entries are made for Kent, London or Cornwall.[7]

It has been argued that Kent was excluded from the plan because its hidage was calculated on a different administrative basis to that of the rest of Wessex, and that London was excluded because of its size.[8]

It is not militarily easy to accept these propositions. If it is conceded that the Burghal Hidage list originated as a defensive plan for Wessex, then the only acceptable explanation for the exclusion of any of its areas should be a military one. Cornwall, for example, was possibly omitted because its 'Welsh' sympathies rendered it politically unreliable or, equally probably, because the River Tamar provided a better line upon which to base the defence of Wessex. In the context of 'fortress Wessex', the defence of London would have meant little to Alfred *per se*. On the other hand he would have regarded Southwark through different eyes. Its loss would have opened the northern frontier of his kingdom to the enemy and would have spelt disaster. We may therefore judge that the overall West Saxon plan for the defence of Wessex would have included priority arrangements for the retention of the Southwark stronghold.

What, then, about the defence of Kent? If the West Saxons had at this stage chosen to advance to the shores of the Wantsum for the defence of Kent, they would then have lain some 65 miles or, at best, a march of two and a half days from Southwark, exposing this key feature in their defensive strategy to a sudden onslaught by the Danes of East Anglia and their allies. Moreover, they would have been at the end of a long line of communication, vulnerable to the sort of attack from the continent which Haesten's two divisions were to deliver in 892. For these reasons, and doubtless also remembering the experience of his predecessors, the king seems to have decided to abandon eastern Kent, if indeed he had ever reoccupied it.

A tactic of this nature would only have been fully successful if it were accompanied by the sort of scorched earth policy which the Saxons were later to pursue against the Viking army in the Wirral. There is some evidence that they acted similarly in Kent, not least by denuding the area of grain, cattle, horses and shipping which might otherwise have fallen into the hands of the enemy. It is noteworthy, for example, that the Viking host in its flight from Rochester in 885 is said to have left behind 'all the horses they had brought with them from Francia'.[9] It had previously been the custom of raiding parties to steal or requisition these upon arrival. Likewise the great Viking army which was soon to land in the Romney Marsh went first to Boulogne, where they obtained additional shipping 'so that they transported themselves across, horses and all, in one journey'.[10] It is sometimes suggested that these additional vessels were needed to replace those worn out during the arduous continental operations in which they had been engaged during the past decade, but replacements of this essential nature would surely have been ongoing, else the war-band would have been immobilised. It is more probable that the Danes were already aware of the conditions awaiting them upon arrival and took the precaution of landing with full resources. It is equally feasible that on this occasion many of their longships would have required modification for the safe loading, passage and disembarkation of their animals.[11]

If, as we are suggesting, the West Saxons deliberately withdrew from east Kent as part of their 'fortress Wessex' defence policy, the question remains, at what point, or on what line, did they see the defence of eastern Wessex commencing? A hint of the answer is to be discovered in the location of an earthwork on the Sussex/Kent border, some 13 miles north of Hastings, which has been broadly identified as *Eorpeburnam*,[12] one of the thirty *burhs* of Wessex. Lying at this eastern extremity of fortress Wessex, it was conceivably one of the last of the Burghal Hidage strongholds to be set in place. This may in part be the reason why, when the Danes came ashore in 892, they found it only partially constructed. It was, according to the chronicler Aethelweard, a fort of primitive structure and occupied 'only by a small band of rustics'. It is likely that this stronghold was to the forefront of Asser's mind when he wrote scathingly, doubtless echoing Alfred's feelings, of circumstances in which fortifications 'were not fulfilled because of people's laziness, or else (having been begun too late in a time of necessity) were not finished in time to be of use to those working on them . . . and enemy forces burst in by land and sea'.[13]

An obvious riposte would be of course that their behaviour was in parallel with that of those in authority who, confronted with imminent invasion, ordered construction work as part of a national defence plan but failed vigorously to pursue its progress. It reflects badly on the command structure set in place by the king.

One favoured site for the location of this hapless fortification is Castle Toll, an earthwork lying on the end of a mile-long peninsula, jutting out from the forest into the Romney Marsh, about 1½ miles north-east from the village of Newenden.[14] Excavations have revealed that construction work on the original site was incomplete. This was a potentially formidable ditch, 15 metres wide but dug to a depth of only .3 metres. This work was then abandoned and a smaller ditch, nine metres wide, was dug to an improved depth of two metres on the line of the initial, larger work. This reduction in the original scaling suggests that earlier standards of construction may have been sacrificed in order to hasten the completion of the renewed fortification, possibly on its reoccupation after the Danes had evacuated it in favour of a site some 4 miles downstream at Appledore.

In those days there was a highway, 2 or 3 miles west of Newenden, traces of which may still be discovered; this was the service road constructed by the Roman army for the purpose of extracting iron from the thickly forested areas of the Weald. It ran from Rochester, through Maidstone, Staplehurst and Benenden, to Hastings, yet another *burh* stronghold. It would be strange if the West Saxons had not made full use of the mobility offered by this highway, possibly mounting their infantry on the horses retrieved from Kent, in order to cover its full length. The road had other attractions to offer to the Saxons. Another Roman road from Benenden, skirting the northern edges of the Romney Marsh, permitted movement eastwards to Ashford and Canterbury. At its northern end this was crossed yet again by two popular trunk roads, the ancient Pilgrim's Way which followed ridgeway routes from central Wessex to Canterbury, and the Roman Watling Street, upon which Rochester was situated, astride the Medway.

It would therefore appear that *Eorpeburnam*, despite its seemingly isolated and vulnerable locality, was specifically sited not merely for the purpose of guarding against enemy infiltration of the marshes, but also in the knowledge that it could be speedily reinforced along the Roman iron road, either from Rochester or Hastings or from any other supporting stronghold along its length. In that sense, well fortified, stocked and garrisoned, it would have provided stability to the right flank of a force posted by Alfred to close the gap between Rochester and the northern edge of the *Andreaswald* forest. The left flank, with responsibility for blocking the Medway to enemy warships, would have rested on the garrison at Rochester, which had already distinguished itself by its sturdy resistance to the Third Army when besieged by it in 885. It is conceivable that it was upon this line, which we may term the Medway Gap, that Alfred based the eastern defensive line of 'fortress Wessex'. It is likely that he gave it support in depth by siting his headquarters, with a reserve force, at Crayford, where Watling Street crosses the River Darent, 20 miles east of Southwark. Further, with his navy at his command, he was in a position from here to secure the open river flank of his forward position.

Before we conclude this glance at the state of Alfred's military preparedness on the eve of renewed Viking landings, it is necessary to recognise the extent to which West Saxon overall strategy was affected by the reorganised military system which emerged during these years. The detail with which we have been provided is based on one brief, ambiguously phrased and much quoted sentence:

> The king ... divided his army in two, so that always half his men were at home, half out on service, except for those who were to garrison the *burhs*.[15]

In the simplest terms it was a scheme designed to give teeth to the king's carefully prepared *burh* defence plan, and at the same time to provide him with a field force capable of mobilising at speed and sustaining itself in the field for considerable lengths of time. It was a system whereby, in the case of each stronghold he established, a number of men, calculated to a specific formula of five men to each pole of measurement and based on the total length of the *burh* walls, would be nominated for garrison duties; the duties of the remainder would be rotated so that half their number would be at home, working in the fields or employed in their particular specialist industry, and the other half would be on military duty in the field or on standby, ready for call-out.

Alfred's new defence structure was an understanding arrangement designed to take note of the peasant mentality which had been at the root of many of his past failures in the field. It recognised the demands of farming and the normal cycle of agriculture and took account of the individual's natural dislike, on call-out, of leaving his family at home, frequently undefended; but it went deeper than this. The *burhs* were mutually supporting and were expected to move to each other's aid in the event of attack; they provided a base into which families could withdraw in case of trouble; they provided the means of guarding standing crops and cattle from predatory bands and a base into which stocks of grain could be removed or indeed permanently stored. Perhaps more importantly than anything else, by their very presence, they encouraged the field forces to look beyond domestic defence and pursue the enemy without fear of jeopardising their home localities.

The underlying theme of Alfred's *burh* scheme was 'aggressive defence', a policy which he also appears to have injected into the operational handling of his field force by introducing an element of mounted infantry. There has been a vigorous debate regarding the totals of mounted troops which may have been involved and about the date of their introduction. There are those who argue, for example, that as early as 877 – when it is reported that Alfred with 'his *fyrd* rode from Wareham after the mounted host up to Exeter' – he was in fact heading a mounted contingent. It is a theory which, when examined against the military circumstances of the West Saxons at that time, is open to considerable argument. There is nothing in the unusually full accounts surrounding the battles of Ashdown and *Ethandun* to suggest that the West Saxon forces on those two occasions were even partially mounted. Nor it should be added is there any evidence to suggest that they were not. However, the presence of West Saxon mounted infantry as an integral part of their army is well documented during the campaigning years 892–6; unfortunately the essential piece of knowledge, the ratio of foot soldiers to horsemen, is nowhere stated.

There are, however, various factors which would have restricted the numbers of horsemen, the most important of which would have been the size of the manageable total; this factor would have been regulated by their command structure, the level of training and general administration, and the nature of the opposition. Thus without examining at length all the administrative problems involved, it is clear that there would have been a militarily economic proportion which would have given maximum satisfaction in terms of battlefield and administrative efficiency. In other words, Alfred's mounted infantry would have formed a sensible number in proportion to his foot soldiers and the degree to which we see his army wholly mounted, or as a mixed body of horse and foot, or as wholly infantry, depends entirely upon the nature of the operation to which they were to be committed.

*   *   *

The detailed reports of continental affairs provided by the *Anglo-Saxon Chronicle* in the years following the Danish raid on Rochester are a reflection of the importance which King Alfred attached to information of this nature. He kept a close watch both on the European economic climate and on the constant shifting of power, in particular the widespread changes evoked by the death of Charles the Fat in January 888. He was well aware that successful resistance to Danish aggression stemmed from the quality of leadership at the top and that, as the war-bands were deprived of resources on the continent, either through defeat in battle or by the failure of crops, the Danes would once again turn their attention across the Channel to the fertile fields of England. For this reason, Alfred required Viking operations in neighbouring continental states to be logged meticulously and he followed their progress year after year. He noted the passage of the Third Army up the Seine in 886 and its arrival at Paris. He would have heard with incredulity how Charles the Fat, after a year of their presence, was so eager to speed the raiders' departure that he unblocked the river to hasten their progress upstream, gave them permission to ravage Burgundy and then undertook to collect a tribute which would be paid to them on their return. During the next few years the raiders exploited his peculiar generosity to the full and drained the upper reaches of the river of its treasures. At this moment their fortunes changed. They now determined to move elsewhere and, in their search for a more lucrative territory, they were heavily defeated by the Bretons at St Lo, after being bloodily rebuffed at Paris by King Odo. In 891 they were defeated yet again, on this occasion by Arnulf, King of Eastern Francia, at the battle of the Dyle, where they lost sixteen royal standards. Arnulf did not pursue his success but withdrew to Bavaria and in 891–2, his Danish opponents moved into winter quarters at Louvain. But fate had not yet finished with them. The harvest failed and the spectre of famine was now added to their troubles.

This natural disaster also impacted upon the activities of another band of Danish marauders, led by the legendary but ill-reputed Haesten, notorious for his deceitfulness, 'his naked savagery and animal cunning'.[16] As a young man he had distinguished himself by slaying in one battle two Frankish heroes, one of them Count Robert the Strong, father of the equally gallant Odo. Haesten had for many years based his activities in the delightful and prosperous valleys of the Rivers Loire and Sarthe, where he made a living by plundering and burning mainly ecclesiastical property. As a result of his activities these areas were becoming increasingly fortified and in 882 he withdrew to the coast, after signing a profitable peace treaty with Louis III. Haesten is thought then to have played some part in the attack on Wessex in 885 but his subsequent whereabouts remained uncertain until the years 890–1, when he is known to have been at Argoeuves, on the Somme. In the following year he was at Amiens. Doubtless, during this period of operations in northern Francia, he renewed his contact with the Third Army, with whom he was now to act in collusion in a joint assault on Wessex.

The combined Danish fleet set sail from France in 892 in two divisions. The first division, sailing in 250 ships, descended upon Appledore, as we have heard, after having penetrated up the Lympne as far as *Eorpeburnan*. The navigation of the river cannot have been easy and the route must have been well reconnoitred. The second division, carried in eighty ships and under the command of Haesten, sailed around the Kent coast and made a landing on the Swale marshes, where they constructed for themselves a fortification at Middleton (today Milton Regis). Earthworks at nearby Castle Rough are traditionally said to be the remains of Haesten's stronghold but it seems to have been too small. A strong argument is also made for another, more probable, location at Bayford Court, where a moat, extending for 1,000 feet or more, encloses the remains of an earthwork on three sides.[17]

The position adopted by Haesten in the lower waters of the Thames, centrally located and with the ability to call upon the support of the nearby Danish settlers of East Anglia, would suggest that he was the senior commander of the combined force. There is, however, some indication that the settlers north of the Thames did not respond to his presence in the numbers that he had anticipated, perhaps because Alfred had been aware of some such happening and had already extracted hostages and pledges of good behaviour from the East Anglian community. This act may have reduced the scale of the settler response to Haesten but in the event it did not deter them from sending him a substantial contingent. If we are to understand the *Chronicle* correctly, this unit played its full part alongside the new arrivals from the continent.

The purpose of the Danish tactic of dividing their forces and landing simultaneously in north and south Kent is open to only one interpretation. Haesten anticipated that the West Saxon forces would move forward to the shores of the Wantsum to defend Canterbury and perhaps recover Thanet, and by this deployment of his landing forces he hoped to sever their communications with mainland Wessex. If the East Anglian Danes had at this stage decided to join him in force, this would have led automatically to the Viking occupation, one might say reoccupation, of Kent and once again to the return of their control of the Wantsum. Alfred, whom we may judge from the wording of the *Chronicle* was lying back on his newly established frontier of 'fortress Wessex', was quick to appreciate what was happening:

> He assembled his army and advanced so that he was encamped between the two Viking armies at a point where he had the best access both to the forest stronghold [at Appledore] and to the river stronghold [at Milton], so that he could reach either one if they chose to make for any open country.[18]

It is probable that the encampment he selected lay at Bredgar, on the northern escarpment of the Downs. It was here that the ancient 'salt' trackway from the Swale descended to the *Andreaswald* forest. This crossing-place, a few miles from the Pilgrim's Way and Rochester, was of earlier tactical importance, where Caratacus is thought to have skirmished with advancing Roman legions in AD 43. The important Bredgar Hoard was also found here.[19] From this high ground, which provides long views of the Hoo Marshes, the Swale and the low hills of Sheppey, it is conceivable that the king could have kept both the Viking fleet and the fortification at Milton in sight, and watched shipping traffic moving back and forth across the Thames.

It was a classic 'stand-off' position. The Danes at Milton were reluctant to emerge from their base in strength, fearful of its destruction should they do so. The West Saxons were equally concerned that, if they laid siege to the Milton fortification, they would open themselves to attack from Appledore, which they continuously harassed with troops 'from the English army and from the *burhs*'.

It was patently a situation which could have lasted for a long time and, although the chronicler conceals the fact from us until a later paragraph, Alfred clearly determined to resolve it by negotiation. At one moment he is reported to us as encamped on the North Downs, with Haesten at Milton; at the next, Haesten has arrived at Benfleet, on the coast of south-east Essex, and the king is leading an army into the west country. We then learn that, at some stage about which we have been uninformed, Haesten's two young sons had been received into the Christian faith and that Alfred and his son-in-law, the loyal Aethelred of Mercia, had sponsored them as godfathers. We are also told that the king had given Haesten 'a good deal of money', implicitly as part of the baptism ceremonial. In exchange the Dane had given Alfred 'hostages and oaths' which, almost immediately and surely not unexpectedly, he was to break. Whether we like it or not, and the chronicler by his method of presenting his facts has surely judged that we will not, we can only assume that this was, once again, a good old-fashioned Danegeld transaction, where peace was purchased for hard cash. Nevertheless it had the desired effect and proved to be sound common-sense, if we accept the use of cash in this manner as a sound military option. Haesten slipped away to Benfleet at some time before Easter 893, leaving his southern division to resolve its own destiny.

The mounted infantry from Appledore now set out to fight their way across country to join their commander at his new base, while the main body of the division made its way by sea. The mounted infantry did not have an easy time. They were making a wide sweep, picking up a large amount of booty as they progressed, when they were intercepted at Farnham by the king's son Edward. He was a young man who was already beginning to display his leadership qualities. He attacked the enemy at once and with vigour.

He came clashing in dense array into collision with the foemen . . . There was no delay, the young men leapt against the prepared defences, and having slipped on their armour they duly exulted, being set free from care by the prince's arrival, like sheep brought to the pasture by the help of the shepherd after the customary ravaging. The barbarian king was wounded then, and they drove the filthy band of his supporters over the River Thames. . . .[20]

The Danes were compelled to cross the Thames at a point where there was no ford, and in their disarray they abandoned their plunder. Their rate of march was slowed by the presence of their wounded leader and they sought shelter on Thorney Island, one of the islands of the River Colne, located about 6 miles from its confluence with the River Thames. Today, Thorney stands in the shadow of Heathrow airport, just south of West Drayton station.[21]

It was here that Edward caught up with them and surrounded their position. At this moment the worst of West Saxon discipline revealed itself in an incongruous series of events. The prince's army had not only consumed all its provisions but had also been in the field for its allotted time. They therefore lifted what might have been a decisive siege and turned for home, without waiting for the relief division which was already marching towards them under the command of Alfred himself. The Danes did not take the opportunity of immediately slipping away because their king was in no fit state to be moved. They were right not to be concerned, for Alfred did not arrive anyway. He was, quite correctly, alarmed by the news that Danish armies, drawn from Northumbria and East Anglia, had chosen this moment to open a two-pronged attack on Devon. At once he turned west towards Exeter with all the English army, save for a detachment which continued eastwards in pursuit of the Appledore Danes.

Edward in the meantime was quickly joined by Aethelred of Mercia and the two men determined to redeem the outcome of the disastrous Thorney Island affair by carrying the fight to the Danish army now concentrating at Benfleet. They marched out of London at the head of a composite force made up of contingents from the militia of Wessex, the trained garrison of London and reinforcements from the west. They found Haesten away on a plundering mission but a large part of his great army was at home. The Saxons stormed the fortification, put the Viking army to flight, 'and seized everything that was inside it, in the way of goods, women and children as well, and they brought everything to London, and they either broke up and burned all the ships, or brought them to London or to Rochester'.[22]

It was a shrewd, hard blow which should have been delivered many months earlier. Some evidence of their success was discovered in the middle of the nineteenth century when workmen preparing the foundations of a new railway bridge at Benfleet discovered the remains of a number of ships, 'many of which were charred, and in and about them lay great quantities of human skeletons'.[23] The West Saxon assault on the Viking base marked the beginning of a new, more aggressive policy, with increasing responsibility passing into the hands of younger commanders.

Among the women and children captured during the raid was the Danish chieftain's wife and their two young sons. In due course they were brought to Alfred and he gave instructions for them to be released. It was a kindness that did nothing to stem the growing Danish pressure on the West Saxon alliance but it may have been appreciated, for the name of Haestan now disappears from our pages. West Frankish tradition reports him killed while fighting against Raoul of Burgundy in 931.[24] However, whatever his degree of further participation, his army now pulled back eastwards to a new camp at Shoebury where, in the summer of 893, it received large reinforcements from East Anglia and Northumbria. Then, when it had regrouped, it marched westwards, thrusting along the axis of the Thames Valley until it reached the River Severn, where it turned northwards to Buttington, an area which is said locally to have been settled some three years earlier by Danes infiltrating up the river from the Bristol Channel.[25]

King Alfred was right in his appreciation of the true threat to Wessex posed by the Danish seaborne attack on the west country. The involvement of the Danish settlers from East Anglia and from Northumbria permitted only one interpretation: it was a diversionary measure, designed to distract attention from the impact of Haesten's two divisional landings in the east. If his two armies had been permitted to link together and had been successful in isolating Alfred in eastern Kent, a simultaneous landing in Devon by Danes from Northumbria and East Anglia could have posed tremendous military problems to the West Saxons, particularly if the enemy force upon its arrival had been able to persuade the Cornishmen to join them. The king's prompt action denied them this opportunity but he must have been concerned that the Danish break-out from Essex must in some way be concerned with the west country landings.

The reaction of the West Saxon commanders to the Danish westward march was so instantly comprehensive that it could only have been preplanned. Ealdorman Aethelhelm of Wiltshire at once set off in pursuit of the Danes at the head of a force of mounted infantry.[26] His task would have been to harry the enemy, to maintain contact with them and report the direction of their progress. He was closely followed by the loyal ealdorman Aethelnoth of Somerset[27] leading an army from western Wessex. This, it may be concluded, was comprised of foot soldiers. At the same time a combined force was assembled from 'every *burh* east of the Parret, and both west and east of Selwood, and also north of the Thames and west of the Severn, and also some part of the Welsh people'. Inevitably, this must have taken a considerable time to muster, presumably gathering at some forward assembly area which was operationally central for all those called upon to send contingents. It then hastened to the battle zone under the command of Aethelred of Mercia. A mobilisation on this scale, with such rapidity, determination and widespread, ready response, would have been unthinkable in earlier times.

The combined force finally ran the Danish army to ground at Buttington, on the east bank of the River Severn. Here they surrounded it on three sides, with the opposing bank being covered by an allied Welsh army under Mervyn of Powys.[28] In this manner they held it under siege for several weeks. By the end of that time, the Danes had been reduced to such straits of starvation that they were compelled to kill and eat their horses, having taken these with them into their stronghold. The remains of this earthwork, described in the *Montgomeryshire Collections*,[29] were at one time to be seen in an area now covered in part by the local churchyard and the old vicarage grounds. The line of Offa's Dyke enclosed it to the east and on its southern and western sides there ran 'a strong bank and broad deep ditch', the latter sloping away to swampy ground lying between the fort and the river. The northern defences of the stronghold are said to have been destroyed during the construction of the Welshpool to Shrewsbury road.

Those besieging the fort apparently made no effort to breach its walls but the Danes, confronted with their diminishing resources, were finally driven by desperation to break out eastwards through the English lines, and make a dash for their base in Essex. We are not told the numbers of the Danish army engaged in this operation but its strength cannot have been overly large, perhaps just a mounted party of some 500 men or so. The circumstances of the siege, with men and animals sharing the same fortification, would surely have prohibited more. It is noteworthy that in 1838, 'some 300 human skulls, with portions of skeletons,' were discovered buried in lines of circular pits in the south-east corner of the churchyard. Local tradition holds these to be the remains of the Danes killed in the siege at Buttington but the possibility that their number also included English dead should not be forgotten.

Before speculating on the purpose of this attack, it is necessary first to look at the nature of the continuing raids on West Mercia which the Danes now prosecuted. After returning to Essex from their disaster at Buttington, they did not delay. They received immediate reinforcements, as they had done previously, from East Anglia and Northumbria, and commenced preparations for a speedy return westwards. Then, before the summer was over and 'having made safe their women their ships and their property', they set forth once again to 'a deserted city in the Wirral, which is called Chester'. The English were unsuccessful in their efforts to overtake them and, before they could catch up with them, the Danes had occupied a fortification there, probably the remains of the old Roman fortress. The Saxons surrounded it

> for two days or so, and seized all the cattle they had left outside, and killed the men whom they had been able to cut off outside the fortification, and burned all the corn in the whole neighbourhood or else used it up for their horses.[30]

This gesture by the English was seemingly designed to render the position untenable by the Danes, leaving them dependent during the winter of 893–4 on either finding scant pickings from the Wirral or on obtaining supplies from Anarawd of Gwynedd and his Northumbrian allies. The Danes then devoted the whole of the following year to the pursuit of a campaign in Wales. At the conclusion of that time, doubtless leaving both the population and its treasures exhausted and Anarawd disillusioned with the value of his Viking alliance – 'from which he had got no benefit, only a great deal of misfortune' – they returned to their new base at Mersea, on an island off the Essex coast, 'travelling over the land of the Northumbrians and the East Angles so that the *fyrd* could not overtake them'. Here they were soon to be rejoined by the fleet returning from its abortive raid on Exeter.

The third and last Danish raid in this sequence of events opened in the autumn of 894, when they rowed their ships up the Thames from their island headquarters on Mersea. It is possible to imagine the wary and speculative Saxon eyes which watched them pass. Aware that the river was blocked by the West Saxon river stronghold at Southwark, they turned northwards, passing up the valley of the River Lea and through the Hackney Marshes to a point some 20 miles from London, probably near Hertford. Here they made camp and built themselves a winter fortification, where they were allowed to remain untroubled until the summer of the following year. It was not until the harvest of 895 was ripening that action was taken to remove them. A force composed mainly of men from the London garrison attacked the Danish stronghold, but without any great success. It was at this moment that Alfred arrived and 'encamped in the vicinity of the *burh* while they [the locals] reaped their corn, so that the Danes could not deny them the harvest'. He simultaneously gave orders for a double fort to be constructed astride the River Lea so as to block the river, deny its use to the Vikings and immobilise the longships lying upstream.

The Danes, confronted with this blockade, now broke out westwards, leaving their vessels to the Londoners who salvaged what they could and burned what could not be moved. The Danes were followed discreetly along their way by an English force which appears to have been content to keep them under simple observation. There is no record of any fighting. Yet again the raiders headed for the Severn, spending the winter of 895 and the spring of 896 at Bridgnorth. This was the final escapade of this army for in the following summer it dispersed: some of its numbers returned to their homes in Northumbria and East Anglia, and 'those without property got themselves ships and went south across the sea to the Seine'. In this manner the final phase of Alfred's last war drifted to an uncertain end. 'Thanks be to God,' wrote a chronicler, recording their departure, 'the Army had not too much afflicted the English people.'

He might also have added his thanks to King Alfred, the instrument of their salvation.

CHAPTER 9

Warrior King

What though the radiance which was once so bright
Be now forever taken from my sight,
Though nothing can bring back the hour
Of splendour in the grass, of glory in the flower;
We will grieve not, rather find strength in what remains behind.
William Wordsworth, *Intimations of Immortality*

King Alfred died on 26 October 899. He had just reached fifty years of age but in terms of medieval longevity he was an old man. Asser's biography presents us with a picture of a monarch stricken by illness, who suffered unremittingly. It suggests that the affliction that had laid Alfred low at his wedding celebrations in 868 was to trouble him all his life. This, however, is an image difficult to reconcile with that of the young man who, 'like a wild boar'[1] led the decisive uphill charge against Halfdan's shield-wall at Ashdown, rolling it backwards to seal a famous Saxon victory. A medical diagnosis of the king's sickness, to which we have already made reference, takes a more acceptable view of his condition.[2] It is clear, the author writes, that

> the king was able to fight, study, pursue his leisure interests, worship and govern, in short to live a very full life. Either we are to understand that Alfred was of such fortitude that he continued doing all of this whilst very ill, that is, with all his symptoms present, or, more plausibly, that his illness was intermittent. The former seems quite incredible. Asser, in his admiration for the king, treats us to the occasional exaggerated notion.

Nevertheless it is fair to believe that constant dread of the recurrence of his symptoms troubled him greatly and, when his tactical decision-making is considered, we should never forget this factor which may frequently have affected his choice of options.

A silver penny from the reign of Alfred's brother Aethelred I. The reverse side (right) shows the name of the moneyer – coincidentally another Aethelred. (British Museum)

Prior to 878 Alfred was involved in some ten major operations against the Vikings. Five of these were battlefield encounters, namely Ashdown, Basing, *Meretun*, Wilton and *Ethandun*. The first three took place when his brother Aethelred was king, but Alfred himself was king and sole commander at the battles of Wilton and *Ethandun*. The battles of Ashdown and *Ethandun* were major West Saxon victories but the scale claimed by the chroniclers should be read in the light of the Danish predilection to withdraw from the field rather than suffer heavy casualties. Alfred's defeat by Halfdan at the battle of Wilton was the first occasion upon which the king paid Danegeld to the enemy. Halfdan honoured the agreement: he withdrew to Reading while the money was being collected and, once it had been paid, fell back down the Thames to London. By this means Alfred bought himself some five years of peace. Regrettably, he did not use it to any great purpose but his first experience of paying off the Danes was not entirely unsatisfactory. He was not so fortunate in later years but he does seem to have persuaded himself to regard the payment of Danegeld as an acceptable tactic if it furthered his aim of creating 'fortress' Wessex.

Modern Cricklade, which developed out of one of Alfred's fortresses along the River Thames. (Aerofilms)

A notable feature of the Alfredian campaigns, particularly during the years up to 878, is the number of occasions on which Danish armies were allowed to escape from seemingly hopeless situations. Guthrum's break-out from Wareham, his negotiated withdrawal from Exeter (the terms of which he was quickly to dishonour), and after *Ethandun* his permitted lengthy stay at Chippenham when Alfred, having persuaded the Dane to be baptised, showered him and his compatriots with 'riches', are but three examples. Yet another, crucially important, example – his paying-off of Haesten in 893 – was yet to follow. In view of the uncertain West Saxon military situation in his early years, and the manifestly unsuitable defence organisation which the king inherited, it is possible to find a valid excuse for these apparent political and military failures. Likewise,

Alfred knew his countrymen and how far and fast he could carry them with him. In nearly all these instances, however, even if he had acted with the ruthlessness which was later to be displayed by his successors, it must remain doubtful that he would have changed the course of the events which followed.

Thus the peace agreement reached by Alfred and Guthrum after the battle of *Ethandun* appears to have been a diplomatic success for the king as much as a military one. On the other hand it could be argued on his behalf that it, and other similar agreements into which he entered in this phase of operations, not only saved many West Saxon lives but ultimately bought him six years of peace in which to carry through the many reforms Wessex so sorely needed. In these six years he was enabled to establish river fortress barriers across the Thames at Cricklade, Wallingford, Sashes, Southwark and elsewhere; to commence the tactical siting and construction of *burh* strongholds; to establish an intelligence gathering organisation to keep him abreast of military events and ideas on the continent; and to set in place an education programme which in large part may be judged to have had a military purpose, for it was his wish that as many of his senior officials as possible should learn to read and write in order to improve his communications with them. If they did not do so they could no longer hold office.

Some eight years later Alfred and Guthrum signed the decisive treaty that defined the boundary between Saxon England and the southern Danelaw. By that time Alfred had invigorated the Wessex defence mechanism and expanded his influence into Mercia; he had consolidated his grip on the major coastal estuaries and on the Thames, in the lower reaches of which he had by now based elements of his newly designed and reorganised fleet; he had largely set in place his system of *burh* strongholds and had taken possession of London, the future security of which he delegated to his son-in-law Aethelred, governor of Mercia. Responsibility for the shires of eastern Wessex he granted to his son Edward.

This was the command structure which operated in 892 when a Danish army under Haesten landed in Kent in two separate divisions, one in the north at Milton Royal near Sheppey, the other at Appledore near Lympne in the heart of the *Andreaswald* forest. The fighting which then took place has been discussed in the previous chapter. But it is a classic example of Alfredian tactics and for this reason various aspects are worth re-examining, particularly where the scope and scale of his opposition are concerned.

Haesten was a piratical raider with no great reputation as a soldier. He had recently suffered a series of defeats on the continent, first on the outskirts of Paris at the hands of King Odo and then in 891 by Arnulf, King of East Francia. He was by common definition a marauder, notorious for his deceitfulness, 'his naked savagery and his animal cunning'. Prior to landing in Kent, Haesten and his 'army' had spent an unprofitable winter in Louvain. The local harvest had failed and the spectre of famine had been added to his other problems. It was probably during these times that he contacted the host which was to provide the 'second division' of the operation he was about to undertake in Kent.

His plan, briefly, was a two-pronged attack, a popular ploy with the Danes, so as to isolate eastern Kent from Wessex. The southern division, with horses and transported in 250 ships, was to penetrate the Lympne estuary. Haesten, for his part, with eighty ships, undertook to land in northern Kent. The disparity in strength between the two divisions of the invasion force needs no emphasis. Haesten's comparative weakness suggests that, before setting out, he had already received undertakings of reinforcements from Danish settlers north of the Thames and from East Anglia. Alfred had anticipated this possibility[3] and extracted oaths of neutrality from the Northumbrian and East Anglian settlers, together with an additional six preliminary hostages from the East Angles who were nearest to the action and most likely to interfere. Nevertheless it was clear that the settlers had no intention of honouring these oaths, for 'as often as the other host sailed forth in full force, then went they with them, or on their own account'.

At this juncture Alfred offered his opponent 'a good deal of money' to withdraw across the Thames estuary to Benfleet on the north bank. For both men it was seemingly a good bargain. Haesten, at considerable financial profit, extricated himself from what promised to be a tricky situation and was quickly joined in Essex by both the seaborne and mounted contingents of his southern division. His army was now intact but he had been persuaded to abandon Wessex. For Alfred's part, Wessex had been left virtually unscathed, despite the weight and careful planning of the assault Haesten had delivered upon it. Moreover, the West Saxon army remained intact, ready for further eventualities. How much King Alfred was aware of events yet to come we are not told, but the very thought begs the question whether Haesten himself was the author of the Viking master plan, or whether he was summoned from the continent simply to provide foot soldiers for a campaign initiated by the Danish settlers of the Danelaw in east and north-east England, in particular Northumbria and York.

The King of Northumbria at that time was Guthfrith, a Christian who died at York in 895. In the years leading up to Guthfrith's death, the warships of the Northmen were pronouncedly active around the coasts of Wessex. In the year 893 alone, if we accept the figures of the *Anglo-Saxon Chronicle*, a total of some 470 ships' crews were deployed in Wessex coastal waters. This total included a fleet of 140 warships that landed in Devon in an assault clearly planned to coincide with Haesten's attack on eastern Kent. Aethelweard, in his *Chronicle*, tells us that this latter attack was headed by the pirate Sigefrith, 'from the land of the Northumbrians'. Thus in 893 we have a simultaneous, two-pronged assault on the West Saxons: one, in the east, with Northumbrian and East Anglian support, under the command of Haesten, a pirate notorious for the ferocity of his continental raids; the other, in the west, under the leadership of Sigefrith, another pirate. It can be no exaggeration to state that an intervention on this scale, involving the use of 470 ships over the period of the year, could not have been planned and set in hand without a co-ordinating body, nor without the full knowledge and co-operation of Guthfrith himself.

Guthfrith was feeling increasingly vulnerable to the growing strength of Alfred's position in southern England and to the onward march of the West Saxon king's influence in Mercia and South Wales. The Northumbrian king's problems were further enhanced by the growing unpopularity of the Viking settlers in Ireland, many of whom were being compelled to cross the Irish Sea to settle in Wales. Guthfrith had been able to strengthen Northumbria's position by entering into an alliance with the Rhodri family of Gwynedd. Like him, they viewed West Saxon diplomacy and the advance of their Welsh alliances with considerable distrust. Guthfrith's chief ally in north Wales, at this point, was Anarawd of Gwynedd, a Rhodri brother, whose territory held great strategic importance for the Northumbrians, for it lay just south of the Wirral and extended across north Wales to include the Isle of Anglesey, thus providing unhindered access to the Irish Sea, linking the interests of Dublin with York. In this pattern of associations, the importance to Northumbria of already established Danish bases on the Severn, such as Buttington, need hardly be stressed.

In 893 Anarawd, as a firm member of the Northumbrian alliance, was engaged in harassing operations against his neighbour, Cadell of Deheubarth,[4] with the probable intention of disorganising Welsh resistance to the Danish armies then moving to assemble in the areas of the Bristol Channel and the Severn estuary. Clearly if the armies of Sigefrith and Haesten could successfully have met together at this time in the Severn estuary, their combined presence would have struck a mortal blow to Alfred's efforts to bring the Welsh kingdoms to his side.

These facts and possibilities were doubtless all present in King Alfred's mind when news reached him of Sigefrith's landings in the west country. Alfred's grasp of the situation as it swiftly developed is remarkable for its clarity. He initiated three pieces of action, the need for which had seemingly already been foreseen. First, he turned around the entire English army then under his command and marched to the west country to the relief of Exeter, whose garrison was under siege. Secondly, he detached a contingent – presumably as many men as he felt could be spared – to join with the garrison from London and the 'help which came from the west'; they marched, under his son Edward and Aethelred of Mercia to contain Haesten at Benfleet. He was thus seemingly already alert to the possibility that Haesten planned to move to join Sigefrith in the Severn estuary area. Thirdly, he alerted a force of mounted infantry, supported by other levies, to intercept Haesten whenever he might move. These men, drawn from garrisons east of the Parret, north of the Thames and west of the Severn, together with allies from west Wales, came from a widespread area and were indicative of the seriousness of the situation which Alfred now saw confronting his kingdom.

The chroniclers provide us with very meagre detail of the outcome of these events. The host besieging Exeter 'retired to their ships' upon Alfred's arrival but we remain uninformed of what happened next, other than a later statement, during the confrontation between the English army and Haesten at Buttington, that the king was still 'occupied west in Devon against the pirate host'.[5] He was evidently there for a period of several months. Indeed it is not until the annal of the following year that we learn that the Viking army that had besieged Exeter was now ravaging the coast of south-east England, 'up into Sussex, near Chichester, [where] the townsmen put them to flight and killed many hundreds of them and captured some of their ships'. The presence of the king is not mentioned again until he appears in the Lea Valley, east of London, in 895 when he blockaded Danish warships in the upper reaches of the river and frustrated their escape into the Thames.

Equally, we remain uninformed about any action he may have taken against Sigefrith, the Danish commander of the landing party in north Devon. Smyth[6] argues that Sigefrith went on from there to Dublin before returning to Northumbria, and presumably met with Northumbrian forces in north Wales. We are not told what persuaded him to do this: we can only conclude that he was discouraged either by the speed and scale of Alfred's reaction to his arrival or that, if it had been his intention to meet with Haesten, he had been foiled in his plan by one reason or another.

Haesten, in his westward march, 'went up the Thames until he came to the Severn, then up along the Severn'. It is fair to deduce that he had a predetermined purpose for doing this, for the Thames Valley seems to have been bristling with military activity at this moment and, if his final destination had been Buttington, taking the diagonal route to there from London would have been both quicker and safer. He was hotly pursued on his way by ealdormen Aethelhelm of Wiltshire and Aethelnoth of Somerset. He had no time to dally and, in the absence of Sigefrith, he turned north to Buttington, where he could expect help from local Danes and the Northumbrian army.[7] It was here that the West Saxons from the west country and their Welsh allies caught up with him, later to be joined by Aethelred of Mercia with 'a mighty army'. Haesten was then besieged and his men:

> became distressed for lack of food, and had devoured most of their horses, the remainder perishing with hunger; then they sallied forth against the men encamped on the east side of the river and fought against them, and the Christians had the victory . . . and very great slaughter was made there of the Danes and the remnant that escaped were saved by flight.[8]

The subsequent behaviour of the remnants of Haesten's army reflected the damage to Northumbrian ambitions caused by the destruction of the Viking base at Buttington. The survivors, having made their escape, fled back with all speed to their stronghold in Essex where they gathered reinforcements from East Anglia and Northumbria and, almost without delay, returned to the north-west, marching day and night, to occupy the old Roman fortress at Chester in the Wirral. Their purpose in heading for Chester, an inhospitable area which is widely thought to have remained derelict since the Roman occupation,[9] remains mystifying. It can only have been to re-establish, after the battle at Buttington, a Northumbrian military presence in north-west Mercia for the benefit of their allies and potential settlers. Plainly this was no cornucopia of plenty: the district contained little in the way of food supplies, for the English army that had harried them all the way from Essex required only two days to burn the corn and round up the cattle in the area before withdrawing to a less impoverished environment.

Anarawd was one of the first to feel the impact of this act of attrition. The Viking army, having exhausted its meagre food supplies, wasted little time in moving from the Wirral to go foraging in Wales and it was not long before the disillusioned King of Gwynedd turned to Alfred for protection. The outcome of these events was that the previously ambitious and better organised Danish operations in northern Wales soon deteriorated into piratical raids deep into

Welsh territory, without much official Northumbrian support. Their actions served simply to antagonise the Welsh people and in 894 the Danes withdrew. They collected together such booty as they had accumulated and 'crossed Northumbria and East Anglia (so that the English army could not reach them) until they came to the eastern part of Essex, to an island out in the sea called Mersea'.

Alfred's last war was the ultimate testing-ground for the series of defensive arrangements the king had set in hand for the creation of 'fortress Wessex': his *burh* defences, which came to be known as the Burghal Hidage system, with its well-known manpower formulae for military and agricultural provision; his river fortifications and estuary strongholds, designed to curtail the enemy's ability to penetrate the coastline and the frontiers of Wessex; complementary to these, his newly created and carefully deployed navy; his defensive arrangements in the Medway Gap designed to seal the dangerously exposed eastern extremity of his kingdom; even his ready acceptance of the payment of danegeld as a military option. All of these, together with his diplomatic successes among his Welsh neighbours and his concentration upon the gathering, particularly in mainland Europe, of the latest intelligence of the enemy and the most up-to-date military practice, provided him with a secure base from which he could progressively bring military aid to his allies in their efforts to regain their territories lost to the Danes. By the year 907 his daughter Aethelflaed, the Lady of the Mercians, had occupied and refortified the city of Chester, extending the wall of the Roman fortress to encompass the castle area.

It is sometimes suggested that Alfred's concept of *burh* strongholds was being practised in Europe some twenty-five years before he initiated the idea in Wessex. This may well be true but it should not be allowed to detract from the intellectual scope of his plan. Military tactics of this nature are as old as war itself. A thousand years before Alfred's last war, Quintus Fabius Maximus, dictator of Rome, was creating village strongholds in central Italy as part of his strategy of attrition against Hannibal. In 1953, during the anti-terrorist Malayan campaign, Field Marshal Sir Gerald Templer, with food control primarily in mind, set in hand a similar system, on this occasion of newly sited villages, defended by wire against terrorist operations, and bolstered by an armed and carefully selected Home Guard, supported by police and occasionally by regular troops. The principle in each case was the same: to deny sustenance to an unpredictable, mobile and hard-hitting enemy.

In the title of this work, we have referred to Alfred as a warrior king. A 'warrior' may be defined as someone 'experienced or distinguished in fighting in

King Alfred's statue at Wantage, erected in 1877. (A.F. Kersting)

an armed force'.[10] Experienced, Alfred certainly was; distinguished, as an adjective applied to his soldierly qualities, might be more difficult to accept. On the other hand he was a firm and innovative leader, whose mind was never closed to the benefits of political or military compromise, nor did he fear it, even if this meant yielding Danegeld to a hated enemy. In the years of the axe and the broadsword, a distinguished warrior could well have found this attitude unacceptable. But as an experienced warrior and a distinguished ruler, the term 'warrior king', my readers may agree, fits him well.

It is doubtful if the importance of his reign was immediately recognised by contemporary historians. The chronicler's curt reference to his death in 899 suggests that it was not: 'In this year King Alfred died on 26 October: he ruled for twenty-eight and a half years. Then, Edward, his son, succeeded to the kingdom.[11] He was buried at Winchester but over the centuries the actual burial-place of this great English hero has been lost. It was not perhaps until the mid-nineteenth century, in the wave of interest aroused by the millenary year of his birth, when memorials were erected in his memory at Wantage, Winchester, Pewsey and other places, that he was awarded his rightful place in English history by his many Victorian admirers. The statue in Wantage, erected in 1877, is inscribed with words which, it may be thought, admirably reflect his achievements:

Alfred found learning dead

and he restored it

Education neglected

and he revived it

The Laws powerless

and he gave them force

The Church debased

and he raised it

The Land ravaged by a fearful enemy

from which he delivered it

Alfred's name will live as long

as mankind shall respect the past.

Notes

The following abbreviations have been used:

ATG: *Alfred the Great: Asser's Life of King Alfred and other contemporary sources*, ed. and trans. Simon Keynes and Michael Lapidge (Penguin, 1983)
ASE: *Anglo-Saxon England*, F.M. Stenton (Oxford University Press, 3rd edn, 1971)
EHD: *English Historical Documents*, vol. 1, *c.* 500–1042, ed. D. Whitelock (Eyre & Spottiswoode, 1979)
AAE: *An Atlas of Anglo-Saxon England, 700–1066*, D. Hill (Blackwell, 1981)
ASC: *Anglo-Saxon Chronicle*, trans. G.N. Garmonsway (The Chaucer Press, 1953, repr. 1984)

Introduction

1. *The Chronicle of Aethelweard*, ed. A. Campbell (Nelson, 1962), 3rd book, i, 26.
2. ASC, 'The Laud Chronicle', 787, 55.
3. EHD, I, 845.
4. ASC, 833, 63.
5. To hold 'possession of the place of slaughter' was a more tactful way of saying 'gained the victory'.
6. ASC, 851, 65.
7. C. Plummer, *The Life and Times of Alfred the Great* (Oxford, 1902).
8. G. Craig, 'Alfred the Great: a Diagnosis' *Journal of the Royal Society of Medicine*, vol. 84.
9. R.H. Hodgkin, *A History of the Anglo-Saxons* (Oxford, 1952), vol. 2, 265.
10. C. Plummer, *Two of the Anglo-Saxon Chronicles, Parallel* (Oxford, 1892), 107.
11. ATG, 'Alfred's Translation of Gregory's Pastoral Care', 125.

1. Alfred of Wessex

1. ATG, Introduction, 13. See also Smyth (1995), i, 3–8, for a discussion on this subject.
2. ASC, 851, 65.
3. ATG, *Asser's Life of King Alfred*, i, 67.
4. Woden was the great chief of Valhalla.
5. ATG, *Asser's Life*, xxii, 74.
6. ATG, *Asser's Life*, vi, 69.
7. ASC, 888, 83.
8. K. Manchester, *The Archaeology of Disease* (University of Bradford, 1983), 8–9.
9. ATG, *Asser's Life*, xxiii, 75.
10. This likelihood is supported by Professor A.P Smyth, in his work *King Alfred the Great* (Oxford, 1995), i. 11.
11. EHD, I, 611, 853.
12. The length of time spent by Alfred in Rome is obscure and much debated.
13. EHD, I, doc. 219, 8.
14. EHD, I, *Annals of St Bertin*, doc. 23, 856: the annals for this year are noted by

Professor Whitelock to have been written by Prudentius of Troyes; he became Bishop of Troyes in 843.

15. Ibid.

16. ATG, *Asser's Life*, xii, 70.

17. Ibid.

18. ATG, *Asser's Life*, xvi, 73.

19. This is by no means the last we hear of this lively young lady, who left a considerable mark on English history.

20. ASC, 860, 67.

21. A.P. Smyth, *King Alfred the Great* (1995), iv, 107.

22. ATG, *Asser's Life*, xxii, 75.

23. EHD, I, 747.

24. The Venerable Bede, *A History of the English Church and People* (Penguin, 1968), 206.

25. Ibid.

26. EHD, I, 845.

27. N.P. Brooks, 'England in the 9th Century: The Crucible of Defeat', *Transactions of the Royal Historical Society*, 29 (1979), 14–15.

28. Ibid.

29. Alfred the Great (trans.), 'Gregory's Pastoral Care' as in ATG, 125.

30. H.G. Hodgkins, *A History of the Anglo-Saxons* (Oxford University Press, 3rd edn, 1952), vol. 2, 620.

31. ATG, *Asser's Life*, cii, 107.

32. Boethius, 'Consolation of Philosophy', as in ATG, 131.

33. Sometimes associated with a tribal area which existed in the neighbourhood of present-day Gainsborough in Lincolnshire.

34. G. Craig, 'Alfred the Great: a Diagnosis', *Journal of the Royal Society of Medicine*, vol. 84, 303–5.

35. ATG, 'The Will of King Alfred', 173–4.

2. *'Devils of the Sea'*

1. EHD, I, doc. 194, 845.

2. See Appendix A for a background to the story of the Lothbrok family.

3. E. Joransen, *The Danegeld in France* (Augustana Library, 1923), publication 10, 27.

4. As in FM Viscount Montgomery of Alamein, *A Concise History of Warfare* (Collins, 1972), 6, 86.

5. Joransen (1923), 29.

6. Joransen (1923), 37.

7. Sir Frank Stenton, *Anglo-Saxon England* (Oxford University Press, 3rd edn, 1971) viii, 241–2.

8. E. Linklater, *The Conquest of England* (Hodder & Stoughton, 1966), iii, 19.

9. ASC, 853, 66.

10. A.P. Smyth, *Scandinavian York and Dublin* (Irish Academic Press, 1987), 17–22.

11. ASC, 866, 69.

12. R.A. Hall, *Jorvik, Viking Age York* (York Archaeological Trust, 1987), 14.

13. Smyth, *Scandinavian York*, 22.

14. EHD, I, doc. 4, 282.

15. ATG, *Asser's Life*, ch. 29, 77.

16. ATG, *Asser's Life*, ch. 30, 77.

17. Stenton, *Anglo-Saxon England*, viii, 248: the Danes were primarily seeking Mercian neutrality.

18. As in D. Hill, *An Atlas of Anglo-Saxon England, 700–1066* (Blackwell, 1981), 11.

19. Dorothy Whitelock, 'Fact and Fiction in the Legend of St Edmund', *Proceedings of the Suffolk Institute of Archaeology* (1969), 223.

20. ASC, 870, 192.

21. EHD, I, 192, note 6.

22. Another waterway which could have benefited the Danes should here be mentioned, for it underlines the range of opportunities the Vikings had at their disposal. The riverine link between the Wash and the city of York follows the course of the Witham, the Roman-built Fossdike and the River Trent. Even today, given a fair wind, it is possible to reach

Naburn Lock, 8 miles from York, in two tides. For further reading see John Seymour, *The Companion Guide to East Anglia* (Collins, 1970).

23. A tree at which Edmund is traditionally said to have been slain stood in the park at Hoxne until 1849, when it fell. Upon being broken up, an ancient arrow head was found embedded in its trunk. Whitelock (1969) is in no doubt, however, that Hellesdon, not Hoxne, is the site of Edmund's martyrdom. Modern DNA testing might perhaps help to decide.

24. Smyth (1987), 15–24.

3. The Opposing Forces

1. *King Alfred's Old English Version of Boethius' de Consolatione Philosophiae*, ed. W. Sedgefield (1899, repr Darmstadt, 1968), 40; as in EHD, I, doc. 237, 918.
2. *The Chronicle of Aethelweard*, ed. A. Campbell (Nelson, 1962), 45.
3. Professor Gwyn Jones, *A History of the Vikings to 1066* (OUP, 1968), 194.
4. EHD, I: 500–1042, Dorothy Whitelock (Eyre & Spottiswoode, 1979).
5. ASC, 884, 79. The chronicler relates that Alfred attacked a Danish army at Rochester, who 'were there deprived of their horses'. Asser (ch. 66) is more specific and relates that the enemy, on returning to their ships, left behind 'all the horses they had brought with them from France'.
6. ASC, 896, 90.
7. EHD, I, 1, 318.
8. *Viking Treasure from the North West*: selected papers from *The Vikings of the Irish Sea*, Conference, Liverpool, 18–20 May 1990, ed. James Graham-Campbell (Liverpool Museum, 1992), no. 5.
9. John Peddie, *Hannibal's War* (Sutton Publishing, Stroud, 1997), v, 95.

10. See Appendix A, Roman and Ancient Roads.
11. J.H. Clapham, 'The Horsing of the Danes', *English Historical Society* (1910), 25, 289.
12. P.H. Sawyer, 'The Density of the Danish Settlement', *University of Birmingham Journal* (1957), vi, 5.
13. Gwyn Jones, 218.
14. Sawyer, 'Danish Settlement', vi, 5.
15. John Peddie, *Invasion, The Roman Conquest of Britain* (Alan Sutton Publishing, 1987), ii, 40.
16. Asser's *Life of King Alfred*, and other contemporary sources, translated with notes and introduction by S. Keynes and M. Lapidge (Penguin, 1983), ch. 42.
17. See also Appendix D and p. 69 on the military strength of *burh* garrisons.
18. ATG, *Asser's Life*, 35, 78.
19. Bernard S. Bachrach, 'Some Observations on the Military Administration of the Norman Conquest', *Anglo-Norman Studies*, ed. R. Allen Brown (Boydell Press, 1985), 11.
20. Ibid.
21. Ibid., 15.
22. EHD, I, iii, letter 193, 842.
23. A not very unusual tactic, but this is not to detract from Alfred for employing it. Fabius used it against Hannibal in the Second Punic War, and Alfred could have learnt of it during his time at school in Rome.
24. ASC, 874, 73.
25. C.W. Hollister, *Anglo-Saxon Military Institutions* (Oxford, 1962), vii.
26. Sir Frank Stenton, *Anglo-Saxon England* (Oxford, 3rd edn, 1971), ix, 90.
27. EHD, I, 501; Richard P. Abels, *Lordship and Military Obligation in Anglo-Saxon England* (London, British Museum, 1988), 5, 110.
28. ASC, 878, 75.

29. ASC, 877, 75.

30. ASC, 860, 67.

31. EHD, I, 794; see also Abels (1988), 17. When St Adhelm learned that St Wilfred had been exiled from Northumbria after a quarrel with King Aldfrith, he wrote a letter admonishing the saint's followers that, if they abandoned their lord in his adversity, they would be regarded as 'deserving of ridicule and hateful jeering, and of the clamour of execration'.

32. DB: 1, 56.

33. ATG, *Asser's Life*, 52, 83.

34. ATG, *Asser's Life*, 91, 101.

35. David Hill, 'The Burghal Hidage – the Establishment of a Text', *Medieval Archaeology* (1969), 13, 91–2.

36. ASC, 893, 85–6.

4. Wessex under Siege

1. ASC in EHD, I, 187.

2. ASC, *The Parker Chronicle*, 836.

3. ATG, 12, 70.

4. Bede, *A History of the English Church and People* (Penguin, 1968), 70.

5. ASC, 851, 65.

6. See p. 72.

7. Stenton, ASE, vii, 204.

8. ASC, *The Parker Chronicle*, 853.

9. ASC, 865, 69.

10. W. Stuart Best, 'Relations between Wessex and Cornwall in Early Days', *Dorset Natural History and Antiquaries Field Club*, vol. 77, 110.

11. Stenton, ASE, xiii, 439–40.

12. ATG, 35, 78.

13. See Chapter 2.

14. Also as a harbour for his surplus longships, not all of which would have been required to support his advance.

15. Stenton, ASE, viii, 250.

16. J.R.L. Anderson, *Upper Thames* (Methuen, 1974), 79.

17. ATG, 35, 78.

18. John Man, *History and Antiquities of the Borough of Reading* (Snare & Man, 1816) 1, 3.

19. ATG, 35, 78.

20. ATG, 36, 78.

21. Aethelwulf, ealdorman, soldier and Mercian aristocrat, appears to have been a doughty servant to Alfred throughout the young king's early life. We are constantly meeting him but Professor A.P. Smyth, in *King Alfred the Great* (Oxford, 1995), I, 4, points out that there were at least five perhaps six Mercian ealdormen of the same name at that time. The man who died at Reading was a particularly loyal and gallant supporter.

22. EHD, I, letter 193, 842.

23. ATG, 37–8, 78–9.

24. ASC, 871, 71.

25. See Chapter 3.

26. ASC 871, 71.

27. H.W. Timperley & Edith Brill, *Ancient Trackways of Wessex* (Phoenix House, 1965) 75–8.

28. Map references: Marden, SU 0857; Marten, SU 2860; Martin, SU 0619.

29. Timperley & Brill (1965), 79.

30. David Hinton, *Alfred's Kingdom, Wessex and the South, 800–1500* (Dent, 1977), 2, 33.

31. ASC , 871. The statement that Aethelred was buried at Wimborne is contested by Dorothy Whitelock (EHD) who quotes ASC, version C, which gives Sherborne as his place of burial.

5. 'That oft-defeated King'

1. Revd Canon J.M. Fletcher, 'The Tomb of King Aethelred in Wimborne Minster', *Proceedings of the Dorset Natural History and Archaeological Society*, 16, 25.

2. Fletcher, *Dorset NH&AS*, 16, 34.

3. ATG, *Asser's Life*, 42, 80–1.

4. Ibid.

5. *The Chronicle of Aethelweard*, ed. A Campbell (Nelson, 1962), 37–40.

6. ASC, 72, 871.

7. See Chapter 4.

8. ATG, *Asser's Life*, 42, 81.

9. Ibid., 82.

10. ASC, 75, 875.

11. Ibid.

12. N.P. Brooks, 'England in the Ninth Century: The Crucible of Defeat', *Transactions of the Royal Historical Society* (1979), 29, 10–11.

13. J. Hutchins, *History and Antiquities of the County of Dorset* (Nichols, 1851), 78.

14. G.J. Bennett, 'Wareham: its Invasions and Battles', *Proceedings, Dorset NH&AS*, 13, 91.

15. ATG, *Asser's Life*, 49, 82–3.

16. For a discussion on this see ATG, *Asser*, notes 89, 108; also p. 283, note 2.

17. The *Anglo-Saxon Chronicle* states that Alfred 'rode after the mounted army with the English army'. This is sometimes taken to suggest that the West Saxon force was mounted. This may have been so but there is no firm evidence to suggest that Alfred possessed a mounted arm at this moment.

18. These are among the most dangerous waters surrounding the British Isles, to the extent that the Romans, in the early days of their occupation of Britain, established an overland route between Weymouth and the Parret estuary in the Bristol Channel.

19. ASC, 876, 75.

20. Ibid.

21. ATG, 52, 83. For the propaganda aspect of Asser's writings see R.H.C. Davis, 'Alfred the Great: Propaganda and Truth', *History*, (1971), 56, 169–81.

22. Revd J. Collinson, *The History and Antiquities of the County of Somerset* (Crutwell, 1791), 86–7.

23. ASC, 874, 74–5.

24. ATG, *Asser's Life*, 54, 83–4.

25. P.A. Rahtz, 'Cannington Hillfort, 1963', *Proceedings of the Somerset Archaeological & Natural History Society*, 113, 65–8.

26. ATG, 'The Will of King Alfred', 175.

27. W.H. Stevenson, *Asser's Life of King Alfred* (OUP, 1904), 41–2, 256–61.

6. *Wessex Reconquered*

1. ASC, 878, 75.

2. In the days of the East India Company a sepoy was paid, in part, by an allotment of salt. Hence the expression, to be 'worthy of his salt'.

3. EHD, I, letter 165, 793–4.

4. Richard P. Abels, *Lordship and Military Obligation in Anglo-Saxon England* (British Museum, 1988), 232–3.

5. ASC, 878, 76.

6. See Chapter 5.

7. W.H. Stevenson, *Asser's Life of King Alfred* (Oxford, 1904).

8. Camden's *Britannia* (1586).

9. J.E. Jackson, 'Selwood Forest', *Wiltshire Archaeological Magazine* (1887), 23, 279.

10. R.H. Hodgkin, *A History of the Anglo-Saxons* (Oxford, 3rd edn, 1952).

11. ATG, *Asser's Life*, 92.

12. W.H.P. Cresswell, *Dumnonia and the Mouth of the Parrett* (Barnicott & Pearce, 1922), 74.

13. *Ethandun* has been defined as 'waste, bare or uncultivated hill or downland'. See J. Gover, A. Mawer and F.M. Stenton, *Place-Names of Wiltshire* (Cambridge, 1939). This suggests that the battle was fought on the downs and not around the village.

14. D. Whitelock, *The Beginnings of English Society* (Penguin, 2nd edn, 1954), 81.
15. ATG, 'Introduction', 55.
16. This bivallate, 6 acre hillfort, defended by steep slopes, is today overgrown by thick woodland and is not instantly recognisable.
17. Sir Richard Colt Hoare, *The History of Wiltshire* (1822).
18. Walbury Camp, it should be noted, near which the battle of *Meretun* was contested, lay on the boundaries of Berkshire, Hampshire and Wiltshire.
19. G.B. Grundy, 'The ancient highways and tracks of Wiltshire, Berkshire and Hampshire and the Saxon battlefields of Wiltshire', *Archaeological Journal* (1918), 75, 178–81.
20. A. Burne, 'Ancient Wiltshire Battlefields', *Wiltshire Archaeological Magazine* (1950), 397–412.
21. 'Excursion on 23rd August 1877', *Wiltshire Archaeological Magazine*, 17.
22. E.A. Rawlence, 'On the site of Ethandun', *Antiquaries Journal* (1921), I, 105–17.
23. Stevenson, *Asser's Life*.
24. Now locally known as 'Robin's Bower'.
25. A. Burne, *More Battlefields of England* (Methuen, 1952), 38.
26. ATG, *Asser's Life*, 84–5.
27. Ibid., 85.
28. This phrase is pure propaganda: common sense rather than compassion was the ruling factor.
29. Aller: map ref. ST4029.
30. This is considered a doubtful claim by the *Victoria County History*: a similar font was unearthed from the churchyard at Kingston Deverill which is traditionally claimed to have come from the original Saxon wattle church of St Andrew.
31. This is the ceremony of discarding baptismal clothing.
32. See note 28 above.

7. Fortress Wessex

1. ATG, *Asser's Life*, 57, 85.
2. EHD, I, 31.
3. ASE, viii, 250.
4. Ibid., 254.
5. J.M. Hassall & D. Hill, 'Pont de l'Arche: Frankish Influence on the West Saxon Burh?' *Archaeological Journal*, vol. 27 (1970), 188–95.
6. Ibid.
7. ASE, viii, 259–60.
8. ATG, *Asser's Life*, 80, 96.
9. Ibid.
10. ATG, 'The Letter of Fulco, Archbishop of Rheims, to King Alfred', 331–2.
11. ATG, *Asser's Life*, 101, 107.
12. ASE, x, 344.
13. F.T. Wainwright, 'Aethflaed, Lady of the Mercians' in *Scandinavian England*, ed. H.P.R. Finberg (Phillimore, 1975), 305.
14. R.P. Abels, *Lordship and Military Obligation in Anglo-Saxon England* (British Museum, 1988), 305, n. 130.
15. ATG, *Asser's Life*, 64, 86.
16. R.P. Abels, *Lordship in Anglo-Saxon England*, 5, 108–10.
17. ATG, *Asser's Life*, 91, 101.
18. ATG, *Annals 892*, 114.
19. ATG, 'Gregory's Pastoral Care', 124.
20. ATG, 'The letter of Fulco', 184–5.

8. The Final Campaign

1. ASC, 886, 80.
2. *The Chronicle of Aethelweard*, ed. A Campbell (Nelson, 1962), 44.
3. ATG, *Asser's Life of King Alfred*, 97–8.
4. J.M. Hassall and D. Hill 'Pont de l'Arche: Frankish Influence on the West Saxon Burh?', *Archaeological Journal*, 127 (1970), 191.
5. AAE, 19.

6. D. Hill, 'The Burghal Hidage: the Establishment of a Text', *Medieval Archaeology* (1969), 13, 84–92.

7. Ibid., 84.

8. Ibid., 88.

9. ATG, *Asser's Life*, 87.

10. ASC, 892, 85.

11. For a discussion on these administrative problems, see Bernard Baruch, 'Some Observations on William the Conqueror's Horse Transports', *Technology & Culture* (1935), 25.

12. B.K. Davison, 'The Burghal Hidage Fort of Eorpeburnam: A Suggested Identification', *Medieval Archaeology* (1972) 16, 124–7.

13. ATG, *Asser's Life*, 102.

14. Newenden: MR TQ 8528.

15. ATG, *Asser's Life*, 115.

16. Frederic Amory: 'The Viking Hastings in Franco-Scandinavian Legend', in *Saints, Scholars and Heroes in Medieval Culture in Honor of C.W. Jones*, ed. King & Stevens (University Miicrofilms, 1979), 265–86.

17. F.C.J. Spurrell, 'Early Sites and Embankments on the Thames Estuary', *Archaeological Journal* (1885), 43, 25.

18. ASC in ATG, 115.

19. John Peddie, *Invasion: The Roman Conquest of Britain* (Sutton, 1987), 73–4, 76.

20. *Aethelweard*, ed. Campbell, 49.

21. F. Stenton, 'The Danes at Thorney Island in 893', *English Historical Records*, 27 (1912), 512–13.

22. ASC in ATG, 115.

23. Spurrell, 'Early Sites'.

24. Amory, 'The Viking Hastings', 282.

25. ASC in ATG, 115.

26. *Aethelweard*, ed. Campbell, 50.

27. It was Aethelnoth, ealdorman of Somerset, who had come to the aid of King Alfred when he sought refuge on the Isle of Athelney.

28. ASC in ATG, 116–17: see also note 29.

29. T. Morgan Owen, 'The Battle of Buttington, with a brief sketch of the affairs of Powys and Mercia', *Montgomeryshire Collections*, 7, 260.

30. ATG, 'Annal, 893', 117.

9. *Warrior King*

1. ATG, *Asser's Life*, 38, 79.

2. G. Craig, 'Alfred the Great: a diagnosis', *Journal of the Royal Society of Medicine* (1991), vol. 84, 304.

3. ASC, 893, 84.

4. T. Morgan Owen, 'The Battle of Buttington, with a brief Sketch of the Affairs of Powys and Mercia,' *Montgomeryshire Collection*, 7, 260.

5. ASC, 893, 87.

6. A.P. Smyth, *King Alfred the Great* (Oxford, 1995), v, 123–4.

7. Morgan Owen, *Montgomeryshire Collection*, 7, 260.

8. ASC, 894, 88.

9. Graham Webster, 'Chester in the Dark Ages', *Chester and North Wales Historical Society* (1951), vol. 38, 43–5.

10. *The Concise Oxford Dictionary* (Oxford, 9th edn, 1995).

11. ASC, 899, 91–3.

APPENDIX A
The Lothbrok Family

It would be inaccurate to describe Ragnaar Lothbrok as a mere pirate, for the scale of his operations, conducted against powerful European nations on the continental Atlantic seaboard, placed him well beyond such a simple categorisation. He might perhaps be defined as a privateer in the Drake mould, for he is thought to have had Norse as well as Danish royal connections and much of his plunder may have been fed into princely treasure chests. Whether this was so or otherwise, the territorial ambitions subsequently displayed by his sons leave us in little doubt of the quest for conquest they inherited from their father. His origins are equally obscure, one eminent nineteenth-century historian identifying him as the legendary Viking Ragnaar Sigursson, named *Lothbrok* because of the 'hairy breeks' (hide leggings) he traditionally wore in battle and which were supposed to endow him with some form of magical protection.

Despite doubts about his early history, it can be stated with a degree of certainty that it was Ragnaar Lothbrok who in the year 845 headed a raiding party of 120 warships up the Seine against the Paris of Charles the Bald. His army, during the course of the operation, was severely afflicted by a plague of dysentery and some annalists claim that the Danish commander was himself infected at this time and died as a consequence. The proposition, however, is largely denied by the records of contemporary English and Irish chroniclers, who provide evidence of his presence in the ensuing decade in the waters of northern Scotland, the Western Isles and the shorelines of the Irish Sea. The name Ragnaar Lothbrok is to be found, probably carved by a travelling scholar in the twelfth century, on the wall of the 5,000-year-old chambered tomb of Maes Howe in Orkney. It reads:

> This mound was raised before Ragnaar Lothbrok's . . .
> His sons were brave, smooth hide men though they were . . .
> It was long ago that a great treasure was hidden here,
> Happy is he that might find that great treasure.

The words bear the implication that members of the Lothbrok family were present on the island at some time and played a major role in the looting of the burial site, perhaps during the years of exile from their homeland by Horik, King of Denmark.

At this time the influx of Scandinavian raiders into the Irish Sea gave increasing importance to the seaport of Dublin, ideally situated at the mouth of the River Liffey, and it was here that Ragnaar is said in due course to have based himself. His presence was not uncontested, either by the local population or by the flood of Norwegian raiders who, like him, were now probing westwards in considerable numbers. A host of traditional tales, each of which differs from the others, relate how,

The twelfth-century Ragnaar Lothbrok runic inscription from Maes Howe, Orkney. (Historic Scotland)

in one of these encounters with his fellow Scandinavians, in about 852–6, Ragnaar was either killed in battle or tortured to death as a prisoner. One account relates that he died while raiding ashore on the Isle of Anglesey; another that he lost his life in a naval encounter with a rival Norseman on the sheltered waters of Carlingford Lough; a third tradition, which appears in different forms, tells of his death from being flung into a pit filled with poisonous snakes.

Upon Ragnaar's death, his eldest son Ivar the Boneless retained command in Dublin. Once again, the true date and circumstance of this man's arrival in the city are obscure. Some historians argue that he preceded the arrival of his father by a period of some years; others suggest that Ragnaar appointed his son as ruler upon the eve of his departure for the fighting in which he died.

Upon his succession to power, Ivar soon found his suzerainty challenged by one Olafr, the warrior son of a Norwegian king. Olafr shared Ivar's vision of the commercial and military potential of Dublin and its hinterland and had determined to acquire an interest in it. Unusually, rather than opt to resolve their differences by war, with the resulting wastage of their military and manpower resources, both men astutely joined together to forge a powerful military and political partnership. The *Annals of Ulster* for the year 871 record a naval force under their joint command, numbering a formidable 200 ships.

While Ivar was establishing himself in this manner in Ireland, Arab chroniclers relate that some of Ragnaar's other sons were engaged in a 'piratical voyage' along the coast of France and Islamic Spain. Events were to indicate that they may have had deeper motives for this adventure for, by the end of the decade, a thriving slave-trade with Spain and the Islamic Mediterranean had become a key factor in the economic life of Dublin. This market was substantially enhanced in 871 when Olafr and Ivar returned from Britain after what would prove to be their final operations on the British mainland, bringing with them a 'multitude of men, English, Britons and Picts', thus providing a welcome boost to their slave-market. It was a watershed period, for within two years Ivar was to die in battle and Olafr returned to Norway to succeed his father to the throne.

We have not yet examined the Lothbrok family's English connection. Almost predictably, this is obscured by yet other Scandinavian traditions which fancifully set the responsibility for Ragnaar's death upon the head of Aelle, King of Northumbria. The popular tale of the snake-pit is yet again revived, but this time set against the background of Northumbria, and the Viking leader is said to have threatened as he died that the wrath of his sons would be quickly visited upon those responsible for his torture. There is no evidence to suggest any basis of fact for this tradition. Nevertheless in 863 the Lothbrok sons Halfdan and Ubba, joined their elder brother Ivar in a carefully planned and systematic assault on the English mainland.

In the autumn of 863 Ivar set out from Dublin for what may well have been a preliminary reconnaissance of Northumbria. Two years later a powerful Danish task force, described as 'a heathen army' by the *Anglo-Saxon Chronicle*, landed in Thanet, subdued eastern Kent and secured the strategically important waters of the Thames estuary and the Wantsum Channel. It cannot be said with any certainty that Ragnaar's sons took any part in this operation, but they probably did. There can be no doubt that the assault on Thanet opened the way in the following year for Halfdan's invasion of East Anglia with his Great Army, and they 'took winter quarters from the East Anglians, and there were provided with horses, and they made peace with them'.

Twelve months later Ivar joined his two brothers Halfdan and Ubba in East Anglia and then the 'host went from there, over the mouth of the Humber to York in Northumbria'. They took possession of the city on 1 November 866. The campaign by Ragnaar's sons for the subjugation of Anglo–Saxon England had begun.

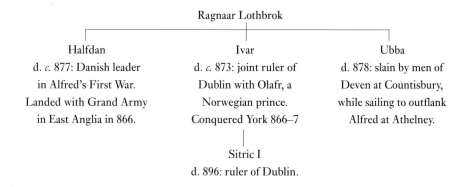

Ragnaar Lothbrok

Halfdan	Ivar	Ubba
d. *c.* 877: Danish leader in Alfred's First War. Landed with Grand Army in East Anglia in 866.	d. *c.* 873: joint ruler of Dublin with Olafr, a Norwegian prince. Conquered York 866–7	d. 878: slain by men of Deven at Countisbury, while sailing to outflank Alfred at Athelney.

Sitric I
d. 896: ruler of Dublin.

APPENDIX B

Main Roman and Ancient Roads in England Militarily in Use by Vikings

Source: Ivan D. Margary, *Roman Roads in Britain* (London, 1957)

ITINERARY	COMMENT
1. **Watling Street**: Richborough – Canterbury – Rochester – London – St Albans – Towcester – High Cross , thence in a series of straight alignments to Wall, near Litchfield, and thence to Wroxeter, where the main route ends	Watling Street would have been of prevailing use to the Vikings throughout their military presence, witness the strategic value of Canterbury, then adjoining the shores of the Wantsum Channel.
2 **York**: Tadcaster – Adel – Ilkley – Skipton – Ribchester – Preston.	This route would have assisted the Danish links with Dublin. The Danes would have been aware, like the Romans, of the parallel presence and usefulness of the Rivers Ouse and Ribble.
3. **York**: Tadcaster – Cleckheaton – (where the road connects with the above serial through the Aire Gap) – Slack – Castleshaw – Manchester – Northwich – Chester.	This road linked York with the Viking territories in each of Anglesey, Caernarvon and across the Irish Sea, in Dublin, Dublin, probably by means of naval bases at Chester or the Ribble Valley estuary areas.
4. **Ermine Street (1)**: London – Braughing – Chesterton (*Durobrivae*) – Lincoln.	Ermine Street provided a useful road link between Danish forces located throughout eastern England. It also provided, with the ancient Icknield Way, a militarily important link between north and south.

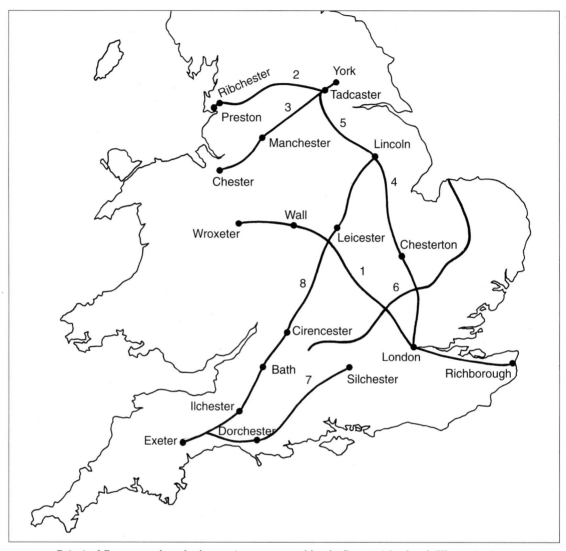

Principal Roman roads and other ancient routes used by the Danes. (Aardvark Illustration)

5. **Ermine Street (2)**: Lincoln – Doncaster –
   Castleford – Tadcaster – York.

6. **Icknield Way**: an ancient trackway, used and
   improved by the Romans, which provided a
   route, when combined with the Roman road
   from Silchester (see 7), from the borders of
   Norfolk to Dorset.

   The Icknield Way passes within a few miles
   of Cambridge, from whence Guthrum
   marched to Wareham in Dorset. He seems
   to have used this combination of trackway
   and Roman road.

7. **Silchester**: from here, via Old Sarum, to Badbury, thence to Hamworthy, in Poole Harbour, and to Wareham; also from Badbury via Dorchester to Exeter.

–

8. **Fosse Way**: Provides a through, straight road from Exeter, via Bath, to Lincoln.

Guthrum would almost certainly have used this road having made his peace with Alfred at Exeter, to withdraw to Mercia.

The Isle of Athelney

Extract from *The History and Antiquities of the County of Somerset*, by Reverend John Collinson (1791)

Between this hamlet [Ottery] and the church of Ling is the famous isle of Athelney, being a spot of rising ground on the north side of Stanmoor, bounded on the north-west by the River Tone, over which there is a wooden bridge, still called the Athelney Bridge. The name given by the Saxons to this land was the Isle of Nobles, by contraction Athelney.

This spot, which was anciently environed with almost impassable marshes, will be for ever memorable for the retreat of Alfred from the fury of the Danes, who in tumultuous numbers had overrun the eastern part of his dominions. The register of Athelney sets forth that Alfred, after having bravely encountered his enemies for five successive years, was at length reduced to the necessity of fleeing from them, and taking refuge in the little isle of Athelney. The place that lodged him was a small cottage belonging to St Athelwine, formerly a hermit here, the son of King Kynegilsus. After his emersion from this retirement and the total defeat of his enemies, he founded a monastery for Benedictine monks on the spot which had given him shelter and dedicated the same to the honour of St Saviour, and St Peter the apostle, appointing John (a native of old Saxony) the first abbot, and endowing the establishments with the whole isle of Athelney.

William of Malmesbury gives us a romantic account of this island and monastery. 'Athelney', says he, 'is not an island of the sea, but is so inaccessible, on account of bogs and the inundations of the lakes, that it cannot be got to but in a boat. It has a very large wood of alders, which harbours stags, wild goats and other beasts. The firm land, which is only two acres in breadth, contains a little monastery and dwellings for monks. Its founder was King Alfred who, being driven over the country by the Danes, spent some time here in secure privacy. Here, in a dream, St Cuthbert appearing to him and giving him assurance of his restoration, he vowed that he would build a monastery to God. Accordingly he erected a church, moderate indeed as to size, but as to the method of construction singular and novel: for four piers, driven into the ground, support the whole fabrick, four circular chancels being drawn round it. The monks are few in number, and indigent; but they are sufficiently compensated for their poverty by the tranquillity of their lives and their delight in solitude.

Some allusion to the vision of St Cuthbert above-mentioned is supposed to have been intended by a little curious amulet of enamel and gold, richly ornamented, that was found in 1693 in Newton Park, at some distance northwards from the abbey. On one side of it is a rude figure of a person sitting crowned, and holding in each hand a sceptre surmounted by a lily, which Dr Hickes and other antiquaries have imagined to be designed for St Cuthbert. The other side is filled by a large flower, and round the edge is the following legend: AELFRED MEC HEIT GEVVRCAN; that is, Alfred ordered me to be made. This piece of antiquity is now in the museum at Oxford, accompanied with the accounts of doctors Hickes and Musgrave.

APPENDIX D

The Garrisons of the Shires

	Shire	Burh	Hides	Total
1.	SUSSEX	*Eorpeburnan*	324	
		Hastings	500	
		Lewes	1300	
		Burpham	720	
		Chichester	1500	4344
2.	HAMPSHIRE	Winchester	2400	
		Christchurch	470	
		Southampton	150	
		Portchester	500	3520
3.	DORSET	Bridport	760	
		Wareham	1600	
		Shaftesbury	700	3060
4.	DEVON	Lydford	140	
		Halwell	300	
		Exeter	734	
		Pilton	360	1534
5.	SOMERSET	Bath	1000	
		Axbridge	400	
		Watchet	513	
		Lyng	100	
		Langport	600	2613
6.	WILTSHIRE	Wilton	1400	
		Chisbury	700	
		Malmesbury	1200	
		Cricklade	1500	4800
7.	BERKSHIRE	Wallingford	2400	
		Sashes	1000	3400

	Shire	Burh	Hides	Total
8.	OXFORDSHIRE	Oxford	1400	
9.	SURREY	Eashing	600	
		Southwark	1800	<u>2400</u>
			TOTAL	27071

Bibliography

Abels, Richard P., *Lordship and Military Obligation in Anglo-Saxon England* (British Museum, 1988)

——. *Alfred the Great: War, Kingship and Culture in Anglo-Saxon England* (Addison-Wesley Longman, 1998)

Amory, Frederic, 'The Viking Hasting in Franco-Scandinavian Legend', *Saints, Scholars and Heroes: Studies in Medieval Culture*, ed. King and Stevens (University Microfilms, 1979)

Anderson, J.R.L., *Upper Thames* (Methuen, 1974)

Bachrach, Bernard S., 'Some observations on the Military Administration of the Norman Conquest', *Anglo-Norman Studies*, ed. R. Allen Brown (The Boydell Press, 1985)

——. 'Some observations on William the Conqueror's Horse Transports', *Technology & Culture*, vol. 25

Bede, *A History of the English Church and People* (Penguin Classics, Harmondsworth, 1968)

Bennett, G.J., 'Wareham: Its Invasions and Battles', *Proceedings, Dorset Natural History and Archaeological Society*, vol. 13

Best, W. Stuart, 'Relations between Wessex and Cornwall in Early Days', *Dorset Natural History and Antiquaries Field Club*, vol. 77

Brooks, N.P., 'England in the Ninth Century: The Crucible of Defeat', *Transactions, Royal Historical Society* vol. 29 (1979)

Brown, David, *Anglo-Saxon England* (The Bodley Head, 1978)

Burne, A., 'Ancient Wiltshire Battlefields', *Wiltshire Archaeological Magazine*, vol. 53 (1950)

——. *More Battlefields of England* (Methuen, 1952)

Camden's *Britannia* (1586)

Campbell, A. (ed.), *The Chronicle of Aethelweard* (Nelson Medieval Texts, London, 1922)

Chevalier, Raymond, *Roman Roads* (1989)

Clapham, J.H., 'The Horsing of the Danes', *English Historical Society*, vol. 25 (1910)

Codrington, Thomas, *Roman Roads in Britain* (Sheldon Press, 3rd edn, 1928)

Collinson, Revd John, *The History and Antiquities of the County of Somerset* (R. Crutwell, 1791)

Craig, G., 'Alfred the Great: a diagnosis', *Journal, Royal Society of Medicine*, vol. 8 (1991)

Davis, R.H.C., 'Alfred the Great: Propaganda and Truth', *History*, vol. 56 (1971)

Davison, B.K., 'The Burghal Hidage Fort of Eorpeburnan: A Suggested Identification', *Medieval Archaeology*, vol. 16 (1972)

Dymond, Charles W., 'On the Identification of the Site of Buttingtune, of the Anglo-Saxon Chronicle, Anno 894', *Montgomeryshire Collections*, vol. 31

Fletcher, Revd Canon J.M.J., 'The Tomb of King Ethelred in Wimborne Minster', *Proceedings, Dorset Natural History and Archaeological Society*, vol. 16

Garmonsway, G.N. (trans. and ed.), *The Anglo-Saxon Chronicle* (J.M. Dent & Sons, repr. 1978)

Graham-Campbell, James (ed.), 'Viking Treasure from the North West', *The Vikings of the Irish Sea*, paper 5 (Liverpool Museum, 1992)

Gresswell, W.H.P., *Dumnonia and the Valley of the Parrett* (Barnicott & Pearce, 1922)

Grundy, G.B., 'The ancient highways and tracks of Wiltshire, Berkshire and Hampshire and the Saxon battlefields of Wiltshire', *Archaeological Journal*, vol. 75, (1918)

Hall R.A., *Jorvik, Viking Age York* (York Archaeological Trust, 1987)

Hassall, J.M. and Hill, D., 'Pont de l'Arche: Frankish Influence on the West Saxon Burh?', *Archaeological Journal*, vol. 127 (1970)

Hill, D., *An Atlas of Anglo-Saxon England, 700–1066* (Blackwell, 1981)

——. 'The Burghal Hidage – The Establishment of a Text', *Medieval Archaeology*, vol. 13 (1969)

Hinton, David H., *Alfred's Kingdom, Wessex and the South 800–1500* (J.M. Dent & Sons, 1977)

Hodgkin, H.J., *A History of the Anglo-Saxons* (Oxford University Press, 3rd edn, 1952)

Hollister, C.W., *Anglo-Saxon Military Institutions* (Clarendon Press, Oxford, 1962)

Humble, Richard, *The Fall of Anglo-Saxon England* (Arthur Barker, 1975)

Hutchins, J., *History and Antiquities of the County of Dorset* (J.B. Nichols, 1861)

Jackson, J.E., 'Selwood Forest', *Wiltshire Archaeological Magazine*, vol. 23 (1887)

Keynes, S., and Lapidge, M. (trans.), *Alfred the Great: Asser's Life of King Alfred and Other Contemporary Sources* (Penguin, Harmondsworth, 1983)

Kirby, D.P., 'Asser and the Life of King Alfred', *Studia Celtica*, vol. 6 (1971)

Jones, Gwyn, *A History of the Vikings to 1066* (Oxford, 1968)

Joransen, E., *The Danegeld in France*, publication 10 (Augustana Library, 1923)

Linklater, Eric, *The Conquest of England* (Hodder & Stoughton, 1966)

Man, John, *History and Antiquities of the Borough of Reading* (Snare & Man, 1816)

Marsden, John, *The Fury of the Northmen* (Kyle Cathie Ltd, 1993)

McTurk, R.W., 'Ragnarr Lodbrok in the Irish Annals?' in Almquist and Greene (eds) *Seventh Viking Congress*, 93–123

Montgomery of Alamein, FM Viscount, *A Concise History of Warfare* (Collins, 1972)

Owen, T. Morgan, 'The Battle of Buttington, with a brief Sketch of the Affairs of Powys and Mercia', *Montgomeryshire Collections*, vol. 7

Peddie, John, *The Roman Conquest of Britain* (Alan Sutton, Stroud, 1987)

Rahtz, P.A., 'Cannington, Hillfort, 1963', *Proceedings, Somerset Archaeological and Natural History Society*, vol. 113

Rawlence, E.A., 'On the site of the Battle of Ethandune' *Antiquaries Journal*, vol. 1 (1921)

Richards, Julian D., *Viking Age England* (English Heritage, 1991)

Sawyer, P.H.T., 'The Density of the Danish Settlement in England', *University of Birmingham Historical Journal*, vol. VI (1957)

Smyth, Alfred P., *King Alfred the Great* (Oxford, 1995)

——. *Scandinavian York and Dublin* (Irish Academic Press, 1987)

Spurrell, F.C.J., 'Early Sites and Embankments on the Thames Estuary', *Archaeological Journal*, vol. 43 (1885)

Stenton, Sir Frank, *Anglo-Saxon England* (Oxford, University Press, repr. 1988)

——. 'The Danes at Thorney Island in 893', *English Historical Records*, vol. 27 (1912)

Stevenson, W.H., *Asser's Life of King Alfred* (Oxford University Press, 1904)

Sturdy, David, *Alfred the Great* (Constable, 1995)

Timperley, H. and Brill, E. *Ancient Trackways of Wessex* (J.M. Dent & Sons, 1965)

Wainwright, F.T., 'Aethelflaed, Lady of the Mercians' in *Scandinavian England*, ed. H.P.R. Finberg (Phillimore, 1975)

Webster, Graham, 'Chester in the Dark Ages', *Journal, Chester and North Wales Historic Society*, vol. 38 (1951)

Whitelock, D. (ed.), *English Historical Documents*, vol. I *c. 500–1042* (Eyre Methuen, 2nd edn, 1979)

——. *The Beginnings of English Society* (Penguin Classics, Harmondsworth, 2nd edn, 1954)

Index

Page numbers in italics refer to illustrations and maps.